THE BATTLE OF WATERLOO

JEREMY BLACK

THE BATTLE OF WATERLOO
A NEW HISTORY

ICON BOOKS

This edition published in the UK in 2010 by
Icon Books Ltd, Omnibus Business Centre,
39–41 North Road, London N7 9DP
email: info@iconbooks.co.uk
www.iconbooks.co.uk

First published in the USA in 2010 by Random House,
an imprint of The Random House Publishing Group,
a division of Random House, Inc., New York.

Sold in the UK, Europe, South Africa and Asia
by Faber & Faber Ltd, Bloomsbury House,
74–77 Great Russell Street,
London WC1B 3DA or their agents

Distributed in the UK, Europe, South Africa and Asia
by TBS Ltd, TBS Distribution Centre, Colchester Road,
Frating Green, Colchester CO7 7DW

Published in Australia in 2010 by Allen & Unwin Pty. Ltd,
PO Box 8500, 83 Alexander Street,
Crows Nest, NSW 2065

ISBN: 978-184831-155-8

Book design by Christopher M. Zucker

Printed and bound in the UK by
CPI Mackays, Chatham ME5 8TD

For Charles Esdaile

CONTENTS

PREFACE

A most destructive and murderous fire was opened on our
column of round, grape, musquetry, rifle and buckshot
along the whole course and length of their line, in front, as
well as on our left flank. . . . The officers and men being as
it were mowed down by ranks.

IT IS 1815 INDEED, but not the French at Waterloo on 18 June.
Instead, this is Lieutenant Gordon of the British army reporting on
the resounding British defeat at New Orleans on 8 January by
American forces commanded by Andrew Jackson. This passage provides a key context for this book: that of warfare in the period, and
not only that of Napoleonic Europe. Waterloo is used to discuss the
changing nature of war, the rise and fall of Napoleon's empire, and
the influence of the French Revolutionary and Napoleonic Wars on
the nineteenth century.

Waterloo was an iconic battle for the British, a triumph of en-
durance that ensured a nineteenth-century world in which Britain
played the key role. It was also a defining moment for the French,
bringing to an end both the reign of Napoleon I and the Second
Hundred Years' War between Britain and France, a conflict that had

started in 1689. Further, the battle was important for a host of other participants, from Prussia, the state that was to be the basis of modern Germany, to the Netherlands and Belgium, whose fate it decided until the Belgian revolution of 1830, and to minor German principalities such as Hanover, Brunswick and Nassau, each of which also sent troops to the Duke of Wellington's army.

The echoes of the battle can still be felt across Britain and the anglophone world, and also more widely. While writing this book, I visited Rostock in Germany, where there is an impressive memorial to Gebhard Leberecht von Blücher, the Prussian commander at Waterloo. In England, I visited the 175-foot Wellington Monument (begun in 1817 and completed in 1854) in Somerset, a site that can be seen by all travellers on the glorious Great Western Railway route to the West Country; caught a glimpse of Waterloo Cross in Devon; travelled to Waterloo station, the terminus of one of the rail lines from Exeter; passed through Waterlooville in Hampshire; saw a print of a Victorian gathering for the hare coursing Waterloo Cup; sat often at my favourite seat in London overlooking, as it so happens, Waterloo Place; and, thanks to the success of the film *Mamma Mia!* (2008), was aware of frequent renditions of the ABBA song 'Waterloo'. Lunch in Parliament, moreover, enabled me to see again *The Meeting of Wellington and Blücher After Waterloo,* a crowded but grand painting by Daniel Maclise (1806–70). Now largely unknown, in part due to the demise of history painting, Maclise was much applauded in his day as a great artist and received £7,000 for this painting, finished in 1861, and for *The Death of Nelson* (1864). These works for the Houses of Parliament, built anew after being burned down in 1834, were thought an appropriate inspiration and backdrop for the empire's legislators. This list of celebratory references is eclectic, of course, but resonant of a strong layer of commemoration.

I am most grateful for the opportunity to give the Wellington Lecture at the University of Southampton in 2000, and also to speak at the 1998 Wellington Conference held at that University. I would also like to thank Charles Esdaile for discussing the battle with me and for commenting on an earlier draft. It is a great

pleasure to dedicate this book to Charles. We were colleagues together at Durham in the early 1980s and then went separate ways
in career terms, but we have remained friends and share a strong
commitment both to military history and to the need to understand
the political contexts of war. Charles is a major inspiration for all
those who work on the period. I have also benefited from advice on
an earlier draft by Ian Beckett, Rick Schneid and Dennis Showalter,
and on particular points from James Chapman, Malcolm Cook,
Odile Cook, James Friguglietti, Bill Gibson, Rob Johnson, James
Kay and Bob Tennant. Howard Cohn has proved an exemplary copy
editor.

   Those who read a book on Waterloo want to hear of battle, not
rail timetables, and it is to this we must turn. Alongside the discussion of military capabilities, options and contingencies, it is important to recall the human suffering, not least because, otherwise, the
historian can become too detached from what he is writing about.
Captain John Hill of the 23rd Foot (Royal Welsh Fusiliers) of the
British army, wrote to his brother-in-law after the battle:

> The front wound still continues to discharge very much, he
> is a most confounded ugly fellow . . . as big as a tea-cup. . . .
> I got the grape shot in my shoulder and five other wounds
> in my face. . . . Honesty [his horse] got three shot. . . . He
> bled to death.[1]

There is uncertainty over the casualty figures, which, itself, is a
comment on the nature of war in the period. This problem is accentuated by the numbers of troops who used the opportunity to leave
their armies, which was particularly an issue for the routed French
but was also serious for the Prussians after their defeat at Ligny two
days earlier. At Waterloo, Wellington's army suffered about 16,200
killed, wounded, or missing out of 69,700 men, about 23 per cent.
Over 3,500 men were killed. Their Prussian allies suffered about
7,000 casualties at Waterloo, or about 14 per cent. French casualties have been estimated at about 31,000 killed or wounded, with
several thousand more men captured. The large number of troops

who deserted after the battle made the impact of Waterloo on France's main army more serious. Earlier, on 16 June, the battles of Quatre Bras and Ligny had also been costly, with Wellington's army suffering 4,600 casualties, the Prussians 18,800 and the French 17,800. In this case, as in others, Wellington's army refers to the Anglo-Allied forces under Wellington's command, forces that were British, Dutch, Belgian (at the time, part of the Netherlands) and German.

Individual accounts of the battle drive the reality of these losses home, although they suffer from many flaws, not least the extent to which they offer a partial perspective, namely that of a narrator who could only see and experience part of the battle and who sought to do so in the exhausted aftermath of the day. Personal memoirs also face the problem of the process of construction,[2] and this was noted at the time. In 1814, Sergeant Thomas Morris noted:

> The drum-major of a regiment in our brigade, who, though he had not been within the smell of powder, wrote an elo-quent and affectionate letter to his wife in London, giving her a detailed (but purely imaginary) account of the affair, describing very minutely his own exploits . . . highly pleas-ing to the good wife, who took occasion to show it to some of her friends, who advised her to send it to the editor of one of the daily papers, who immediately gave it insertion.[3]

Contradictory accounts pose serious difficulties for scholars. As Rory Muir noted of the battle of Salamanca in 1812 between Wellington and French forces:

> While the sources are plentiful, they do not always fit neatly together; indeed, they are riddled with contradictions, incon-sistencies, gaps and uncertainty. Normally the historian deals privately with these problems. This method is inescapable in addressing a large sweeping subject if the narrative is not to lose its momentum and the reader to miss the thread of the

argument. However, it can also mislead the reader by suggesting that our understanding is far more securely based than is the case.

Muir wrote more specifically of the British cavalry charge on the French left, 'How can an account written more than twenty years after the event be so clear, comprehensible and detailed, when letters written within days are generally confused and fragmentary?'[4] This book seeks to balance such problems with the desire to make the course of the battle understandable. The key point is to remember that the Waterloo campaign was not some war game or historical reenactment, but a series of battles in which men suffered and endured.

THE **BATTLE** OF **WATERLOO**

I.

EIGHTEENTH-CENTURY WARFARE
AND THE CHALLENGE OF REVOLUTION

AT WATERLOO, THE ARMY that apparently encapsulated change, the French army of the Emperor Napoleon, was stopped by another, the British army of Arthur, Duke of Wellington, that was essentially an eighteenth-century force in its composition, culture and methods. This contrast needs emphasising because it undercuts much of the standard analysis of military history, with its repeated stress on the positive consequences of change and its ranking of military capability in terms of the welcoming of change. This is an issue that is pertinent for warfare and that we will also address more generally in Chapter 11.

Waterloo, of course, was more than an eighteenth-century victory over the Napoleonic aftermath of the French Revolution, yet that description captures an important aspect of the battle. It is therefore appropriate to begin by considering eighteenth-century ancien régime (old regime, pre-1789) warfare before turning to the impact of the French Revolution, which broke out in 1789. The space this book devotes to conflict before the Napoleonic Wars might appear surprising, but it is important to remember that standard modern linear perceptions of warfare as a condition experiencing continual change, with past episodes appearing anachronistic

due to very different conditions, notably weaponry, were not pertinent for the period of this book and, indeed, are of only limited
value for modern warfare.

By modern battle standards, both ancien régime and French
Revolutionary/Napoleonic combat relied on close-quarter fighting
by soldiers who could see each other. In terms of the proximity of
the combatants, Waterloo encapsulated this point, even if gunpowder smoke ensured that they could not see clearly, and indeed this
smoke led both to confusion and to a high level of unpredictability
at the level of individual combatants. This confusion and unpredictability affected the accounts they left and help explain discrep-
ancies between them.

In Europe, the weapons of the various armies (and navies) of the
period were similar, and differences between the weapons did not
generally account for victory or defeat. The key infantry deployment was linear, as the standard weapon, a flintlock musket
equipped with a bayonet, led to long, thin linear formations based
on a shoulder-to-shoulder drill designed to maximise firepower.
This ensured that casualty rates could be extremely high, particularly as a result of the exchange of fire at close quarters between lines
of tightly packed troops. Low muzzle velocity led often to wounds
without the victim being knocked over, but these wounds were
dreadful, because, the more slowly a projectile travels, the more
damage it does as it bounces off bones and internal organs. As a
result, the real point of drill and discipline was defensive: to prepare
a unit to remain intact and tractable to its commander, in the face
of death and injuries and regardless of the casualties. Waterloo
provided numerous instances of this, notably from 4:00 P.M. to
6:00 P.M., with the British squares exposed to deadly French
artillery fire in support of repeated cavalry attacks.

Despite the bayonets on the firearms carried by infantry, hand-
to-hand fighting on the eighteenth-century battlefield was relatively uncommon, and most casualties were caused by shot, which
indeed remained the case at Waterloo. The hand-to-hand fighting
that occurred at Waterloo reflected the breakdown of conventional
tactics, notably in the struggle for particular strongpoints such as

La Haie Sainte. Alongside the relative infrequency of hand-to-hand fighting, the accuracy of muskets and, indeed, of most musketeers was limited, which led to deployment at close range. In 1985, the historian Arthur Ferrill discussed how the Macedonian leader Alexander the Great (r. 336–323 B.C.), popularly regarded as the greatest general in antiquity, could have beaten the British at Waterloo in A.D. 1815, an argument that was an ironic commentary on the apparent timelessness of conflict between the two periods. Ferrill conceded that the classical world lacked firearms, but he argued that the effectiveness of the latter in 1815 was not a quantum leap greater than those of the projectile weapons of the classical period, namely arrows, spears and slings.[1]

Indeed, the difficulties created by muskets, which had both a short range and a low rate of fire and had to be resighted for each individual shot, were exacerbated by the serious and persistent problems associated with poor sights, eccentric bullets, heavy musket droops (firing short), recoil, overheating and misfiring in wet weather. As most guns, both muskets and cannon, were smoothbore, with no rifling (grooves) in the barrel, part of the explosive force of the gunpowder charge was dissipated, so that the speed of the shot was not high, while its direction was uncertain. Nonstandardised manufacture (a result of craft-production techniques), as well as wide clearances, meant that the musket was difficult to aim or hold steady, and the ball could roll out if the barrel was pointed toward the ground. To counteract these problems, training stressed rapidity of fire (to build up the volume of shot) and thus drill and discipline.

Yet what could be achieved was affected by serious difficulties at the tactical level. In particular, given the poor state of communications, coordination along the long front line of troops posed a problem. An increase in the number of officers and noncommissioned officers helped address the issue at the tactical level, although this tactical solution could not secure matters of general command, especially of responding to the unpredictable flow of battle. In responding to this flow, commanders relied on mounted couriers to communicate orders, but the couriers sometimes suffered accidents or were wounded, problems that affected Wellington's army at Waterloo.

At best, the command situation was generally slow and, at worst, serious problems could arise when couriers failed to deliver orders or they were misunderstood. The latter were especially serious, as it was impossible to check orders except by the long process of dispatching and receiving couriers. Such issues of command effectiveness recurred frequently during the Waterloo campaign, including at Waterloo, and were a particular problem for commanders trying to move their forces and to coordinate advances. Indeed, because Wellington rested on the defensive at Waterloo, this problem gave him an advantage.

Whatever the strengths and weaknesses of command and of individual commanders, there were major issues in fighting effectiveness. As Waterloo demonstrated, combat readinesss was not simply the sum of what individuals could do with their weapons. Unit action was crucial, and therefore unit cohesion was a key factor in fighting effectiveness. Rather than employing individually aimed fire, soldiers fired by volley, in a process designed not only to maximise the continuity of fire, but also to establish a relative superiority that could help sway the conflict. Within the pattern of volley fire, there were variations in the order in which ranks or platoons fired, and these variations remained the case during the Napoleonic Wars. In particular, there were contrasts between firing by rank and platoon, although such contrasts were far less significant than those, in both defensive and offensive formations, between lines, columns and squares. Whatever the method, the speed of fire was enhanced from the eighteenth century by the use of paper cartridges, with the ball, powder and wadding in a single package. This packaging made reloading easier and allowed each soldier to carry more ammunition.

Another instance of variety between armies was the stress placed on the battlefield use of artillery, either for counterbattery fire (bombarding the opposing cannon) or for firing on opposing troops. The latter was a practice developed by Napoleon, who massed cannon successfully to that end, but had also been a practice advocated and used by ancien régime commanders such as Frederick II

(Frederick the Great) of Prussia (r. 1740–86). Wellington, in contrast, generally used his artillery for close support and made very few attempts to create 'grand batteries', the one exception being at his victory over the French at Vitoria in 1813. At Waterloo, Wellington certainly did not create such a battery, and this was understandable due to his determination to mount a strong defence along the entire line and not simply in the central section.

Cannon were deadly, firing both round shot – solid cannonballs – and canister shot (also called case-shot) – canisters that shattered on impact, spreading their contents. But cannon were affected by muzzle explosions, defective caps and unexpected backfiring, although the key problems were poor accuracy (by later standards) and the fact that cannon could not fire indirectly. They could not be placed behind cover but had to be trained directly on their targets. Mortars and howitzers, in contrast, with their high trajectories, could provide indirect fire, although their range was affected by these higher trajectories, and the absence of aerial reconnaissance seriously limited the value of indirect fire. This lack of reliable information would have been a factor had it been possible for Napoleon's cannon (as it was not) to bombard Wellington's troops on the reverse (hidden) slopes, which he used so skillfully at Waterloo to provide cover.

The absence of smokeless powder meant that all firearms were badly affected by smoke. After the first shots, battlefield visibility was limited, a major factor at Waterloo, and one that contributed to a confusion that commanders sought to counter with tight formations. The problem of battlefield visibility put a premium on the fire discipline required to delay shooting until a short range had been reached. Moreover, short-range infantry fire was more deadly than longer-range fire as velocity was lower in the latter case, while the musket balls spread out far more.

On the ancien régime battlefield, the infantry was generally flanked by cavalry units, but over the eighteenth century as a whole, the proportion of cavalry in European armies declined as a result of the heavier emphasis on firepower, as well as the greater per capita cost of cavalry. There were also particular supply problems for cavalry, with the need for large quantities of fodder, which was bulky to transport. Cavalry was principally used on the battlefield to fight cavalry, although, having defeated the other side's cavalry, it then often turned on the defending infantry. In ancien régime warfare, frontal attacks on unbroken infantry in defensive positions were uncommon and, when tried by the French against the British at Minden (1759), spectacularly unsuccessful. Infantry units, unless they could rapidly reform into defensive squares, were exposed, however, to attack by cavalry in flank and rear and squares were more vulnerable to attack if the troops had just fired at another target.

Cavalry played a crucial role in some ancien régime battles, such as the British victory over the French at Blenheim (1704) and the Prussian over the French at Rossbach (1757), and cavalry-infantry coordination, or at least combination, could be important. At Fraustadt (1706), a Swedish army defeated a Saxon force twice its size, the numerous Swedish cavalry enveloping both Saxon flanks, while the relatively small Swedish infantry force held off attacks in the centre. Much depended on the terrain and cover. Due to the many hedges on the battlefield, Roucoux (1746) was very much an infantry battle, while at Waterloo the dense cover and terrain to the front of Wellington's far left discouraged the French from launching attacks there, but the very opposite was the case in the open terrain between Hougoumont and La Haie Sainte.

In general, although the Prussian general Blücher demonstrated the continued role of cavalry at the battle of Leipzig in 1813, it was less important than it had been in the past. The degree to which the social prestige of being an officer in cavalry units nevertheless remained high reflected the extent to which values did not necessarily reflect practicalities. The British heavy cavalry units were socially particularly prestigious. Despite this, the infantry was the key arm in the British army.

Napoleon did not benefit greatly at Waterloo from the strength of his cavalry, which was more numerous than that in Wellington's army by about 15,600 to 13,350, although this lack of benefit owed something to their inappropriate use and, in particular, to the failure to operate combined-arms attacks successfully. The French cavalry was also affected by the nature of Wellington's position as they could not get effectively at the British troops on a wide front until the French infantry had cleared the way by taking either Hougoumont or La Haie Sainte. At Waterloo, there were major cavalry attacks on infantry, by the British heavy cavalry on the disordered corps of Jean-Baptiste Drouet, Count d'Erlon, and by the French cavalry on British foot soldiers in the afternoon. This latter was not in preference to an attack on the British cavalry, which was not deployed in a way that left it exposed.

Unbroken infantry was more vulnerable to artillery fire than it was to cavalry attack, especially because of the close-packed and static or slow-moving formations that were adopted in order to maintain infantry discipline and firepower as well as the cohesion that enabled infantry to fight on despite casualties. The use of artillery increased considerably during the eighteenth century and by 1762, Frederick the Great, who had not initially favoured the large-scale use of artillery, was employing massed batteries of guns. The development in the mid–eighteenth century of a new system of fabricating cannon – casting them solid and then drilling them out, rather than casting a hollow barrel – improved effectiveness by decreasing windage (the gap between the barrel and the shot). This improvement made it possible to use smaller charges and thus to lighten barrels and increase mobility, although the improvement also meant that bigger pieces could be used in the field. Moreover, during the century, cannon became both more mobile and standardised. The leaders in this field were, in the 1750s, the Austrians, who enhanced the mobility of field pieces by reducing their weight. From the late 1760s, the French, thanks to the brilliant innovation of General Jean-Baptiste Gribeauval, assumed pride of place in artillery. This was the service from which Napoleon rose to prominence.

The greater standardisation of artillery pieces led to more regular fire, and this encouraged the development of artillery tactics, away from the largely desultory and random bombardments of the seventeenth century toward more efficient exchanges of concentrated and sustained fire. Artillery fire therefore acquired the key characteristics of its infantry counterpart. Grape and canister shot proved particularly deadly at Waterloo: these consisted of a bag or tin with small balls inside, which scattered as a result of the charge, causing considerable numbers of casualties at short range to infantry, horses and cavalrymen.

The notion of ready improvement, however, has to be qualified by an appreciation of the difficult trade-off in field artillery between mobility and weight. Heavier field pieces provided more effective fire support, as with Napoleon's Grand Battery at Waterloo, but that effectiveness depended, in part, on the battle being relatively static, since heavy cannon could not be moved rapidly. When the cannon's targets were stationary, they were highly vulnerable. In the British army, the Twenty-seventh Regiment, the Inniskillings, deployed on the afternoon of Waterloo at the crossroads to the north of La Haie Sainte, lost well over half its numbers to French cannon fire. During the battle, the Grand Battery was only briefly attacked by British cavalry, and then unsuccessfully, so that it was able to continue firing on the British lines.

Far from being unchanging prior to the outbreak of the French Revolution, warfare saw a tactical and operational responsiveness to circumstances, not least the war-making of opponents. Thus, during the Seven Years' War (1756–63), which is known in America as the French and Indian War, warfare was shaped by the fluid dynamics of the contending armies, as everyone sought to avoid the mistakes of the previous year's campaigning season. This rapid learning curve indicated the variety and flexibility of ancien régime warfare.

Just as this warfare is misleadingly seen as inflexible, so there is also an emphasis on conventions of fighting that suggest that it was restrained and limited. Among officers of the period, there was indeed a pseudo-chivalry that reflected their sense of being members of a common profession and, in large part, an aristocratic caste, as well as conventions of proper conduct, conventions that played a role for some at Waterloo. In 1758, Lord George Sackville, who was to direct British strategy during the War of American Independence, reported of the opposed British and French forces in Germany, 'Our sentinels and advanced posts are in perfect harmony and good humour with each other, they converse frequently together and have not yet fired though officers go out of curiosity much nearer than there is any occasion for.' The following year, Captain William Fawcett of the British army noted that the advanced posts of the two forces in Germany were very close,

> which afford a sight extraordinary enough, to those who are not acquainted with the formalities of war. The French, to do them justice, are a very generous enemy and above taking little advantages: I myself am an instance of it, amongst many that happen almost daily: Being out a coursing a few days ago, I was galloping at full speed after a hare . . . into a thicket, where they had a post of infantry, and must infallibly have been taken prisoner, if the officer commanding it had not showed himself; and very genteelly called out to stop me. We frequently discourse together.[2]

Such episodes have tended to characterise the image of warfare prior to the French Revolution, with particular attention devoted to the British and French at the battle of Fontenoy in Belgium in 1745, and the willingness there to let the other side fire first. Indeed, as an important instance of restraint, the treatment of prisoners improved.[3]

Nevertheless, indications of restraint are less than the full picture, which looked toward the harsh Prussian treatment of the retreating French at Waterloo. Soldiers in ancien régime armies were often brutal in their treatment of each other and of civilians. After the Battle of Dettingen in 1743, British soldiers even plundered and stripped their dead and wounded compatriots, to say nothing of the defeated French.

Moreover, the horrors of the fighting were readily visible and, in this, Waterloo also followed in a long tradition. The use of case-shot against close-packed rows of soldiers, or the pursuit of fleeing infantry by cavalry, both of which were seen at Waterloo, had brutal consequences, and consequences that were seen as brutal. In addition, the primitive nature of medical care had deadly results.

The horror of war seen at Waterloo was anticipated by many battles, such as Minden (1759), another British victory over the French, from which Richard Browne of the British army wrote to his father:

> I thought formerly I could easily form an idea of a battle from the accounts I heard from others, but I find everything short of the horrid sense and it seems almost incredible that any can escape the incessant fire and terrible hissings of bullets of all sizes, the field of battle after is melancholy, four or five miles of plain covered with human bodies dead and dying, miserably butchered dead horses, broken wheels and carriages and arms of all kind . . . in the morning on the ground in our tents was pools of blood and pieces of brain.[4]

The following year, William Fawcett remarked on the commonplace and coarsening nature of killing.

> The destruction of two or three hundred poor wretches is looked upon as a mere trifle here, wherever there is any point to be carried, which is thought of consequence . . . 500 or 1,000 fine fellows, in full bloom and vigour ordered to march up, to possess themselves of an eminence, an old house, or windmill, or other particular piece of ground, with a certainty of one half of them at least, being, at the same time, exposed to certain death, in the doing of it.[5]

The ancien régime background to the warfare of the French Revolutionary and Napoleonic period, the warfare that culminated at Waterloo, was therefore both harsh and changing. While rulers and ministers sought to cope with the consequences of the wars of 1740–63, and engaged in highly competitive international relations, commanders tried to gain a capability advantage by responding to what they saw as developments.

In this process, the prestige of Prussian methods was particularly important, which looked toward the episodic wars between Prussians and French from 1792 to Waterloo, conflict that was resumed in 1870–71, 1914–18 and 1939–45. The campaigns of Frederick the Great were studied by contemporaries, while Prussian military manoeuvres were widely attended by those interested in military matters, including, in 1783, Louis-Alexandre Berthier, later Napoleon's chief of staff and minister of war. In 1792, Robert Jenkinson (subsequently, as second Earl of Liverpool, prime minister at the time of Waterloo and indeed until 1827), after observing a Prussian army review, commented, 'the celerity and precision with which all their movements are performed are inconceivable to those who have not seen them. Every operation they go through is mechanical.'[6] The more critical French envoy in London referred to 'new hordes of disciplined slaves.'[7]

Western commentators were less aware of new French ideas, as well as of the impressive effectiveness that the Russians were displaying at the expense of the Turks in 1768–74 and 1787–92. Under the pressure of failure in the Seven Years' War, it was in France that much rethinking took place. French reforms encompassed tactics, operational ethos, organisation, administration and the individual arms. In terms of firepower, Gribeauval, who became inspector-general of the artillery in 1776, standardised artillery, employing eight-gun batteries, with four-, eight-, twelve-pound cannon and six-inch howitzers. The mobility of cannon was increased by stronger, larger wheels, shorter barrels, better casting methods and lighter weight. Their accuracy was improved by the introduction of elevating screws, inclination markers and graduated rear sights and the issue of gunnery tables. As with muskets, the rate of cannon fire rose through the introduction of prepackaged rounds and mobility increased when horses were harnessed in pairs, instead of in tandem.

The theory of war advanced to take note of these and other developments. In his *De l'usage de l'artillerie nouvelle dans la guerre de campagne* (1778), Chevalier Jean du Teil argued that the artillery should begin battles and be massed for effect. Napoleon's thoughts on the use of massed cannon were drawn from du Teil, and he studied in 1788 at the artillery school at Auxonne, which was commanded by du Teil's brother, Jean-Pierre. Another supporter of such massing,

Jacques, Count de Guibert, who had fought at Rossbach and Minden, advocated, in his *Essai général de tactique* (1772), living off the land in order to increase the speed of operations, as well as the establishment of a patriotic citizen army. Napoleon was to praise Guibert's writings, which, with their stress on movement and enveloping manoeuvres, and their criticism of reliance on fortifications, prefigured his generalship. In 1787–89, Guibert served as director of the French Higher War Council.

There was also pressure in France for a less fixed sequence of moves in manual drill, and for a drill that enabled troops to be more flexible, which was seen as a basis for enhanced effectiveness. Some military discussion was long-standing, particularly that of tactical questions, specifically over the rival merits of line and column formations. These rival merits were to be an issue at Waterloo, where French columns attacked British lines, and the deployment of these columns was sometimes presented as a cause of French failure. Earlier, in the eighteenth century, in contrast to the customary emphasis on firepower and linear tactics, Jean-Charles, Chevalier de Folard, and François-Jean, Baron de Mesnil-Durand, two influential French commentators, emphasised the shock and weight of a force attacking in column: ordre profonde, not ordre mince. Manoeuvres in 1778 designed to test the rival systems failed to settle the controversy, and the new French tactical manual issued in 1791 incorporated both.

There was also interest in France in the development of the division as a unit composed of elements of all arms and therefore able to operate independently. Such a unit could serve effectively, both as a detached force and as part of a coordinated army operating in accordance with a strategic plan. The system of combat divisions, which became a standard wartime procedure for the French in the 1790s, gave generals the potential to control much larger armies than the 60,000 to 70,000 troops that had been considered the maximum effective force in midcentury.

The American War of Independence (1775–83), in which France intervened on the American side from 1778, also indicated the extent to which ancien régime warfare was neither limited nor static. This war spanned much of the world, with bold attempts at power projection, such as the French fleets and armies sent to North America and India in 1780. British resilience was also a key dimension. Like much else, this resilience linked the French Revolutionary War with what came earlier.

Breaking out in 1789, the French Revolution was in part a product of French military failure. First, the French government had badly lost domestic prestige as a result of defeat in battle, notably Rossbach at the hands of Frederick the Great in 1757, and its inability to confront Prussia and Britain in the Dutch crisis of 1787. The latter was an episode that in fact fell short of war but in which equations of military strength, international support, and political resolution all proved mutually supporting. Second, although it considered doing so in 1789, the government did not use the army to suppress the disaffection and opposition that led to and accompanied the Revolution. Indeed, the opposite occurred: the French army was unable to maintain order and prevent violent insurrectionary episodes, and notably so in Paris, the centre of government, in both 1789 and 1792.

An increasingly more radical government and politics in France led to the mustering of a counterrevolutionary international coalition, and war between the two broke out in 1792. Initially, it seemed that the Revolution might fail, with Prussian and Austrian forces successfully invading eastern France. In the event, the Prussian army, already greatly concerned about its supplies, was checked at Valmy by a larger French army supported by effective artillery and then fell back. Its commander, Charles William Ferdinand, Duke of Brunswick, who was to be mortally wounded at the battle of Auerstädt in 1806, was brother-in-law to George III of Britain and the father of Frederick, Duke of Brunswick, who was mortally wounded at the battle of Quatre Bras on 16 June 1815.

The French forces exploited their successes in late 1792, invading the Rhineland, Belgium (then the Austrian Netherlands) and Savoy, then part of the Kingdom of Sardinia. This exploitation was a victory for the larger numbers of the French troops, for the potential these large numbers offered for the battlefield tactic of a bold advance employing columns of massed infantry, as at Jemappes, the battle fought southwest of Mons on 6 November 1792, that led to the overrunning of Belgium, and for political resolution. In contrast, there was a degree of uncertainty about opposition to the French, especially on the part of the Prussians. Prussia, Austria and, in particular, Russia all proved more interested in partitioning Poland out of existence in 1793 and 1795. The resolution displayed by the Seventh Coalition in 1815 was a marked contrast.

By 1796, despite Britain, the Dutch and Spain entering the war against France in 1793, the French had conquered the Low Countries (Belgium and Netherlands) and western Germany, and had knocked Prussia and Spain out of the opposing coalition. In 1797, Austria was forced to accept terms, in particular as a result of Napoleon's defeat of Austrian forces in northern Italy and his advance toward Austria.

These French victories are easier to list than to explain, in part because a number of possible explanations have been offered. They range from tactical, specifically the superiority of columns over lines; to organisational, especially the division system and the provision of plentiful artillery; to numbers, the large number of troops produced by the conscription of the levée en masse; to the enthusiasm of a popular revolution. These issues are all subsumed for many by the argument that the French represented a modern and modernising way of war, one characterised by total goals and means, not least a mobilisation of all the resources of society. In turn, this mobilisation is held to explain success over ancien régime states and militaries that lacked such resolution and effort, and whose warmaking was characterised accordingly.

While apparently persuasive, many aspects of this interpretation have been picked apart by scholarship concerned to demonstrate the complexity of war making in the 1790s. This scholarship is not simply a case of the revenge of the particular on the general; it also raises profound questions about the way in which the image of military change frequently serves as a substitute for reality. For example, alongside the theory of a radical break at the time of the French Revolution, it is necessary to note the extent to which the French army was already changing from midcentury. It would also be inappropriate to argue that the French alone were capable of devising aggressive tactical and operational methods, as the campaigning of the Russian army abundantly showed and as the Prussians were to make tellingly clear at Waterloo. Moreover, the British navy was probably the most proficient force in the 1790s (certainly more so than its French counterpart), and it abundantly demonstrated both the value of professionalism and the extent to which success in battle was not dependent on radicalism, whether in politics or in war.

This navy also enabled Britain to project its power, seizing French colonies in the 1790s as well as those of the Dutch and Spaniards once they became France's allies, such as Cape Town from the Dutch in 1796 and Trinidad from the Spaniards. The strategic and geopolitical consequences of British naval strength were even more far-ranging. Napoleon struck at Egypt in 1798, in an attempt both to retain his own military position at home (as Julius Caesar had invaded Britain in 55 and 54 B.C.) and also to establish French power on the route to the Orient. After capturing Alexandria, Napoleon defeated the Mamelukes at Shubra Khit and at Embabeh, the Battle of the Pyramids, victories for French defensive firepower over the shock tactics of the Mameluke cavalry. Fearing a threat to India, not least because of their struggle with Tipu Sultan of Mysore, the British mounted a powerful riposte. This included Horatio Nelson's defeat of the French fleet at the Battle of the Nile (1798) and, after Napoleon had abandoned his forces and returned to France, the landing, in 1801, of a British expeditionary force near Alexandria that defeated the French in a defensive battle and then forced their surrender.

The ability to combine British forces from both Britain and India in Egypt, and to secure an outcome, was a testimony to a range of power that looked toward more fully fledged strategies of global power in the two world wars of the twentieth century. The differences were of course numerous, but the possibility of making such a comparison underlines the unique nature of European war making on the world scale. It also suggests that narratives of military modernisation should focus on Britain, and its capabilities and goals, and not on France.

Allowing for this, the warfare of the 1790s was important to the style of battle Napoleon was to adopt at Waterloo. The characteristic battlefield manoeuvre of French Revolutionary forces and the most effective way to use the mass of new and inexperienced soldiers, most of whom went into the infantry, was as the advance in independent attack columns. This approach was best for an army that put an emphasis on the attack, and it was easier to train hastily raised troops to fight in columns. Little time was required, and the formation offered a psychological benefit of packing the recruit in with others, which established a sense of security in the midst of battle. Column attacks were particularly successful against the Austrian linear defensive formation, although at Jemappes this was only after initial failures and at the cost of losses heavier than those of the defenders.

It is necessary, however, to distinguish between shallow columns and deep columns, and between columns of manoeuvre and columns of attack. The French Revolutionary armies did not apply these principles in practice zealously, for levels of training suffered in the early 1790s, especially with the new armies. Anyway, everything tended to break down when combat began. Nevertheless, there is a need, when considering both the battles of the 1790s and those of the Napoleonic period, to distinguish between the image of some enormously broad and deep column formation, with men packed tightly together, and what was probably more common, a less coherent and dense formation. There was also a difference between battalion columns and brigade (division) columns. The former were a single block of men, say fifty wide by twelve deep. In contrast, the latter could be made up in many differing ways, with variations on possible formations achieved by varying the spacing of the individual battalions and lines of battalions. Whatever the organisation, in general, column attacks, such as those mounted by the four divisions of d'Erlon's corps on Wellington's left in the early stages of Waterloo, required substantial numbers of troops.

The French used concentration at two levels, tactical and operational. In the first, their opponents tended to be vulnerable because these opponents emphasised traditional close-order linear formations, while the French system allowed for more men to be concentrated in a smaller area than before, which increased the chance of a breakthrough. At the operational level, the French struck at the Austrian 'cordon system', which distributed units across a wide front in order to hold territory and so reduced the number of troops that could be concentrated at any one point in order to repel attack. The French did this when they invaded Belgium in November 1792, leading to their victory at Jemappes, and Napoleon was essentially trying to repeat this feat in 1815. To make that point is not to criticise him for a lack of originality, but, instead, to note the extent to which similar circumstances (albeit against different opponents) led to similar responses.

The large number of separate armies that the French deployed during the French Revolutionary and Napoleonic Wars needed substantial quantities of troops. These separate armies were required so that France could operate on the series of fronts that the number of her opponents made necessary. As a consequence, Napoleon faced a key dilemma in 1815; he had an unprecedented number and combination of opponents, but could not field the armies required to fight them all. To that extent, his previous campaigning was of scant relevance, with the campaign of 1814 being the closest to that of 1815.

More generally, substantial quantities of troops were also required to man the various divisions of individual armies, and these divisions were necessary for the methods of envelopment, encirclement and convergence that were so important for French Revolutionary and Napoleonic warfare. Furthermore, the greater number and dispersal of units in the French Revolutionary and Napoleonic Wars ensured that command and coordination skills became more important, although the introduction of the corps-division-brigade structure countered the increase in the number of units and their dispersal.

Returning to the tactical level, column advances were more flexible than traditional linear formations and the rigid drill these formations used. Furthermore, as the units became more experienced, the supply of equipment improved, and vigorous generals rose to the fore in the 1790s, French forces became steadily more effective, providing a pool of talent Napoleon could still call on in 1815. In tactical terms, the French were helped by their turn toward light infantry, so that a substantial force of skirmishers, using individually aimed fire, weakened the opposing lines before the French attack. Deployed in open order, the skirmishers were not vulnerable to volley fire or cannon but were able to use individual fire to inflict casualties on the close-packed lines of their opponents. This fire damaged enemy morale and could also disrupt its formations. Other armies had previously used light infantry in a largely separate capacity on the battlefield, but the French integrated close-order and open-order infantry, so that each infantry battalion had the capacity to deploy its own skirmishers.

Yet, as with the use of rifles by the American Revolutionaries, it is important not to exaggerate the impact of a particular weapon, tactic, or deployment. None was unique to the French (the Russians, for example, being expert in the use of columns), and each, moreover, faced particular problems. Thus, if the advance of the head of a column was stopped by defensive fire, as the British were often to succeed in doing, for example to d'Erlon's corps at Waterloo, this check could have a disastrous consequence. Furthermore, columns were vulnerable to surprise cavalry attacks; this was to be the eventual fate of d'Erlon's advance. Skirmishers were vulnerable to cavalry, although far less so in broken terrain, and were not unique to the French. They were also employed by the Allies, although not as the French used them. Waterloo was to demonstrate the deficiencies of both French columns and skirmishers in breaking or disrupting British units.

In the 1790s, the impressive French battlefield artillery was also important, not least with the development of horse artillery. More generally, the French combination of mobile artillery, skirmishers and assault columns was potent, an original and disconcerting ad hoc combination of tactical elements matched to the technology of the time and the character of the new republican soldier.

The politics of revolution ensured that systems of command in France differed from those of the ancien régime, with a more 'democratic' command structure in terms of social background, although the election of officers was rapidly abandoned as too extreme. The French benefited from young, energetic and determined commanders, as the Revolution created an officer class dominated by talent and connections, as opposed to birth and connections. The emphasis on republican virtue, seen in 1792–94, was replaced by a stress on professionalism, merit no longer being regarded, as it had been then, as a dangerous sign of individualism.

This emphasis on merit greatly benefited Napoleon personally. Moreover, his chief of staff at Waterloo, Marshal Nicolas Jean-de-Dieu Soult, also had his career made by the Revolution. Born in the same year as Napoleon and enlisting as a private in the Bourbon army in 1785, Soult became a general in 1794. The extent to which both the Revolution and serving under Napoleon made men's careers in the army helped explain the zealous support Napoleon enjoyed in 1815. Conversely, many of his marshals proved willing to serve Louis XVIII in 1814–15, and Louis was accompanied into exile at Ghent by General Auguste-Frédéric Marmont and Marshal Claude Perrin (called Victor), two of Wellington's opponents in the Peninsula.

Initial confusion in military administration after the French Revolutionary War broke out in 1792 was followed by a measure of new organisation, as the Revolutionary government struggled to equip, train, feed and control the new armies. This organisation owed much to Lazare Carnot, head of the military section of the Committee of Public Safety, and, like Napoleon, a product of the reformed royal army of the years prior to the Revolution. Carnot, who was to return to serve Napoleon as minister of the interior during the Hundred Days in 1815, had in 1793–94 improved the equipment, artillery and staff organisation of the armies, ended the election of officers, and melded together veterans and unseasoned recruits. The process of forming the new armies and using them successfully was instrumental in the transition from a royal army to the nation in arms. The way was open for the ruthless boldness Napoleon was to show as he made his reputation in Italy in 1796–97.

2.

NAPOLEON'S GENERALSHIP

NAPOLEON DOMINATED THE MILITARY imagination of the Western world for most of the nineteenth century, and he remains a key figure to this day in military history and works on leadership. This dominance might seem ironic as his career ended in total failure, but Napoleon's generalship was long held up as the pinnacle of military achievement, and not only by the French.

Born on 15 August 1769, Napoleon Bonaparte, or Napoleone di Buonaparte, was a Corsican who, in 1785, became a second lieutenant in the artillery under Louis XVI. Thus he owed his first great break to the fact that Louis XV bought Corsica from the Republic of Genoa in 1768 and that the French army then suppressed a rebellion there. Napoleon's career took off as a result of the French Revolution, which provided many opportunities for talented opportunists like him, not least a major war. Napoleon made his name in 1793 when his successful command of the artillery in the siege of Toulon by the revolutionary forces played a key role in driving British and royalist forces from the crucial Mediterranean port. This episode was his sole clash with the British prior to Waterloo, a situation that was far from unique among senior French commanders but that, nevertheless, contrasted with the careers of many others.

Promoted to Brigadier General in December 1793, Napoleon, like many of the French Revolutionary generals, was young and ambitious. He was made artillery commander for the French army in Italy the following February, but he suffered from the political instability in France, and was briefly imprisoned in 1794. In turn, on 5 October 1795, Napoleon employed artillery firing at point-blank range, the famous 'whiff of grapeshot', to help put down a rising in Paris.

As a reward, Napoleon was appointed by the grateful government, that of the ministers known as the Directory, to the command of the Army of Italy. Here, he developed and demonstrated in 1796 the characteristics of his generalship: self-confidence, swift decision-making, rapid mobility, the concentration of strength at what was made the decisive point, and, where possible, the exploitation of interior lines. Napoleon's tactical grasp and ability to manoeuvre achieved the outcome that French forces on this front had failed to secure since the outset of the war in 1792. He knocked Sardinia (Piedmont) out of the war and brought repeated victory over the Austrians who dominated northern Italy. Napoleon's siting of the artillery was particularly important to his successes in battle.

Victory in northern Italy crucially associated Napoleon with military success and played a central role in the Napoleonic legend – seen, for example, in the paintings, by Jacques-Louis David and others, of Napoleon as a glorious leader. Meanwhile, in 1796, the suppression by his forces of a popular revolt at Pavia in Italy served both as an assurance of his revolutionary vigour and a reminder that this was a conflict of rival cultures as well as politics. The destruc-tion of the revolt entailed summary executions and the burning of villages.

Napoleon's invasion of Egypt in 1798 was less successful, being undercut by the British navy, especially in the shape of Nelson's victory at the Battle of the Nile, which left the French forces blockaded in Egypt. However, on 9 November 1799, having abandoned his army and returned to France, Napoleon was able to seize power from the Directory in a coup, becoming First Consul and General-in-Chief. In 1804, he promoted himself to Emperor. As such, Napoleon was in a position not only to act as an innovative general, but also to control the French military system and direct the war effort. He enjoyed greater power over the army than any French monarch since Louis XIV, who succeeded Louis XIII in 1643 and reigned until 1715. In many respects, Napoleon was even more powerful than Louis. His choice of commanders was not constrained by the social conventions and aristocratic alignments that affected Louis, and both armies and individual military units were under more direct governmental control than had been the case during the Bourbon dynasty.

In addition, Napoleon was directly in command of the leading French force throughout the wars of his reign, which helps explain why he had not engaged with the British, who were only a secondary opponent on land. This was still the case in 1815, when the main meal for Napoleon was clearly going to be with the Austrians and Russians. This command of the leading French army underlined Napoleon's key military role, at once strategic, operational and tactical. Although he had also to manage many campaigns from a distance, they were always those of subsidiary forces, such as the armies deployed against Wellington in Portugal and Spain.

Once firmly in the saddle, Napoleon pushed through an important reordering of the military administration between 1800 and 1802. The conscription system, which had become less effective in the late 1790s, was strengthened, providing Napoleon with a key capability, but one that was not to be available for the Waterloo campaign, due to the lack of a conscript army in France when he returned from Elba and the fact that he did not think he had the time to raise such an army before invading Belgium.

Moreover, in the early 1800s, Napoleon, in a crucial organisational move, developed the corps as a level above that of the division, which could include all the arms (infantry, cavalry and artillery) and be large enough to operate effectively: both corps and divisions were given effective staff structures. Thus the corps added, to the flexibility of the earlier divisional system, the strength necessary both for the grinding, if not attritional, battles of the period, where opposing forces would not collapse rapidly as a result of well-planned battlefield moves, and also for Napoleon's campaigns of strategically applied force.[1]

Corps operated effectively, both as individual units, as against the Prussians at the battle of Auerstädt (1806), and in concert, and they helped make what is now referred to as operational warfare more feasible. In the Waterloo campaign, the corps were key units, although they were subordinated to army commands under Marshals Michel Ney and Emmanuel de Grouchy, each of which, however, lacked the necessary staff support and, indeed, cohesion to ensure a high level of effectiveness. At Waterloo, Napoleon deployed the First (d'Erlon), Second (General Honoré-Charles Reille) and Sixth (General Georges Mouton, Count de Lobau) Corps, with the Imperial Guard also being corps strength. The reserve corps was divided into two. Two corps, the Third (General Dominique Vandamme) and Fourth (General Maurice-Étienne Gérard), were under Grouchy at Wavre.

It is important not to idealise organisational units and developments, as there was considerable variety in practice, but the corps system nevertheless enhanced military strength, not least by enabling the different arms to be used more effectively. In the 1790s, the French division had been a force of all arms – for example, two brigades of infantry, one of cavalry and a battery of guns. This force structure, however, meant that the artillery and cavalry were split up into 'penny packets' and deprived of much of their striking power. Under the corps system, by contrast, both cavalry and infantry tended to be controlled at a higher level and even grouped into separate formations, for example artillery reserve and cavalry corps, as at Waterloo, providing an important force multiplier. This separation and concentration also, however, created fresh issues for generalship, as at Waterloo, where the French use of both, especially the cavalry, can be criticised, notably for undermining the possibility for combined-arms attacks.

Skilled staff-work was important to Napoleon, as it resulted in the movement by different routes of several individual corps that were still able to support each other. His chief of staff, Louis-Alexandre Berthier, was a crucial figure. Napoleon thus had a better command structure than his opponents, a contrast that helped him to victory over the Austrians in 1805, although his centralised direction of campaigns became a problem when he limited the autonomy of his commanders in the distant Peninsular War with the British in Portugal and Spain from 1808 to 1814. Equally, the Waterloo campaign indicated that the autonomy of detached forces – Michel Ney at Quatre Bras and Emmanuel de Grouchy at Wavre – was a cause of failure, or, at least, contributed to failure. Yet, conversely, it had also proved difficult for Napoleon in his later years to control the large armies that were under his direct command. Moreover, Berthier did not support him in 1815. Instead, having escorted Louis XVIII to Ghent, he went to Bavaria, where, on 1 June, he fell to his death from a window in Bamberg, a victim of either murder or suicide.

Earlier, the French organisational and command structures were vital to Napoleon's characteristic rapidity of operational and tactical movement, while his troops also travelled more lightly than those of Frederick the Great had done. But by 1815, staff-work proved inadequate to the situation Napoleon confronted, which was ironic as Wellington also complained about his staff. The staff needs of the two, however, were different. In part, this reflected the degree to which Napoleon was on the attack, tactically, operationally and strategically. On the Allied side, the prime problem was not poor staff-work but, rather, the absence of a united Allied staff to facilitate better coordination between Blücher and Wellington.

Putting aside the almost mystical readings of his generalship, such as those advanced by many French writers later in the nineteenth century, Napoleon was good at working within the constraints of the weapons and forces available. He also proved adept at relaxing these constraints, not least by taking pains to understand the theorists of the previous generation, by developing appropriate tactics to maximise potential (especially the firepower of massed artillery), by making a major effort to train his troops, and by developing a staff able to increase operational potential.

In his wars, Napoleon concentrated his resources and attention on a single front, seeking in each conflict to identify the crucial opposing force and to destroy it rapidly. This, not the occupation of territory, was his goal. Thus, in 1815, Napoleon primarily wanted to defeat Blücher and Wellington, rather than to capture Brussels.

For temperamental reasons, and because he pursued glory and rapid and decisive results, Napoleon sought battle and the destruction of the opposing army. He attacked both in campaigning and in battle. On 18 June 1815, the key battle for Napoleon was the attacking battle against Wellington and not the defensive battle forced upon him by the Prussian.

Although he fought for much of his reign, Napoleon's individual wars with Continental opponents were fairly brief. Warfare (incorporating diplomacy, preparation and the campaign) might be a long-term process for Napoleon, but war became an event. Thus, for example, wars with Austria in 1805 and 1809 each ended (victoriously) in the year it began, while the war with Prussia that began in 1806 ended in 1807. Such rapid results were the product of sequential conflict with opponents, as well, operationally, as of a concentration of military resources on a single front, a drive for rapid victory in battle, and a speedy follow-through resulting in a quick peace. The Russians, however, proved a more intractable opponent than either Prussia or Austria. The peace with Russia in 1807 that ended the war started in 1805 reflected, in part, the exhaustion of both sides.

Napoleon exploited the mobility of his forces to tactical, operational and strategic effect. On campaign, Napoleon sought a central position in order to divide more numerous opposing forces and then defeat them separately. This was his goal in 1815. Envelopment was used against weaker forces: They were pinned down by an attack mounted by a section of the French army, while most of the army enveloped them, attacking them in flank or, in preference, cutting their lines of supply and retreat, the manoeuvre sur les derrières. Napoleon apparently thought of employing this manoeuvre against Blücher at Ligny, on 16 June 1815, had Ney sent troops against the Prussians' right flank, and, eventually, against Wellington, had he not retreated from Quatre Bras on 17 June. This manoeuvre put opponents in a disadvantageous position if they wished to fight on rather than withdraw. A similar technique was to be employed by the Prussians under Helmuth von Moltke the Elder against the Austrians in 1866 and the French in 1870, on both occasions with considerable success. There was no French attempt at envelopment, however, at Waterloo. Indeed, insofar as envelopment was a prospect that day, it was envelopment of the French once the Prussians appeared on their right flank.

Napoleon was a strong believer in the value of artillery, organised into strong batteries, particularly of twelve-pounders, the production of which was pressed forward in 1805. This effort was in pursuit of the advice of a committee under General Marmont, which in 1802 recommended, as part of the system of Year IX, the replacement of eight-pounders by the heavier twelve-pounders. Napoleon increased the number of field guns and the ratio of guns to infantry.

Napoleon used his cannon as an offensive force. To do so, he made them as mobile on the battlefield as possible, by the utilisation of effective horse-drawn limbers. Napoleon's experience of the devastating massed fire of the more heavily gunned Russians at the battle of Eylau in 1807 led him to press forward his own massing of artillery, greatly increasing the number of cannon in his massed batteries. Against the Austrians at the battle of Wagram two years later, he covered the reorganisation of his attack with a battery of 112 guns, while against the Russians at Borodino in 1812 about 200 cannon were massed, and at Lützen in 1813 the artillery played a major role in weakening the Prussian centre. Napoleon also increased the amount of shot available per cannon in order to make continuous fire possible.

These developments explain the threat posed by the French cannon at Waterloo, where Napoleon had 246 cannon to the British 157, and also look toward the heavy use of artillery in subsequent Western warfare. Had Wellington not been able to deploy his troops on reverse slopes to shield them from direct French fire, the impact of Napoleon's numerous cannon at Waterloo would have been devastating.

Napoleon also massed his cavalry for use at the vital moment, and launched large-scale charges when he saw such a moment, as with Marshal Joachim Murat's charge through the Russian centre at Eylau in 1807. At Waterloo, this attempted use of the cavalry failed, and this failure can be argued to demonstrate the inability of cavalry to charge determined and well-deployed infantry whose formation was unbroken. Already, at Leipzig, on 16 October 1813, the main day of that lengthy battle, Murat had led a mass French cavalry attack of 10,000 men in an attempt to break through the Austrians under Charles Philip, Prince Schwarzenberg, but he was stopped by the opposing reserves. At Waterloo, the French cavalry, however, made still less of an impact, in large part due to the strength of the British defence, but also because there were serious flaws in the French attack, not least the need to move uphill, and the cavalry was unable to charge. In contrast, at Garcia Hernandez in 1812, the Dragoons of the King's German Legion (KGL), exiled Hanoverians in the service of George III of Britain, broke a French square, while at the battle of Aliwal in 1846, the British Sixteenth Lancers charged through a Sikh square and broke it.[2]

In many respects, Napoleon represented the culmination of the military innovations of the French Revolution. He developed the innovations and practices of the 1790s and systematised them. Crucially, however, he was more successful than his predecessors. As a commander, Napoleon was similar to the British admiral Horatio Nelson. Both were dominated by the desire to engage and win, although they could make serious operational blunders, as Nelson did in 1798, when he missed Napoleon en route to Egypt, and in 1805, when he fruitlessly chased the French admiral Pierre-Charles Villeneuve to the West Indies, and as Napoleon did in the Waterloo campaign.[3]

By forcing a battle whose shape was unclear, both Napoleon and Nelson relied greatly on the subsequent mêlée, which rewarded the fighting qualities of individual units, the initiative and skill of subordinates, and, in Napoleon's case, command skills in the shape of the ability to retain reserves until the crucial moment. Both men deserve high praise for having prepared the effective military machines that their victories revealed, but Napoleon's system was to fail at Waterloo. In part this was due to the degeneration of French tactics in the latter period of Napoleon's reign. This decline owed something to the insufficient attention he devoted to tactics and the impact of heavy casualties in 1807, 1809 and 1812, which necessitated a consequent reliance on new conscripts. However, the quality of the opposition was also very important. Partly as a result of this quality, Napoleon lost control of the course of the battle at Waterloo, both insofar as the struggle with Wellington was concerned and with reference to the Prussian advance.

More generally, throughout his career, Napoleon confronted grave problems, not least the number and fighting quality of his opponents and the difficulty of establishing their positions, let alone intentions, the primitive communications of the period, and the need to raise the operational effectiveness of his conscripts. He deserves credit for developing an effective army, but he was unable to match his political goals to the reality of a complex international system with which he needed to compromise.

When he seized power in 1799, Revolutionary France was already at war and under considerable pressure from the Second Coalition and, crucially, the combination of Austria, Britain and Russia. Boldly advancing into Italy across the Great St. Bernard Pass, so that he arrived in the Austrian rear, Napoleon regained the initiative, winning a hard-fought battle at Marengo on 14 June 1800. This was a battle, like many, in which a capacity to respond to the unexpected and to fight through was crucial. The Austrians proved a formidable rival in that battle, and Napoleon's enforced retreat for much of the battle was only reversed because of a successful counterattack mounted by French reinforcements. As at Quatre Bras and Waterloo, reinforcements, as much as reserves, were a key component of victory. The fighting quality of the experienced French forces proved important at Marengo, not least the ability to keep going in adverse circumstances. Rather than seeing this in terms of any particular characteristics of the French army, it is worth noting that the same was true, for example, of Wellington's victories over the Marathas in India in 1803 and at Waterloo.

Thanks in part to the favourable spin he gave to his eventually successful generalship at Marengo, Napoleon's grasp of power was cemented. At Hohenlinden on 3 December 1800, flexibility in defence helped General Jean Moreau defeat the Austrians, but no other major victory was to be credited to any general bar Napoleon, who was a great manipulator of information to the service of his reputation. French successes led to the dissolution of the Second Coalition, with Russia coming to terms in 1800, Austria in 1801 and Britain in 1802. Prussia had already left the struggle in 1795. Napoleon was left dominant in Western Europe, but his determination to gain advantages from the peace, his clear preparations for fresh conflict, and his inability to pursue measures likely to encourage confidence led to a resumption of conflict with Britain in 1803.

In turn, British efforts, not least the payment of the subsidies made possible by the British system of public finance and by British dominance of oceanic trade, led to the creation of the Third Coalition. This coalition was a formidable combination, in some respects prefiguring the Seventh Coalition created against Napoleon in 1815, but the 1805 coalition suffered from a lack of organisational cohesion or unity, in marked contrast to the situation in 1815. In secure control of France and the Low Countries in 1805, unlike 1815, and with a well-prepared army, it proved easier for Napoleon to respond rapidly to circumstances.

He did so by advancing east, outmanoeuvring and forcing the surrender of an Austrian army at Ulm, before destroying an Austro-Russian army at Austerlitz. Napoleon proved a master not only of gaining the initiative through rapid campaigning, but also of moving large forces on the battlefield. At Austerlitz on 2 December 1805, Napoleon benefited from the overconfidence of Tsar Alexander I, the nominal commander of the Austro-Russian forces. A strong Russian attack on Napoleon's right was held in marshy terrain by French infantry, and the French then turned the weak flank of this attacking force to crush the Russians. Marshal Nicolas Soult led the decisive assault, taking a battlefield role he was not to have an opportunity to adopt at Waterloo.

As a comparison with Waterloo, which was more of a battering battle and one where Wellington did not provide Napoleon with a comparable opportunity to inflict casualties, the French had 8,000 men killed or wounded at Austerlitz, the Austrians and Russians 16,000, and about 11,000 Austrians and Russians were taken prisoner. Casualty figures at Waterloo are controversial, but the French suffered about 31,000 killed or wounded, and several thousand more prisoners; the Prussians 7,000, about 14 per cent of its strength; and Wellington's army 16,200, about 23 per cent of its strength. As with Waterloo, a major victory became decisive due to the political outcome: Austria accepted a harsh peace after Austerlitz.

In 1806, Frederick William III of Prussia joined Russia, which, unlike Austria, fought on, but Napoleon, in a far stronger situation than in 1815, was able to attack before Russian reinforcements could arrive. At the battles of Jena and Auerstädt on 14 October 1806, the poorly commanded Prussian forces were defeated. Napoleon crushed what he thought was the main Prussian army at Jena, with French massed artillery and substantial numbers of skir-mishers inflicting heavy losses, as they were not able to do at Water-loo; while, at Auerstädt, Marshal Louis-Nicolas Davout, with the help of 27,000 men of III Corps, held off and finally defeated the main Prussian army of at least 50,000 men.[4] Davout was not to have an opportunity to take such a battlefield role during the Waterloo campaign.

Napoleon's successes in 1805–06 were very different from those of the French Revolutionary forces. There was no equivalent in the 1790s to Napoleon's successful advance into central Europe, nor to the defeat, in 1805–07, of the main Prussian and Russian armies. At the same time, this success provided no indication of what could have been achieved in 1815, as Napoleon was in a far stronger posi-tion in 1805–07. In particular, the Prussians then suffered from deficient training and organisation, poor command, lack of recent war experience and difficult strategic circumstances.[5] By 1815, they were in a much better shape.

In 1807, moreover, the Russians were engaged at Eylau in East Prussia on 8 February, in a battle that very much revealed the degree to which French success was dependent on opposing weak-nesses. Russian attacks pressed the French hard, and repeated French attacks failed to break the Russians, who withdrew during the night. French casualties were heavy (greater than at Austerlitz, Jena and Auerstädt combined), and although Napoleon had gained possession of the battlefield and Russian losses were heavier, he had won neither tactically nor operationally. However, at nearby Friedland on 14 June, the Russians attacked with an inferior force and with their back to a river and lost heavily.

These casualties left the Russians so battered that they needed time to recuperate and to rebuild their army. On 7 July, the Treaty of Tilsit ended hostilities between France and Russia on French terms. Signed two days later, the second Treaty of Tilsit inflicted major territorial losses on Prussia, and it was followed, in 1808, by the Treaty of Paris, which restricted the size of the Prussian army and specified a heavy indemnity. The humiliation involved, as well as the hardships inflicted by occupying French troops, helped explain Prussian anger toward France in 1815, an anger seen in the killing during the pursuit after Waterloo and in the subsequent devastation of France.

In November 1807, the French successfully invaded Portugal, but Napoleon's attempt to seize Spain in 1808 led to a popular uprising there, in marked contrast to the situation in France after Waterloo. In response, Napoleon advanced into Spain, defeating the poorly trained, commanded and outnumbered Spanish forces at Espinosa, Gamonal and Tudela, and entered Madrid. His victories led to the fall of a major city, a pattern Napoleon planned to repeat in 1815. However, his operational triumph in 1808 did not lead to strategic success. Resistance, encouraged by French exactions, continued, and Britain sent forces, helping make the Peninsular War in Portugal and Spain (1808–14) a long-term drain on the French army.

Napoleon had been left dominant in Central Europe by Tilsit, and this dominance was confirmed when Austria was defeated afresh in 1809, with Prussia and Russia looking on. An Austrian invasion of France's major German ally, Bavaria, an ally Napoleon was no longer to have in 1815, was beaten back when Napoleon responded by seizing the initiative and then invading Austria. Napoleon's first major battle there in this war, Aspern-Essling (21–22 May), prefigured Waterloo in some respects. He launched an inadequately reconnoitered, poorly thought out, and overbold attack on a superior Austrian force. The attack was repelled and followed by an assault by larger Austrian forces on the French, who were isolated on the north bank of the Danube with the main bridge to their rear smashed. In the event, the French army was not destroyed, but Napoleon had to abandon the battlefield.

He counterattacked at Wagram on 5–6 July 1809, but despite the fact that he drove the Austrian commander, Archduke Charles, from the field, the Austrian army was not routed. At Wagram, the French flank offensive, a dimension missing at Waterloo, was successful, while the Austrian one was not, and both sides used artillery to great effect. Yet Napoleon focused on a frontal attack on the Austrian centre, in which, as at Waterloo, he did not display any particular skill. Austrian effectiveness in these battles has been seen as a stage in the emergence of modern war, a view that places too great a weight on one campaign, but this effectiveness reflects the extent to which Napoleon was facing more impressive opponents. Support for war then ebbed in Austria, and in October 1809 the Austrians accepted harsh terms in the Treaty of Schönbrunn.

The weaknesses of Napoleon's empire, both politically and militarily, were already apparent. The rising in Spain in 1808 against French control indicated that the policies and politics on offer from Napoleon were scarcely going to assuage opposition. Instead, Napoleon was widely seen as an unwelcome imperialist, and this view prefigured the extent to which the new empires created in the nineteenth century found it difficult to win a lasting foundation of support, with the exception of those, such as the United States in the American West, Britain in Australasia and Canada, and Argentina in the Pampas, able to rely on a marked demographic advantage over their opponents.

The British empire was very different from that of Napoleon. Napoleon's empire was landward and focused on himself, while he gave kingdoms and principalities to his relatives, for example Spain to his brother Joseph in 1808, which was scarcely empire on the British pattern. Napoleon's empire was also dedicated to war, while the relationship between war and the British empire was more complex. The British expanded through war, but they lacked conscription and the accompanying military ethos and did not want the expenditure of sustained conflict. The absence of conscription limited the numbers of British troops available at Waterloo.

Unlike Britain, Napoleon was totally unable to command success at sea, and the impact of the navies under his control proved far less than the sum of their parts. Although he made major efforts to rebuild his navy after defeat at Trafalgar in 1805, he was short of sailors, and his navy crucially lacked the experience that was so important to British success. On land, moreover, battles such as Marengo in 1800 had indicated that French victories could be very hard won, and Napoleon encountered severe difficulties, fighting the Russians at Eylau and Friedland in 1807 and the Austrians at Aspern-Essling in 1809. The extent to which his opponents were able to copy successfully such French organisational innovations as the corps system is controversial, but it is clear that their fighting quality was such that French relative advantages were limited.

Strategy is usually discussed in military terms, but that is simply to operationalise what in fact is a set of political suppositions and drives. It is these aspects of Napoleon's strategy, not his ability to win battles, that explain the key element of 1815, the determination of the other European powers to put aside their differences and to unite in a coalition pledged to fight until Napoleon was removed. This determination was the central strategic factor of 1815, and, paradoxically, it was Napoleon's major contribution to the strategy of that year, rather than the shifts and expedients by which he sought to thwart the Seventh Coalition. In part, this unity reflected the circumstances of 1815, but it was largely a product of the repeated bullying with which Napoleon had treated other rulers in the 1800s and early 1810s and his willingness to tear up peace agreements that he himself had dictated. All the major rulers of 1815 had suffered personally at Napoleon's hands, while the British government felt, with considerable justice, that the emperor's policies and attitudes were responsible both for the failure of peace between the two powers in 1802–03, the resumption of war in 1803, and for the breakdown of British peace feelers in 1806.

The policies of 1815 were to be a comment on Napoleon's earlier

policies. Whereas, in 1793–95, Russia and, finally, Prussia had preferred to concentrate on destroying Poland, rather than on fighting
or persisting in resisting the French Revolution, in 1815 these two
powers compromised over Saxony. For Napoleon and his supporters
in France, the international situation in 1815 was a baleful consequence of his earlier quest for glory and his destructiveness toward
others. Napoleon's attempt in 1815 to overturn this, through ability, will, risk, and the manipulation of events, ran up against not
only the superior resources of his opponents but also the weight of
recent history.

3.

THE BRITISH ARMY

'BY GOD! I DON'T think it would have done if I had not been there.' Wellington's comment to the diarist Thomas Creevey on 19 June captured an important truth about the battle, the last major one in Europe to be personally directed by one of the commanders from frontline positions, but victory at Waterloo was a product not only of Wellington's generalship but also of the improvement of the British army over the previous decade and a half.[1] In contrast, the situation for this army when Napoleon came to power in 1799 was dire. Defeated on land in the War of American Independence, the British army had not fared particularly well against Revolutionary France. Indeed, in 1793–95, the army had failed to hold the Low Countries, putting in a very different performance from what it was to achieve in 1815.

When the British troops arrived in Belgium in 1793, the war had been going on for a year. The French were fighting alone against a coalition that included Austria, Prussia and the Dutch. With German auxiliaries, 17,000 of whom were hired in 1793, playing a major role, the British army in the Low Countries rose to 37,500 troops by late 1794. This army was commanded by George III's second son, Frederick, Duke of York, who would have been available to command at Waterloo (his first cousin, Charles William

Ferdinand, the Duke of Brunswick, died at Quatre Bras) had he not made such a hash of previous commands in the field.

The 1793 campaign is instructive for the light it throws on Waterloo. First and foremost, the value to Wellington of Prussian support in 1815 is readily apparent, because York found himself confronting the problems of cooperating with allied forces operating with a very different agenda. He also suffered in 1793 from the problems of launching an offensive in the face of an undefeated French army, a task that Wellington was spared by Napoleon's decision to attack. York, assisted by Hanoverian and Dutch forces, was ordered to besiege the fortified port of Dunkirk, a potent symbol of Anglo-French hostility. This decision was a mistake as, by abandoning the possibility of an Allied concentration of strength and, instead, dividing from the Austrians in order to mount a siege, the British became a more tempting target for French attack. The focus on Dunkirk looked toward British concern in 1815 about the security of Ostend and the communication and supply routes to Britain. The siege of Dunkirk, however, was delayed by a lack of siege artillery, a problem that had also affected British operations in Belgium in 1744, and on 6 September, a relieving French army pushed back the less numerous British at Hondschoote.

In 1794, the strength of British and Austrian forces in attack was indicated in engagements at Villers-en-Cauchies and Beaumont. In the latter, cavalry attacks on the French flanks defeated advancing columns and inflicted heavy casualties. British success culminated at Willems on 10 May: The French cavalry was swept aside and their infantry broken. Repeated cavalry attacks supported by infantry and cannon broke a French square. However, on 17–18 May 1794, in a battle at Tourcoing near Tournai, a major clash, the French under General Jean-Charles Pichegru used their local numerical superiority to defeat British and Austrian forces, driving them from the field. In contrast to Waterloo, York's army was given inadequate support by its ally, and the British were forced to stage a fighting retreat.

In an anticipation of a might-have-been arising from a different result at Waterloo, York thereafter retreated, pushed back by stronger

French forces. He abandoned Belgium and fell back through the Netherlands during a hard winter. The French were able to benefit from their opponents' retreat by driving them in different directions, the Austrians east and the British north, thus prefiguring what they hoped to do to the British and Prussians in 1815. The British fought well when they engaged in 1794–95, but they were outnumbered and had lost the initiative. Their medical, transport and supply systems proved inadequate, and in April 1795 the remaining British troops were evacuated from Bremen in Germany.

Thereafter, there was a series of unsuccessful British expeditions to the European continent, including one under York to Holland in 1799, which is commemorated in a nursery rhyme about the 'Grand Old Duke of York' marching his men up and down hills. In this expedition, an Anglo-Russian army invaded in August, but was defeated at Bergen and Castricum and obliged to retreat. More generally, the campaigns of the 1790s revealed serious deficiencies in the British army. Commanding the Thirty-third Regiment, Lieutenant-Colonel Arthur Wellesley, the future Duke of Wellington, learned in the Low Countries 'what one ought not to do'. The low level of peacetime capability had been manifested in an absence of large-scale manoeuvres and of adequate training, which caused problems when Britain went to war in 1793, as, more generally, did the need to increase greatly and rapidly the size of the army. Similar problems were to be encountered in the two world wars.

The tactical system adopted by the British in 1792 drew on that of Prussia. It was based on Colonel David Dundas's *Principles of Military Movements, chiefly applied to infantry. Illustrated by manoeuvres of the Prussian troops, and by an outline of the British campaigns in Germany* (1788), in short, on the experience of Continental warfare. This tactical system represented a deliberate rejection of the more flexible tactics of the American War of Independence, and, indeed, Dundas, who was to succeed York as commander-in-chief in 1809–11, belonged to what was termed the 'German' rather than the 'American' school of officership. Dundas placed the organised firepower of the close-order line at the centre of military practice, claiming that such a line could resist cavalry in open country. He was much less concerned with light infantry.

Dundas succeeded York as commander-in-chief when the latter was forced to resign in 1809 after a former mistress, Mary Anne Clarke, falsely accused him of selling promotions. As commander-in-chief from 1795, York had proved a more effective administrator than he was a field commander. He faced a formidable challenge. Britain was up against a strong opponent, and it was necessary both to manage the major expansion in army strength that had begun in 1793 and to cope with the consequences of defeat. In reviving the army, York took particular care to improve the quality of the officers. He could not abolish the practice of purchasing commissions, but he made this practice less deleterious by raising the number of free commissions and by establishing minimum periods of military service as a condition for promotion. The appointment of a military secretary to the commander-in-chief was designed to encourage bureaucratic procedures, especially with regard to appointments and promotions. However, York was unsuccessful in ending absenteeism among officers.

York also encouraged schemes for military education, especially those of Lieutenant-Colonel John Le Marchant for military colleges that would both train cadets and staff officers. The former was opened in 1802 at Marlow and developed into the Royal Military College at Sandhurst; and the second, which opened in 1799 at High Wycombe, developed into the Army Staff College. York was also a supporter of the standardisation of drill. Consistency was a standard theme in his policies, and this emphasis on consistency helped to turn a collection of regiments into an army, a development from which Wellington was to benefit greatly at Waterloo insofar as his British units were concerned. Consistency aided the transfer of troops and equipment between units and improved tactical and operational flexibility. But there was little improvement in some areas of training, such as bayonet training, where a system for the whole army was not introduced until 1857. York also addressed the conditions of the ordinary soldiers, including food, accommodation, medical care and punishment regimes, while the soldiers were provided with greatcoats to keep out the cold.

York returned to his position as commander-in-chief in 1811, but he did not seek operational command. This decision was important to the Waterloo campaign. Unlike the Dutch, who expected William, Prince of Orange, the heir to the throne, to play the key role at Waterloo, both the British and the Prussians relied on meritocratic choices for command. Although he did not take a battlefield role in Waterloo, York deserves some of the praise for the state and success of the British army there, and is appropriately celebrated with a statue in Waterloo Place in London. Earlier, in July 1815, he received the thanks of Parliament for his care of the army.

The British army had already been extensively tested during the Peninsular War, a baptism of fire that led to significant improvements. In November 1807, the French successfully invaded Portugal, a major trading partner of Britain. However, Napoleon's attempt to place his brother Joseph on the throne of Spain in 1808 led to a popular uprising that was exploited by Britain with an expedition of 11,000 troops under Lieutenant-General Sir Arthur Wellesley (the future Duke of Wellington). It landed in Portugal at Mondego Bay on 1–5 August 1808.

Born in 1769, the same year as Napoleon, the thirty-nine-year-old Wellesley was the fourth son of the Anglo-Irish Earl of Mornington. Wellesley had entered the army in 1787, and in 1793 he purchased a commission as major and was promptly promoted to lieutenant-colonel. He first saw action in 1794 in the defence of the Netherlands against the French advance and took part in the subsequent winter retreat. Wellesley's rapid rise to positions of command accustomed him to taking responsibility and making decisions.

In October 1795, Wellesley's regiment embarked for the West Indies, only to be driven back by storms. Instead, his regiment went to India, arriving in Calcutta in February 1797, and his reputation was made there. Wellesley took part in the Mysore campaign of 1799 in southern India, and fought the Marathas in 1803–04 in western India, winning the very hard-fought battles of Assaye and Argaum in 1803, each of which was more difficult in some respects than Waterloo. He returned to Britain in 1805. Having taken part in the Danish expedition of 1807, where he successfully forced the

Danes to hand over their fleet, Wellesley was promoted to lieutenant-general in 1808. An MP from 1806, the well-connected Wellesley was appointed chief secretary in Ireland in 1807. The following June, he expressed his confidence about taking on the French, 'first, because I am not afraid of them, as everyone else seems to be; and, secondly, because (if all I hear about their system is true) I think it a false one against steady troops. I suspect all the Continental armies are half-beaten before the battle begins. I at least will not be frightened beforehand.'[2]

Wellesley's battles with the French in the Peninsular War help explain much about his conduct at Waterloo. At Vimeiro on 21 August 1808, the superior firepower of his army and his flexible generalship defeated attacking French forces under General Jean-Andoche Junot, the newly appointed French governor-general of Portugal. As at Waterloo, Wellesley sheltered his lines of infantry from the French cannon by deploying them behind the crest of a ridge. He placed his riflemen in open order down the slope and used them to prevent the French skirmishers, who advanced before the columns, from disrupting the British lines. The advancing French columns were halted by British infantry and cannon fire before being driven back by downhill charges. The French attacks were poorly coordinated and, having beaten them, Wellesley was on the point of ordering a general attack when he was overruled by a more senior general.

On 27 and 28 July 1809, the French under Marshal Victor attacked the Anglo-Spanish army at Talavera, concentrating their attack on the outnumbered British. Wellesley again employed his infantry firepower to repulse the French columns, but the pursuit of the retreating French threw the British into confusion and fresh French units drove them back. The final French attack on the centre of the Allied line was only just held, with Wellesley committing his reserve, the key element in so many battles of the period, but held it was, although the British suffered 5,400 casualties, more than a quarter of the force.

However, as a reminder of the operational context of tactical achievement, Wellesley subsequently had to retreat in the face of fresh, larger French forces under Marshal Soult, who advanced on his lines of communication. Napoleon's strategy in 1815 did not lead him to seek to do the same: He wanted to do battle, not to out-manoeuvre Wellington into retreating. Yet Wellington's concern about such a move led him to deploy a large force to prevent such an advance past his right flank at Waterloo.

On 27 September 1810, at Bussaco, Wellesley, by now Viscount Wellington, resisted the advancing French under Marshal André Masséna in a good defensive position. The French found the British drawn up on a ridge, from where they repulsed the poorly planned attacks and inflicted nearly 5,000 casualties. On 22 July 1812, Marshal Auguste Marmont was defeated at Salamanca. Noting that the French were overextended, Wellington rapidly and effectively switched from defence to attack and ably combined his infantry and cavalry in the destruction of three French divisions, one of which was ridden down by the cavalry. The following year, at Vitoria (21 June), Wellington again took the offensive, inflicting a serious defeat on the French, for which he was rewarded by being made a field marshal. Beethoven composed 'Wellington's Victory' as a celebration.

The disciplined firepower of the British infantry played a major part in Wellington's victories, although this firepower was not nec-essarily immobile, but, rather, often used as a prelude to a bayonet charge. In doing so, Wellington ably executed fire and movement tactics, achieving a success the French were not to match at Water-loo. The British succeeded in the Peninsula in balancing the well-drilled line, a legacy of Frederick the Great, the extensive use of light infantry in battle, and the conservatism of an emphasis on lin-ear firepower formations with a greater role for manoeuvrability.

In the Peninsula, Wellington was always heavily outnumbered by the French in both cavalry and artillery, but his troops were among the best in the British army, a contrast to the situation among his opponents, and a margin of advantage that did not per-tain at Waterloo. Wellington was also, as he was again to display at Waterloo, a fine judge of terrain. Moreover, he was adept at control-ling a battle as it developed. At Vimeiro, the well-positioned

British line succeeded in blunting the attacking French columns, while at Salamanca, Wellington used his lines in attack with great effect. There was not to be an opportunity for such action at Waterloo until the closing stage of the battle.

In the Peninsula, again reflecting a deterioration that was to be seen at Waterloo, the French employed inadequate battlefield tactics. In place of l'ordre mixte, the interplay of lines, columns and skirmishers that had proved so effective in the 1790s, especially in weakening lines of opposing infantry, they relied on crude attacks in dense columns. Thus the firepower of the British lines was not compromised, and the French themselves provided an easy target for the British.

The decline in the quality of the French army, due to nearly continous campaigning, affected its tactical sophistication, not to mention its morale. Success in battle had greatly turned on the exploitation of the synergy that had been created among the cavalry, close-order infantry, artillery and skirmishers. A combination of attacks by different arms reduced both the enemy's physical means to resist – by silencing his guns with counterbattery or skirmisher fire, by neutralising his command and control by picking off officers, or by using cavalry, especially to force infantry from lines into defensive squares, thereby cutting their frontage and, thus, firepower – and chipped away at his will to resist. In Spain, however, the French experienced great difficulty in trying to achieve this synergy and execute these tactics. Problems with the terrain frequently precluded the efficacious use of their often superior cavalry and artillery. Partly as a result, attacks were often executed sequentially, rather than simultaneously, and by one arm, usually the infantry. Much the same happened at Waterloo, although with fewer excuses for Napoleon.

Any French failure to weaken the British lines, by the use of artillery or skirmishers, before the column attack, was especially serious. This failure owed much to Wellington's reverse-slope ploy, his policy of locating his troops behind the crests of hills in order to protect them from artillery, which was important, for example at Bussaco and Waterloo. Because of this British deployment and, more generally, the breakdown of their 'system' in engagements with British troops, French infantry columns were too often left exposed to fire from intact, unshaken lines, with neither the time nor the space to redeploy, a situation that recurred at Waterloo. The French therefore either had to run for it or to try to bludgeon their way through. The latter, however, was often more than flesh and blood could achieve. A bayonet charge against an adversary who stayed ordered and calm, pulling the trigger and throwing up a hail of lead, was generally ineffective, and the French were in a difficult position because this was frequently the situation they faced. Repeatedly, the French advanced and, having taken casualties, retreated, while the British stood firm.

The Brown Bess, the British flintlock musket, had many deficiencies. These included its stiff trigger, powerful recoil, poor performance if the powder became damp, and the large bore that ensured a loose fit for the musket ball and thus decreased its accuracy. Nevertheless, British firepower was more effective than that of the French. Tests carried out by the Prussian general Gerhard von Scharnhorst in 1813 suggested that, whereas French and Prussian flintlocks were more effective at 100 yards, their British counterparts were better at a greater distance and, therefore, more appropriate for engaging French columns from a distance. Furthermore, the large bore of the Brown Bess meant that it could take all calibers of musket ammunition, while the loose fit of the ball helped make ramming it down the barrel easy and thus contributed to the rate of fire. However, the loose ball meant that accuracy was lost with distance. In addition, despite some suggestions of a rate of fire of up to five times a minute in the hands of a trained soldier, the real rate may have been closer to twice a minute.

Aside from organising effective defensive firepower, Wellington was also very active in counterattacks; and the well-timed bayonet charge, launched when the French were disorganised by their approach march and by British fire, was as effective a tactic as the volley. Medical records of casualties and other sources suggest that the bayonet was essentially a psychological weapon in most Napoleonic engagements, as it had also been under the ancien régime. Firepower caused more casualties and was therefore crucial to the outcome of the battle. Troops tended not to cross bayonets, but the bayonet charge permitted exploitation of the advantage. Such a charge, preceded by a volley, had become a standard British tactic from the late 1750s and was used with effect in the War of American Independence.

With his fine grasp of timing and eye for terrain, Wellington brought the system to a pitch of effectiveness at Waterloo. Yet he complained that because he lacked his Peninsular War army at Waterloo (the regiments had been dispatched to fight in the War of 1812), the battle proved much more difficult than his successes in the Peninsula. Not only had many of the British units at Waterloo not served under him, but, more particularly, many of the British units there had had no experience of battle. This was true, for example, of most of the engineers. To a certain extent, the situation repeated that in the American War of Independence, in which the British suffered from the heavy losses that their army had taken from tropical diseases, especially yellow fever, while capturing Havana from Spain in 1762. As a result, there was a greater reliance in 1775–76 on troops that had not hitherto experienced battle.

In practice, neither the British nor the French were at peak form in 1815, as the French army had suffered greatly from the unsuccessful invasion of Russia in 1812, in troop losses and, even more, in the loss of cavalry horses. Nevertheless, Napoleon had more of his veterans present at Waterloo than Wellington. Such deficiencies put a premium on command skills and, in particular, on making the best use of what was available. Although Wellington failed operationally, on 15–16 June 1815, because he did not understand sufficiently clearly what the French, who had the initiative, were trying to do, the duke proved especially good at making the best use of what he had on the day of Waterloo, both in making his dispositions and in responding to French attacks.

In particular, Wellington was energetic in confronting logistical issues and good at the problems of managing alliance forces, tasks he had had to learn in India, where the British relied on sepoys, native troops in their employ, as well as on native allies, and, even more, the Peninsula, where he had to deal both with the Portuguese and with the various Spanish elements.[3] Alliance dynamics were a key element of the British military effort in 1815, and, had he failed in these, Wellington's skill as a commander of British units would have been of far more limited value, not least as the British alone would have been heavily outnumbered by the French.

In this skill at alliance management, Wellington matched the ability of John Churchill, first Duke of Marlborough, as British commander in the Low Countries from 1702 to 1710. That both men campaigned there underlined the need for consistent qualities if Britain was to be successful. As with Marlborough, Wellington had to be able to manage both the Dutch and those German forces that were either part of his army or fighting alongside it. The Prussians fought alongside the British in both wars.

When, conversely, during the Seven Years' War (1756–63), the British were not allied with the Dutch or the Austrians (then the rulers of Belgium), they had not been able to operate in the Low Countries. Instead, allied with Prussia and Hesse-Cassel, and able to rely on the king's Hanoverian dominions, the British forces had operated farther east, in Germany between the rivers Rhine and Elbe. Their supply routes ran through the German port of Emden. During the American War of Independence, the British had lacked even this possibility.

In 1815, in contrast, Wellington was able to rely on a stronger alliance system, and this permitted him to operate in Belgium. Without this system, such operations would not have been possible other than as coastal raids. At the same time, the alliance system had strategic consequences, not least the need to protect Britain's allies. Wellington had shown in the Peninsula that he was willing to withdraw in the face of French advances, and to abandon Spanish and Portuguese towns, but this flexibility was not really present in 1815, as such losses might lead to local weaknesses for the coalition, especially in encouraging Belgian dissatisfaction with Dutch rule.

As mentioned at the close of the previous chapter, the roots of the strategic situation confronting both Napoleon and Wellington in 1815 owed something to the circumstances of that year, and indeed

to the collapse of Napoleon's alliance system in 1812–14 discussed
in the next chapter, but both were essentially a bringing to fruition
of the earlier alienation of other states from Napoleon, and thus of
his increased isolation. This political dynamic was the key context
for Wellington's operations both in the Peninsula and in 1815. In
each case, there were important direct military consequences stemming from Napoleon's unpopularity, not least in the shape of the
composition of Wellington's army, but the wider political tasking
was more crucial. In 1793–1815, as opposed to the War of American Independence or the War of 1812 (i.e., 1812–15), Britain was
pledged to an alliance strategy, a strategy that made possible,
necessary, and logical the commitment of key British forces to the
Continent. Waterloo was the culmination of this strategy.

4.

THE NAPOLEONIC REGIME FALLS, 1812–14

WATERLOO WAS NOT THE beginning of the end, nor the end of
the beginning, but the end. It was the last stage in a story that had
begun with Napoleon's failure in Russia in 1812. This failure
explained not only the background to Waterloo but also why, even
had Napoleon won that battle, he would still have been in a dire situation. Napoleon was largely to blame for the collapse in relations
with his former allies. In particular, Tsar Alexander I of Russia, who
had been forced to accept French domination of most of Europe
when he met Napoleon for the only time at Tilsit in 1807, was
increasingly concerned from 1810 to 1812 about French strength,
intentions and policies, and, partly as a result, Franco-Russian relations deteriorated.

As with his earlier attacks on Austria, Prussia and Spain, Napoleon resolved to deal with a crisis he himself had played a major role
in creating by invading his opponent and striking at the centre of
its power. He wished to destroy the Russian army in Russia's frontier provinces. He sought to do so with an army so large that it
would guarantee victory. Over 600,000 men were available for the
invasion: 200,000 were French, another 100,000 from territories
annexed to France after 1789, and the remainder allied forces, principally German, including 36,000 Bavarians, 34,000 Austrians,
27,000 Saxons and 20,000 Prussians. This was a far larger and more

cosmopolitan force than Napoleon was to lead in 1815, and the contrast was a measure of the collapse of his situation between 1812 and 1815.

The Russians, however, were already in a stronger position in 1812 (let alone 1815) than in 1807. General Michel Barclay de Tolly had reformed the Russian army, which had been successful in conflicts with Turkey (1806–12) and Sweden (1808–09). Russia emerged from these wars with the gains of Bessarabia and Finland, respectively, and with its flanks strengthened.

On 24–25 June 1812, Napoleon's forces crossed the River Niemen without resistance. Enjoying a depth for defence and room for manoeuvre that Wellington totally lacked in 1815, the Russians fell back, denying Napoleon, who entered Vilnius (now capital of Lithuania) on 28 June, the decisive battle he sought. The French, in pursuit, were faced by growing supply problems – exacerbated by Russian scorched-earth and guerrilla actions – again responses that Wellington could not deploy in 1815, although in Spain he had benefited greatly from guerrilla assistance. In Russia, operating to factors of scale – in numbers, distance and time – very different from those in 1815, Napoleon was hit by the loss of men and horses through disease (including dysentery and typhus), fatigue, heat and hunger, which led him to send increasingly frantic demands to France for reinforcements. The River Dnieper was crossed successfully, but attacks on the Russian forces defending Smolensk failed on 17 August, and the Russians withdrew successfully.

The Russians sought to stop the French advance on Moscow in prepared positions at Borodino on 7 September, a battle involving 233,000 men and 1,227 cannon in total. And as at Waterloo, instead of seeking to turn either of the Russian flanks, Napoleon attacked the Russian front. As at Waterloo, the battle lasted all day. The Russians resisted successive French frontal attacks on their entrenchments, especially the Great Redoubt, which Ney finally captured only after repeated bitter attacks. Other Waterloo campaign commanders were also involved in this battle, Grouchy being wounded in a cavalry charge. Unlike the British at Waterloo, the

Russians had had time to construct redoubts, which strengthened defences already helped by the presence of a small river.

The Russians were eventually driven back without their army breaking, which suggests an answer to the question of what would have happened had Napoleon been more successful at Waterloo. At Borodino, Napoleon refused to commit the Imperial Guard, which might have had a decisive impact, and the Russians abandoned the battlefield at night. Despite the heavier Russian casualties (about 52,000 to about 28,000), it was Napoleon's losses, about a quarter of his army, which were crucial. Borodino was very much a battle of attrition.

The road to the capital was now open, as that to Brussels would have been had Napoleon been victorious at Waterloo. On 14 September 1812, he entered an undefended Moscow, but with just under 100,000 troops and only to find the city set ablaze that night, probably by the Russians. That would not have been the fate of Brussels, but the political situation following the fall of Brussels would have been the same, as the fall of Moscow did not compel Alexander to negotiate, and the capture of Brussels would not have been as serious, since it was not an Allied capital.

In the face of very nasty operational and strategic situations, and with the supply situation continuing to deteriorate, Napoleon abandoned Moscow on 19 October 1812. Heavy snow from 4 November, however, turned the retreat into a nightmare as the French supply system collapsed, and exposure and starvation carried off thousands of French troops. The Russian attempt to cut Napoleon off at the River Beresina (26–29 November) failed, but the French rear guard took heavy losses both there and from there to the frontier. The army that left Russia had suffered more than 300,000 casualties, as well as losing about 1,000 cannon and 180,000 horses. The last was a serious problem for the French cavalry subsequently, not least in the Waterloo campaign.

Opposition to French hegemony required a skillful response, both military and political, but Napoleon had failed to provide this. Strategically, operationally, and, at Borodino, tactically, he had mismanaged the 1812 campaign. His inability to translate the capture of Moscow into Russian acceptance of his hegemony, and his retreat from Moscow with the army ebbing away into the snows, were fitting symbols of the folly of his attempt to dominate all of Europe.

This attempt was increasingly problematic, as, aside from Napoleon's deteriorating diplomatic position, the capability gap in favour of the French army had been closed. The extent of such a gap anyway between France and, on the other hand, Russia and Britain is questionable. In addition, among the powers that became France's opponents in 1813, the Prussians improved their army, making a major effort to incorporate skirmishers into their battle formation, and also developed both a reasonably flexible general staff system and an effective militia. Moreover, Austria adopted the corps system. The improvements in these armies were to affect Napoleon's options in 1815, and this point was readily apparent because of the campaigning over the two previous years.

In 1813, Napoleon wrote, 'War is waged only with vigour, decision and unshaken will. One must neither grope nor hesitate.' The year began, however, with his demoralised and indifferently commanded forces retreating across Poland, very much against Napoleon's will. More seriously, his diplomatic position collapsed. The end of war with Turkey had helped the Russians focus on France in 1812. In March 1813, Prussia declared war on France and by using its Landwehr, a militia that could serve as frontline troops, created a large army of 272,000 troops. An improvement in the Prussian army, compared to 1806, was to be noted in 1813–14, one that looked toward the important Prussian role in the Waterloo campaign in 1815.

After his losses in Russia, albeit in far better circumstances than in 1815, Napoleon faced the task of rebuilding his army. Drawing on a far greater area than he controlled in 1815, and with more time available, he rebuilt his army to a field force of over 400,000 plus artillery, but the new recruits were more like the fresh troops of 1792 than the veterans of his earlier campaigns. In particular, Napoleon was unable to create a new cavalry to match the troops and horses lost in Russia.

More generally, as the number of French veterans was cut by casualties, the percentage of new recruits in Napoleon's army rose. As a result, the proportion of French soldiers accustomed to manoeuvring under fire decreased, and this lack of experience may have contributed to the new French battlefield stress on numbers and straightforward assaults. Napoleon's victories in 1813 over the Prussians and Russians at Lützen (2 May) and Bautzen (20–21 May) were achieved over outnumbered forces, and neither was decisive. Bautzen, instead, led both sides to agree to an armistice. Prussian fighting quality was evident in the casualties inflicted at Bautzen, while Ney's failure to close the trap on Blücher there in part prefigured his failure against Wellington at Quatre Bras in 1815.

Napoleon, however, rejected peace terms in 1813, while, as a result, Austria and Sweden joined his opponents. Napoleon was now heavily outnumbered: by over 600,000 to 370,000 in his total field army. The Allies adopted the Trachenberg Plan: battle with Napoleon was to be avoided while independent forces under his subordinates were to be attacked. This was a policy Napoleon unwittingly facilitated by his willingness to detach forces in order to try to capture Berlin, a political objective that contrasted with the supposed Napoleonic focus on knocking out the opposing army. The Prussians defeated detached French forces at Grossbeeren, the Katzbach river (a victory for Blücher), and Dennewitz (where Ney was defeated), and the Austrians won at Kulm.

Looking toward Grouchy's failure in the Waterloo campaign, Napoleon's inability to train his marshals to operate as independent commanders, and their lack of supporting staffs comparable to those that helped Napoleon, cost the French dearly. The marshals also could not cooperate to fulfill strategic or operational objectives. Again looking toward the Waterloo campaign, the scale of war in 1813 was now too great for Napoleon to control everything, although, exacerbating the situation, his failure in June 1815 to match Wellington's stamina and level of activity was a serious drawback.[1]

Once the Trachenberg Plan was adopted, Napoleon was victorious only at Dresden, where Tsar Alexander and Frederick William III of Prussia insisted on fighting on 26–27 August 1813. This victory owed much to strong attacks by his flank forces, a method Napoleon was not to follow at Waterloo. Nevertheless, this was a tactical, not an operational, envelopment, and certainly not the triumph that the French required were they to win.

As far as the 1813 campaign as a whole was concerned, Napoleon, by failing to concentrate his forces, had allowed their attenuation, and this had preserved neither the territory under French control nor the strategic advantage. Instead, it was Napoleon who had lost the initiative and was outmanoeuvred, his line of retreat threatened by the converging Allied forces. In contrast, on the attack in 1815, Napoleon, having created the possibility of cutting off his opponent's line of retreat had Wellington remained at Quatre Bras on 17 June, was to fail to do so next day at Waterloo.

Napoleon, of course, should not be seen on his own. In 1813, for example, his opponents combined attritional warmaking with operational advantage, each reflecting their increased military effectiveness. At Leipzig, in the climactic 'Battle of the Nations' fought from 14 to 19 October 1813, the French were outgeneralled and outfought in the most serious defeat in battle that Napoleon had hitherto suffered. At the outset of this battle, he exploited the advantage of the interior lines on which he was operating, while his mutually suspicious opponents faced the difficult task of cooperation on exterior lines, although this task also provided the opportunity of encircling the French and cutting their lines of communication. Napoleon, moreover, was unable to exploit the early situation in order to win, and his opponents were not defeated in detail (separately). The battle posed serious problems of command and coordination for both sides, with a range of struggles waged across a considerable area, greater than at Waterloo: Alongside large-scale assaults, there was extensive use of artillery, and also major cavalry attacks, particularly by the French on 16 October. Napoleon's failure that day to commit his reserves against the Austrians under Prince Schwarzenberg, who were under pressure, looked toward his reluctance to commit his reserves at Ligny and until late at Waterloo.

The Allies had advantages in numbers and operational situation at Leipzig that the attacking Napoleon lacked at Waterloo. Indeed, under pressure from greater Allied numbers, which became more of a threat as they converged, especially once the 60,000-strong Army of the North under Jean-Baptiste-Jules Bernadotte (a former French general who later became king of Sweden and Norway) arrived on 18 October, the French were finally defeated. Unable to beat his opponents, whom he nevertheless held off, Napoleon retreated, but the premature destruction of the Elster bridge trapped four corps. Defeat led to 73,000 casualties, as well as the collapse of Napoleon's position in Germany as former allies deserted. At least Napoleon was able to thwart an attempt to block his retreat into France.

The 1813 campaign clearly indicated that symmetry had revived in Western warfare. It was possible to defeat the main French field army, and this without the benefit of the distances and climate of Russia. The aura of Napoleonic invincibility had been wrecked by the Russia campaign, the Austrians had now learned to counter the French corps system by using one of their own, and the Prussians had improved their army, not least by developing a more coherent and comprehensive staff system. Many of the key figures in 1815 took major parts at Leipzig, not least Blücher, as commander of the Army of Silesia, and Prince Schwarzenberg, as commander of the Army of Bohemia, while Ney and Murat took prominent roles in the French army.

The subsequent loss in the winter of 1813–14 of 'New France', areas annexed to France since 1792, was in part because of poor French command decisions. Unwilling to take command in person, Napoleon was also not prepared to appoint a commander-in-chief to coordinate operations on the eastern front, and this failure led to a lack of unity among his commanders. Napoleon also failed to provide a clear objective. The individual French commanders, concerned to conserve the strength of their forces, failed to put much of an effort into preventing the loss of the Low Countries, Alsace, Lorraine, and Franche-Comté, but these losses reduced the area from which recruits and taxes could be raised by the French.[2]

In early 1814, France itself was invaded from the east by Austro-

Prussian forces, while Wellington advanced in southwest France, eventually defeating Soult at Toulouse. There was no winter break to campaigning, and this lessened the French ability to mount an adequate response. There were also serious burdens as a consequence of the need to support the military from France itself rather than from occupied or allied territories. The economic consequences of war, invasion and British blockade, and the fiscal burden of the 1812–13 campaigns, were also very serious, and these problems hit the French levée en masse for the army in 1814. So also did widespread noncompliance with conscription demands and resistance to them, which reflected the unravelling of the regime.

Napoleon, nevertheless, with some success, manoeuvred with skill in 1814 in order to destroy the most exposed Austro-Prussian units. Initial victories, for example at Brienne and Champaubert, led him to reject Allied peace proposals, but numbers told against the French, and Napoleon and his subordinates suffered defeats, as at Laon on 10 March. In place of the 80,000 opposing troops Napoleon had anticipated, there were about 200,000; and his own army was 70,000 strong, not the 120,000 men he had hoped for. Napoleon had the advantage at the battle of Arcis-sur-Aube on 20–21 March, but he was outnumbered, and after defeating another French force at La-Fère-Champenoise on 25 March, the Austrians and Prussians marched on Paris, ignoring Napoleon's position on their flank. Their united army of 107,000 men faced only about 23,000 defenders, and the latter were driven back in the Paris suburbs on 30 March, leading to the opening of negotiations on 31 March. Blücher, the Prussian commander at Waterloo, played a key role in this advance.

Napoleon was still in the field with his troops when Paris surrendered, and a provisional French government deposed him. With his marshals unwilling to fight on, and Ney, as their representative, demanding his departure, Napoleon abdicated unconditionally on 6 April, having failed, as he had hoped, to do so on behalf of his son. Napoleon had told Ney that the army would follow him, but Ney replied, 'The Army will only obey its generals.' Under the Treaty of Fontainebleau of 11 April, Napoleon was given the title of emperor, the small Mediterranean island of Elba as a principality, and a revenue of two million francs from the French government, which, in the event, proved unwilling to pay it. Unwilling to accept failure, Napoleon took poison on the night of 12 April, but it did not prove fatal, and he set off for Elba on 20 April.

A new order was being put in place. Louis XVIII was a brother of Louis XVI, who had been executed in 1793. Louis XVII, the son of Louis XVI, like Napoleon II, the son of Napoleon, never reigned; instead, he died a prisoner of Revolutionary France. Louis XVIII returned to France on 24 April, the sole option for the government of France that did not appear to require the Allied military support that neither Louis wished to rely upon nor the Allies to provide. The Allies agreed to withdraw their armies from France, which seemed the best way to consolidate Louis' position and save money, while the French were to evacuate their forces from elsewhere. The Peace of Paris of 30 May gave France generous territorial terms, including the return of most of her colonies, and her European frontiers as of January 1792. Napoleon appeared banished to history.

Napoleon's failure in 1813–14 was important to both the political strategies of 1815 and to their military counterparts. This failure was both military and political. The campaign of 1814 showed that Napoleon could not defend France, at least if this goal was pursued by resting on the defensive. The situation was certainly more serious for France than that during the Wars of the First and Second Coalitions in the 1790s. First, the Allied coalition in 1813–14, as in 1815, was larger than that in the 1790s: Russia had not joined in the pressure on France in 1792–95 and 1808–09, nor Prussia in 1799–1800, 1805 and 1808–09. Second, the coalition forces were fully mobilised in 1813–14, which meant that Napoleon had no possibility of staging a second Valmy and greatly outnumbering the invading army.

Third, the Allies had shown, both in 1813 and 1814, that they could focus on their objectives and continue to victory, irrespective of French success in particular battles. This point suggested that if Napoleon waited for an Allied invasion in 1815 he would find himself under pressure from converging advances on Paris, some of which he might be able to beat, but without stopping the fall of the capital to others. Moreover, the Allied ability to fight on to victory despite defeats in particular battles implied that even victory at Waterloo would only be a temporary success for Napoleon. Fourth, the 1814 campaign demonstrated the political danger posed by military failure, as support for Napoleon collapsed within the regime itself when Paris was under pressure, with a crucial loss of backing among the army leadership.

Napoleon's political failure in 1813–14, however, was more profound than this collapse of military support, and his failure looked toward the reasons why he probably could not have succeeded in 1815. In 1813 and, even, 1814, the Sixth Coalition had divergent views, and there was a lack of agreement on removing Napoleon and on enforcing territorial changes that would satisfy Britain. These views represented opportunities for Napoleon, but he squandered them. In the summer of 1813, before joining the coalition, Austria, which was hostile to Prussia and Russia, proposed a peace treaty for Central Europe that would have offered Napoleon the left bank of the Rhine (including Antwerp); co-guarantorship of a neutralised Rheinbund; noninterference over Spain, which would have obliged Britain to fight on against France without the benefit of Napoleon having to fight Austria, Prussia and Russia; and diplomatic support over colonial concessions from Britain.

The response to these favourable terms was unhelpful. Napoleon declared all France's annexations inalienable, an unrealistic view, and began military preparations against Austria. Defeat had indeed not curbed his instinctive bellicosity. Napoleon's refusal to negotiate peace, nor to understand that it entailed compromise, delivered in person by an angry Emperor to Klemens von Metternich, the Austrian chancellor, led a reluctant Austria finally to join the Sixth Coalition. This legacy was not the best basis for winning over Austria in 1815.

In early 1814, moreover, Napoleon's good faith in negotiations was found wanting. In response to initial Allied military successes in eastern France, he had proved willing to abandon his earlier demands for a Rhine frontier and much of Italy, but a measure of success for France led him to reverse this willingness. After Napoleon's attitude to diplomacy had ruined the chance to use the negotiations at Châtillon in February to bring peace, the Allies agreed at Chaumont not to conclude any separate peace with Napoleon and, instead, to continue the war and then join in maintaining the peace. On 15 March 1814, Armand-Augustin-Louis de Caulaincourt, the French foreign minister, presented new proposals from Napoleon, which would have left France with the left bank of the Rhine, her colonies, and control over the kingdom of Italy.

Such unrealistic responses weakened any chance that the Allies would fail to ensure the end of Napoleon. Conversely, Napoleon was no longer willing even to read Caulaincourt's letters because his minister insisted on offering unwanted cautious advice. This episode ensured the restoration of the Bourbons, as it suggested to contemporaries that Napoleon could not be relied upon to act in a reasonable fashion and that he had to be removed. Moreover, the Seventh Coalition created in 1815 was to act in the shadow of the unity forced on the powers of the Sixth Coalition by Napoleon's policies.

For Britain, the situation was particularly troubling, as the negotiations in 1813–14 revealed a lack of Austrian support for British interests. There was also concern about Prussian and Russian views. Napoleon, however, had played into British hands in 1814, and there was to be no sign in 1815 that this development of Allied cooperation in 1814 could be readily reversed. This point challenged the logic of Napoleon's attempt to use military success in order to divide his opponents politically in 1815.

The legacy of 1812–14 gave the British another reason for firmness in facing France. Napoleon's strength in 1812 had emboldened the United States to declare war, a step encouraged by his skillful diplomacy.[3] This war had put Britain under pressure in Canada and at sea, as it had not proved possible to send significant reinforcements to North America until 1814. Thus a long-established lesson, that the French would seek to exploit Britain's problems elsewhere and that these problems would be exacerbated by war with France, had been demonstrated in 1812–14. This lesson underlined the determination to ensure a friendly regime in France and, certainly, the exclusion of Napoleon. Accepting his return to power in 1815 was not an option.

5.

THE EMPEROR FIGHTS BACK

'BONEY'S RETURN FROM ELBA, or the Devil among the Tailors', a caricature by George Cruikshank based on a design by C. Humphrey, appeared in London on 21 March 1815, and captured the complete change that Napoleon's return appeared to usher in. Looking far younger than in real life, Napoleon, sword in hand, pushes Louis XVIII of France onto the floor and throws the gathering of European potentates into confusion. Yet there are also signs of resistance. John Bull, the symbol of Britain, promises help to Louis and to sew up Napoleon, and Blücher challenges the latter with a large pair of tailors' scissors, while an unperturbed Tsar Alexander I declares, 'I'll take a few Cossack *measures* to him.'

Napoleon had found his control of the island principality of Elba a frustrating lesson in impotence and one that mocked his greatly inflated sense of his own destiny, and he was only too happy to launch an attempt to regain France. On the evening of 26 February 1815, Napoleon took advantage of the absence of his British escort, Colonel Sir Neil Campbell, who was on a visit to Florence, to leave with a small flotilla and about 1,100 troops. Evading two frigates patrolling on the orders of Louis XVIII, as well as a British brigantine, Napoleon arrived near Antibes on the French Provençal coast on 1 March. The garrison was not welcoming, but soon surrendered in the face of Napoleon's force.

This success began a journey of recovery that culminated in Napoleon being welcomed at the Tuileries Palace in Paris on the evening of 20 March without a shot having been fired. The unpopularity of Louis XVIII, who fled Paris the previous night, was an important factor, but so was Napoleon's ability to grasp the initiative, his rapid advance, and the uncertain response of the French military. Under the direction of the war minister, the experienced Marshal Soult, Louis' army prepared to stop and seize Napoleon; but royal troops proved crucially unwilling to fire on their former leader and compatriots, and notably so at Laffrey on 7 March, when Napoleon deliberately exposed himself to the risk of death in order to master the troops psychologically.

This dramatic gesture proved the key episode in his ability to win over the army. Wellington expressed his confidence that Louis XVIII would readily defeat Napoleon, but at Lyon, a crucial centre of communications, planned resistance under Louis' brother, the future Charles X, collapsed on 10 March. The other key royalist force was to have been led by Marshal Ney, who promised Louis XVIII to bring back the captured Napoleon in a cage, but, in the event, he switched allegiance. Attention focused on Napoleon's advance, and elsewhere there was little military activity. Some members of the Cambrai garrison who supported Napoleon tried and failed to seize the military depot at La Fère in Picardy, but once Napoleon had reached Paris, garrisons across France moved to support the new ruler.

Napoleon was able to reimpose his authority relatively easily. His replacement by Louis XVIII in 1814 had been greeted as a result of the welcome peace brought by Allied victory, while in the leading trading ports, such as Bordeaux and Marseille, there was enthusiasm for the departure of Napoleon, who was seen as bad for oceanic trade, but in 1815, there was also scant resistance to his return. This lack of opposition reflected the little Louis XVIII had done to ensure his own popularity. Moreover, when he faced the crisis of Napoleon's return, he provided no leadership. Napoleon, in contrast, was widely seen as a protector of French independence. Royalists who denounced him as a Jacobin contributed to this impression.[1]

There was, however, also a willingness to resist Napoleon. The royalist region of the Vendée rose for the Crown on 15 May, as it had done in the 1790s, but the Army of the West, including part of the Young Guard, was deployed against it by Napoleon, and the rising was crushed in early June at the battle of Rocheservière. Opposition in the South was also suppressed. There was initial resistance at Bordeaux, Marseille, Nîmes, and Valence to the restoration of Napoleon's authority. After Louis XVIII fled, his nephew, Louis-Antoine, Duke of Angoulême, still opposed Napoleon in the South. On 2 April, the Duke gained an advantage at the passage of the River Drôme, leading him to take possession of Valence and the valley of the Isère, but the next day, he began his retreat in the face of the advance of Napoleonic forces. Angoulême's volunteer militia proved inadequate, and he was obliged to sign a convention on 8 April. Under it, royal forces were disbanded, and the militia told to go home. Soon after, Marseille and Toulon surrendered to Napoleonic forces, while the Duke left France. Meanwhile, the Duchess had failed to sustain opposition at Bordeaux and she embarked on a British frigate.

While destroying hopes of national reconciliation behind the Crown by his return and substituting less realistic hopes of the same behind him, Napoleon, however, courted support by populist measures such as the abolition of feudal titles and the institution of public works. Furthermore, promises of constitutional and liberal government were offered, including freedom of the press and maintenance of Louis XVIII's constitutional assemblies. These steps are emphasised in some recent French works, but not in those produced by non-French writers.

In letters to the Allied sovereigns of the Seventh Coalition, Napoleon pledged to observe existing treaties and affirmed peace with the rest of Europe, but his rhetoric within France toward the other powers was hostile and bellicose. Armand de Caulaincourt, Napoleon's last foreign minister, now returned to office, wrote to his British counterpart, Robert, Viscount Castlereagh, on 4 April, to inform him of the return of Napoleon and that Napoleon hoped for peace; but Caulaincourt was also ordered by Napoleon to create a new league with the lesser powers, including Spain, Portugal, Switzerland and the minor German and Italian states, a proposal which was a testimony to Napoleon's lack of realism. So also was his confidence that the people elsewhere who had known his rule would reject war against France whatever their rulers thought. This diplomacy to peoples, a throwback to the French Revolution, and one accompanied in brutal practice by the harsh demands of French power, led Napoleon to order the publication of appeals to foreigners who had served in his forces to rejoin them. These foreigners included many German, Belgian and Dutch soldiers. Thus, military needs and international attitudes combined for Napoleon.

Napoleon's march through France was not resisted by the forces of the alliance that had brought about his downfall in 1814, as none of these forces were still in France; but once the powers, meeting at the Congress of Vienna, were informed of Napoleon's escape, they determined on action. On 7 March, the delegates knew of his escape from Elba, and on 11 March of his arrival in France. Napoleon's return united the powers, which had been divided over the future of Saxony. Indeed, Louis XVIII had joined Austria and Britain in a Triple Alliance concluded on 3 January 1815, in opposing Russo-Prussian pressure for the Prussian annexation of Saxony, which had remained loyal to Napoleon until nearly the end. This alliance was seen by Talleyrand, the French representative, as a way to create a new diplomatic order in which France could have greater influence in Europe, as well as specific benefits on her frontiers. There was also tension between Prussia and William I of the Netherlands, with the Prussians demanding that the Dutch surrender Maastricht and the lands on the east bank of the River Meuse and refusing to hand over Liège until they did so.

Opportunities for France to become an ally in European power politics were lost with Napoleon's return. Instead, on 13 March, the powers assembled at Vienna declared Napoleon's invasion an illegal act and offered help to Louis XVIII. The presence of Tsar Alexander I and Frederick William III in Vienna eased tensions among the Allies and speeded deliberations. Two days later, the British government ordered Wellington back from Vienna to take command of the

British forces in Belgium, while, aware of potential trouble at home, measures were taken to prevent pro-Napoleon demonstrations in Ireland, the part of the British Isles that was regarded as potentially most disloyal. Across Europe, Napoleon's envoys were promptly sent back by the Coalition powers.

On 25 March 1815, the powers at Vienna renewed their alliance in order to overthrow the restored emperor, promising to support France against Napoleon and inviting Louis XVIII to sign the treaty. Austria, Britain, Prussia and Russia each promised to provide forces of 150,000 men, with Britain being permitted to provide some of its contribution with money to be used to subsidise the forces of allies or to hire troops from rulers lacking the necessary funds. This division of responsibilities was an appropriate recognition of the respective strength of the powers. Lesser states were also allocated contributions, Brunswick and the Hanseatic cities, for example, 3,000 troops each and Mecklenburg-Schwerin 3,800 troops. The allocation of the contingents of the lesser German states between the armies of Austria, Britain and Prussia was a matter of some controversy at Vienna, but in April the German contingents were allocated to Blücher or Wellington, although, in the event, none of the Hansa or Oldenburg troops allocated to Wellington ever arrived.

Moreover, the threat from Napoleon led to a settlement of differences at the Congress, a key event in the formation of the strategic context for the campaign. Had disagreements continued, Napoleon's options might have been better, indeed very much so. Instead, the Prussians and Russians backed down over Saxony, each accepting less than they had thought appropriate, although, by the partition treaty of May 1815, Frederick William III was still ceded about 58 per cent of Saxony. Dissension over Saxony complicated the issue of control over the Saxon contingent in the Allied forces deployed against Napoleon. The Allies also disagreed on whether to restore Louis XVIII or to search for other expedients, such as the Duke of Orléans, who indeed became king in 1830, but all agreed that they did not want Napoleon as ruler nor a French general such as Soult.

Despite having troops in Belgium, the Prussians in the Meuse

Valley, and the British, as a support for the Dutch presence, further west, the Allies had not been able to act sufficiently vigorously to enable them to intervene in France on behalf of Louis XVIII. The commander of the Anglo-Dutch army in Belgium, the twenty-one-year-old William, Prince of Orange, had taken defensive preparations as soon as news of Napoleon's return arrived. Orange had also sent an officer to Paris to offer Louis XVIII military assistance. The French, however, refused the offer, which Wellington and the British government anyway disliked, as they believed it would make Louis XVIII unpopular in France. Napoleon, moreover, moved too fast to permit this option.

The Dutch idea of occupying, with Louis's consent, the French frontier fortresses was militarily more viable whatever its political drawbacks. Such an occupation would have provided much greater depth for the Allied position in the Low Countries, more particularly addressing the challenge Napoleon planned in 1815 – driving the Prussians and the Anglo-Dutch forces apart. This goal was easier if Napoleon only had to advance into Belgium, as the Prussians, it was believed, would wish to preserve their routes to the Prussian possessions in the lower Rhineland, especially the bases of Clèves and Wesel, while the Anglo-Dutch forces were likely to fall back to the west and north.

The relevant French frontier fortresses included Dunkirk, Lille, a royalist centre where the departing Louis XVIII had been pressed not to leave France, Valenciennes, Maubeuge, Beaumont, Philippeville and Givet. These positions were the critical ones for the road system leading toward Belgium. Yet occupying a cover of French fortresses, while it would have provided depth for Belgium, would also have tied up much of the Anglo-Dutch army in defensive positions, and thus have given Napoleon greater opportunity to win any engagement in the field, leaving the garrisons redundant. Moreover, the garrisons would have been unable to provide mutual support, in part due to the relative immobility that garrison status produced. The last was to be a major factor helping the invading Prussians in the Franco-Prussian War of 1870–71.

Although there was to be no forward fortification policy, the

Dutch made a major attempt to strengthen their garrisons in the south. Antwerp, Venlo and Maastricht were provided for lengthy sieges, and the garrison of Maastricht was strengthened by 19,000 troops, including 4,000 that had been prepared for the Dutch East and West Indies. This strengthened the Dutch position in Maastricht against the Prussians and protected the Meuse route against French advance. Gunboats were also placed on the rivers Meuse and Scheldt.

While the Allies planned, a planning that thrust British subsidies to its allies to the fore, Parliament deliberated in London. The Whig opposition attacked the Tory government in Parliament and the press, but the opposition itself was divided. This division was important because it raises questions about assumptions that British policy might have changed, and the crucial financial underpinning of the Seventh Coalition been removed, had Napoleon been successful in the Waterloo campaign. Some prominent Whigs, most significantly Samuel Whitbread, George Tierney, Samuel Romilly and Francis Horner, were against war and pressed France's right to pick its own government, but others were opposed to Napoleon.

On 6 April 1815, a message from George, Prince of Wales, the prince regent for the ill George III, about the government's decision to increase the military was communicated to both houses of Parliament, where it was debated next day. In the House of Lords, the prime minister, Robert second Earl of Liverpool, moved the Address to the Crown, declaring that Napoleon had violated the Treaties of Fontainebleau and Paris, and therefore that fighting him was a just war for Britain. William, Lord Grenville, the last Whig prime minister (in 1806–07), Charles, second Earl Grey, Whitbread's brother-in-law and the next Whig prime minister (in 1830–34), and Wellington's discontented elder brother Richard, Marquess Wellesley, each then opposed to Liverpool, all approved the Address, a significant sign of support for the government, although they also made critical remarks. There were no votes against the Address. It was difficult for opposition parliamentarians, unsure of Napoleon's intentions, to decide how best to commit themselves.

In the Commons on 6 April, Robert, Viscount Castlereagh, the foreign secretary, moved the Address but met opposition from Whitbread, who was against a 'new crusade' to determine the Crown of France, and also from the prominent radical Sir Francis Burdett, who argued that Napoleon was 'the choice of the French nation'. Castlereagh told the House,

> It might be thought that an armed peace would be prefer-able to a state of war, but the danger ought fairly to be looked at: and knowing that good faith was opposite to the system of the party [Napoleon] to be treated with, knowing that the rule of his conduct was self-interest, regardless of every other consideration, whatever decision they came to must rest on the principle of power, and not that of reliance on the man.

Whitbread's amendment was rejected by 220 votes to 37. Never-theless, opposition pressure continued. On 12 April, Wellesley crit-icised the government in the Lords for negligence in letting Napoleon escape, and his speech was seen as looking toward an attempt to create a wide-ranging opposition to the ministry. On 28 April, Whitbread moved an Address deprecating the resump-tion of hostilities simply in order to prevent Napoleon's return, but he was heavily defeated by 273 to 72.

On 22 May, the treaty of 25 March agreed to at Vienna was com-municated to Parliament, and it was debated the next day. Liver-pool defended government policy by arguing that Napoleon could not be trusted, while Grey attacked the justice, necessity and expe-diency of war with France. Yet the bulk of the Whigs backed the government, including Grenville, the only one with experience as prime minister. Another group of MPs, among whom William Wilberforce was most prominent, were undecided about war or sought not to commit themselves in public.

The key points were the majorities. Opposition votes in the Commons rose from 37 on 7 April, to 72 on 28 April and 92 on 23 May, as attendance increased, but ministerial votes increased even more: 220, 273 and 331, respectively, and, as a result, the government majorities rose. Thus, just as the conflict interacted with politics in Paris, where the unpopularity of the new regime was readily apparent, so the war interacted with politics in London, but to the benefit of the government. As a result, it was able to raise an unprecedented amount of taxes. At the same time that Napoleon was preparing to launch his attack on Belgium, Parliament was debating the problem of paying for the war. On 14 June 1815, Nicholas Vansittart, the chancellor of the Exchequer, told the House of Commons, 'Whether we supposed the government of Buonaparte was only established over France by the domineering power of a mutinous army, or whether it was assumed that he was invested with the sovereign authority by the suffrages of the nation at large, it could not affect the measures which it had become necessary for England to adopt.' The budget presented that day made provision for the expenditure of £79,893,300, which was to be met by the renewal of the war taxes as well as by new loans.

The Seventh Coalition was not restricted to the great powers but instead united much of Europe, including such former Napoleonic allies as Bavaria. The Napoleonic alliance system that had collapsed in 1813 – that with Austria, Bavaria, Denmark, Saxony, Baden, Württemberg and Nassau – was not to be revived.

Napoleon would therefore have to fight and would need to avoid a repetition of the campaign of 1814. Such a repetition was what Wellington sought. He argued that the Coalition should begin operations 'when we shall have 450,000 men', including Prussians and Russians, and he was confident that Napoleon could bring no more than 150,000 troops to strike at any one point.[2]

As in 1813 and 1814, Napoleon had to defend his position, and, as then, he sought a mobile defence. The situation appeared more promising for him than in 1814, as the Coalition forces were less prepared. For Napoleon to succeed, it seemed best to attack, profiting from the time it would take for the Allies to deploy their forces, as well as from France's position both on interior lines and protected in part from attack by such natural obstacles as the Alps and the Pyrenees.

Attacking would also enable Napoleon to strengthen his political position in Paris, where he was justifiably worried about his popularity and concerned about the attitude of many of his ministers, especially Joseph Fouché, the minister of police, as well as of the Jacobins. Indeed, Napoleon had essentially staged a military coup, and he enjoyed only limited civilian support. Attacking would also provide Napoleon with the strategic opportunity of disrupting the opposing Coalition, with unknown possible advantages, as well as the operational support of being able to raise supplies from conquered territory, and the tactical ability to use French skills in the attack.

By concentrating on part of the opposing Allied forces, Napoleon could hope to achieve a local superiority in numbers. Given this policy, it was clear where Napoleon should attack. To return to Italy, the scene, in 1796–97, of his triumphs as a Revolutionary general and, in 1800, of his opening campaign as First Consul, would be pointless, as this was not the centre of gravity of the Coalition. If he did so, Paris would be exposed to attack, not least from the Allied forces in nearby Belgium. Indeed, although he had visited Milan in 1807, Napoleon had not campaigned in Italy since 1800.

Joachim Murat, the former Napoleonic marshal who, thanks to Napoleon's favour, had become king of Naples, declared war on Austria on 15 March 1815, proclaiming himself Liberator of Italy. Napoleon, however, would gain nothing from joining him. Not only were the Austrians present in considerable strength in Italy, but the peninsula was also a strategic irrelevance. Furthermore, Murat attacked (and was defeated) before Napoleon was ready to act. If Murat's actions suggested to European observers the chaos that Napoleon might unleash, the return of Joseph and Jérôme, two of Napoleon's brothers, to Paris raised fears that they might seek the kingdoms they had gained through him: Spain and Westphalia. There was even less point for Napoleon to advance into Spain than into Italy.

The key Allied forces – Austrian, Russian, Prussian and British – were all deployed north of the Alps, which provided a range of prospects. Napoleon could have advanced east into Germany against the Austrian and Russian armies, but that would have left Paris as well as his left flank exposed to the Anglo-Dutch and Prussian armies in Belgium. The latter two, moreover, would provide the nearest targets, which gave Napoleon an opportunity to win the war sequentially, both militarily and by unpeeling the Coalition, although this opportunity depended heavily on the Coalition powers responding as he anticipated. In short, Napoleon trusted to his will as much as to a supposed ability to determine events.

Napoleon was able to call on a range of manpower, notably the 200,000 troops in the royal army, many of whom had earlier fought for him and remained loyal, a loyalty most were still to retain after defeat at Waterloo. He could also call on troops on leave, and absent without leave, as well as on volunteers. Repatriated prisoners, discharged veterans, and soldiers recalled from the dubious pleasures of half pay were all called to the army, as were sailors from the navy. The pool of French troops was not limited, as it had been in 1814, by the deployment of many in besieged garrisons.

Napoleon also turned to conscription, although he had not the time to deploy any conscripts for the Waterloo campaign, while the unpopularity of the regime was clearly shown in the difficulty of ensuring support for conscription. Conscription had been abolished, and the Legislative Chamber was unwilling to recall the class of 1815. Napoleon responded by seeking to circumvent the situation and the Chamber, which he correctly identified as a source of élite opposition. To do so, Napoleon classified the class of 1815 as discharged soldiers who had to serve, and he was able to raise about 46,000 men, but none reached his army in the field.

Napoleon's key force was l'Armée du Nord, comprising 123,000 troops and 358 cannon, as other units had to be deployed to protect France's other frontiers and to resist possible rebellion. In combination, these other units were a considerable force of about 105,000 men, and more troops possibly could have been added from them to l'Armée du Nord, but other frontiers could not be left completely bare, while only so many troops could have been redeployed. Numbers were not the only difficulty in fielding l'Armée du Nord, as there was also a serious problem in providing the necessary equipment. This problem reflected the degree to which the army had been neglected under Louis XVIII, with a particular failure to maintain the necessary matériel. As a result, once back in Paris Napoleon had to devote a major effort to secure sufficient weaponry and horses.

Meanwhile, the Allies were preparing for war. While this meant that Austrian and Russian forces had to advance toward France, until they did so, it was necessary for the Prussians and, even more, the Anglo-Dutch army, to focus on the defensive.[3] The most exposed army was the Anglo-Dutch one in western Belgium, an area which had recently become part of the kingdom of the United Netherlands. In response to the new crisis, William, Prince of Orange, was replaced as commander by Wellington, who had been a British delegate at the Congress of Vienna. On 4 April, Wellington arrived in Brussels, finding his new command in a disappointing state.

In part, the poor state of the Anglo-Dutch army was a reflection of the rapidity with which Britain and the Netherlands had rushed to take a peace dividend. The British army had been cut with large-scale discharges, while other units had been sent to North America in 1814 in order to pursue the War of 1812 or were deployed to deal with disaffection in Britain, notably from the Luddites, who violently opposed new industrial technology, or to garrison Ireland. Wellington's British units initially were essentially based on those that had operated in the Low Countries in 1814, operations that had not proved especially successful.

Wellington's army, moreover, was a very mixed one, in background, experience and competence. It included not only the Dutch and Belgian forces of the kingdom of the United Netherlands, many of whom lacked relevant experience, but also forces from the army of George III as king of Hanover (essentially militia), as well as the far more experienced King's German Legion, part of the British Army, drawn from those who had fled Hanover when it was occupied by Napoleon's armies, as well as Nassauers and Brunswickers.[4] After a quarrel between Wellington and William I of the Netherlands, as well as British governmental concern about

the trustworthiness of the Dutch forces, William offered Wellington the rank of field marshal and commander-in-chief of the
Netherlands army, an offer accepted by Wellington on 12 May after
the British government had agreed.

To defend Belgium without knowing the likely axis of French
advance, the Allies had to deploy their forces over a large area to
cover the possible routes of attack. In practice, the French advance
would depend on a paved road, not least in order to transport the
artillery, but, compared to Spain, Italy, and even eastern France,
there were a large number of roads that could be used. In particular,
there were roads to Brussels from Lille in France via Tournai, Ath
and Hal; from Maubeuge in France via Mons, Braine le Comte and
Hal; and from Philippeville in France via Charleroi, Quatre Bras
and Mont St. Jean. Further west, there were roads from Lille to
Ostend via Ypres, and from Lille to Ghent and on to Antwerp, a
route that threatened Brussels from the rear. To the east, there were
routes from France to Namur and Liège. Moreover, the Allies had a
number of areas of interest and places that had to be defended
including the Belgian Channel ports, notably Ostend, the naval
base at Antwerp, the court of the exiled Louis XVIII at Ghent, the
Belgian capital at Brussels, and the strategic positions on the
Meuse: Namur, Liège and, further east, Maastricht.

In practice, from the perspective of both sides, all of these positions were instrumental. As Napoleon's principal objective was the
defeat of the opposing armies, thus the preservation of these armies
was the key objective of the Allies. The places above were secondary
goals for both sides. They established the geography of the conflict
and its initial character as the interplay of places and armies, with
both sides manoeuvring in order to pursue primary and secondary
goals. Indeed, Napoleon's opportunity rested on the degree to
which the Allied protection of secondary goals, in particular of lines
of communication, provided Napoleon with an opportunity to
secure his primary goal of defeating their forces. In his mind, there
was none of the confusion between securing key positions and
inflicting defeats, seen with Hitler and the invasion of the Soviet
Union in 1941.

For the Allies, in turn, it was crucial to get within the French decision loop, as a rapid response to French moves would enable them to concentrate their forces and to engage the French from a position of numerical superiority. This response would also let the Allies protect the places that were deemed essential. However, any Allied concentration that was not near the frontier, if followed by a battle that left Napoleon able to advance, would pose a challenge, as one or other of the Allied armies would probably find it difficult to retreat along secure lines of communication.

Initially, the Prussians proposed that the Anglo-Dutch and Prussian armies retreat to Tirlemont, about twenty-five miles east of Brussels, a position that would take the Prussians nearer to their lines of communication. Wellington, however, thought this proposal militarily and politically unwise, the two combining in the anxiety that the French would be able to take Brussels and, as a result, that the loyalty of the Belgian forces would be affected. Such a concentration would also cut Wellington off from Ostend and the route to Britain. As a result, Wellington pressed for a deployment by both armies south of Brussels. Lieutenant-General Count August von Gneisenau, the Prussian commander pending the arrival of Field Marshal Blücher, was keen to cooperate with Wellington, and agreed.[5] Gneisenau had served in Canada on behalf of George III in the Ansbach forces in 1782–83, and was a veteran of the battles of Jena and Leipzig.

The Prussian decision was to be of great importance for the campaign and one that underlined Gneisenau's significance. A concentration at Tirlemont was not politically viable for the British, not least as it would have left not only the route to Brussels uncovered but also the route thence to the key port of Antwerp, as well as all of Belgium that was farther west. Yet had the Prussians concentrated there, and the British to the south of Brussels, then Napoleon would really have been able to defeat the two armies separately. Conversely, because they both deployed south of Brussels, the Allied armies were close to the French frontier and therefore vulnerable to attack, as was to be shown on 16 June 1815. More specifically, as the events of that day were to indicate, these armies risked contact engagements that they did not want, in order to disengage prior to concentration. The concentration, both of the individual armies and of the two together, moreover, would require marching across the axis of French advance.

By mid-June 1815, Wellington was in command of an army of about 112,000 troops and 203 cannon, with the field force over 90,000 strong. This force had been built up from March as the British government scrambled to respond to the new situation and to Wellington's urgent concern about his strength. On 16 March, for example, four British infantry regiments were ordered for Ostend. Six days later, 20,000 muskets followed for the Dutch infantry. The British and King's German Legion rank and file in Belgium had numbered 14,000 in March; by the close of May they were over 36,000 strong.

Wellington made an urgent attempt to mould his army by reorganising it, notably by adopting a method he had employed in the Peninsular War that entailed mixing formations in order to put the impressive alongside the less impressive down to divisional level. This method was seen as a way to stiffen the less impressive units and thus to improve the defensive strength of the entire army. Wellington's system was opposed by William I of the Netherlands, who wanted the Belgian and Dutch forces concentrated in one corps, but, benefiting from his own notable reputation and from the crisis environment, Wellington got his way. This decision was to be very important to the strength of his army at Waterloo. With time, Wellington was also more successful in obtaining the staff officers he wanted.

Prussia had also been affected by large-scale demobilisation, and the resulting problem of limited military preparedness was accentuated by a serious lack of financial resources, compared to Britain, as well as by the lack of loyalty shown by units raised from areas newly acquired by Prussia, especially Saxony and the Rhineland. Indeed, in May 1815, Blücher, the commander of the Army of the Lower Rhine, sent home 14,000 mutinous Saxon troops, after having seven of their officers shot. This act suggested that the Allied armies were not as strong as their numbers indicated and encouraged doubts about the reliability of the Dutch and, even more, Belgians, most of whom had been under French control for nearly two decades. Many of them had fought for Napoleon. The validity of these doubts is unclear: It assumes that the Belgians and Dutch were willing recruits to the French cause, which is uncertain, although it is possible that group bonding in Napoleon's Grande Armée was so strong that it broke their resistance. There were not comparable doubts in the British army about the German contingents, but there was anxiety about their combatworthiness and concern about their numbers, although the Brunswickers tended to inspire confidence.

Despite the problems with the Saxon troops, Frederick William III adopted a robust attitude, ordering full-scale mobilisation that included the recall of the entire militia. Indeed, by June 1815, Blücher's army was about 130,000 strong and had 304 cannon. Based in eastern Belgium, with its headquarters at Namur, controlling the valley of the Lower Meuse, this army also shared the defence of central Belgium with Wellington, whose headquarters and reserve were at Brussels. The division between the two was not simply an east–west one along a north–south alignment. Indeed, complicating the situation for both Allied armies and providing opportunities for Napoleon, the Prussian I Corps blocked the French advance north on Brussels via Charleroi.

Yet instead of Prussian forces to the north of this corps' area of deployment, there was Wellington's reserve around Brussels, ensuring a southwest to northeast division between the armies. This division meant that the I Corps was not protecting Prussian positions to the north and also suggested that the axis of Prussian withdrawal would be east-northeast along the Prussian lines of communication and where the other Prussian units were located.

The Allies had considered a rapid attack on Napoleon, but it was decided to wait until they had built up their forces. This decision reflected concern about the consequences if Napoleon was successful against a small invasion force, but also the delays that accompanied the buildup of the British and Prussian armies. As a result, plans for an offensive intended for May were postponed, first to

June and then to July. Had Britain not been at war with the United States until the winter of 1814–15, more experienced troops might have been available in Belgium for a rapid advance or in Britain for a swift deployment, but the British would not have attacked without the Prussians, and the latter were not ready. Moreover, the delay to July owed much to the desire to wait for the buildup of Austrian and Russian armies able to invade France from the east, the route already taken by the invading forces in 1814.

The Allied armies in Belgium were Napoleon's target, as their defeat would provide both the appearance and the reality of success. He aimed to use a central position in order to defeat his enemies in detail. To do so, he planned a secret concentration south of the junction of Wellington's and Blücher's armies, followed by a rapid advance designed to defeat them separately before advancing on Brussels.

The French, indeed, achieved considerable surprise, in that their axis of principal attack was unclear. Because the Allies did not mount patrols across the frontier, they were short of necessary intelligence, in part also because of failures in the chain of command. Lieutenant-Colonel Friedrich von Wissell, commander of the First Regiment of Hussars of the King's German Legion, reported from Tournai that the French were preparing to attack, but his report was not believed.[6] Nevertheless, Blücher knew of the French buildup southwest of Charleroi and of Napoleon's arrival in the area and, on 14 June, Colonel Sir Henry Hardinge, Wellington's representative at the Prussian headquarters, sent the duke a letter informing him that the Prussians were expecting an attack next morning near Charleroi. To that extent, Napoleon had failed to achieve complete surprise. Blücher benefited not only from sighting patrols but also from the defection of General Count Louis Bourmont, the commander of the Fourteenth Infantry Division, who defected at 5:00 A.M. on 15 June, causing confusion in Gérard's IV Corps. Napoleon told Caulaincourt on 21 June that, but for this defection, he would have destroyed the Allied forces at the outset, but this was an absurd claim reflecting his frenetic postbattle desire to blame others for letting him down.[7]

The invasion was launched at 3:30 A.M. on 15 June, with the French converging on the Belgian town of Charleroi, the key crossing point on the River Sambre between Mauberge and Namur. The town was held by the Prussians, but not in strength. They were heavily outnumbered. Prussian infantry behind the barricaded bridge at Charleroi saw off a hussar attack, but, at about 11:00 A.M., engineers and marines of the Imperial Guard arrived with Napoleon. The troops carried the barricade, and the sluggish Napoleon was soon able to sit on a roadside chair and watch his troops march north from Charleroi.

The Allied response to the invasion was mixed. The Prussian I Corps, under Lieutenant-General Hans von Ziethen, made a skillful retreat. Ziethen was instructed to gain time to allow the Prussian army to concentrate but not to mount a serious resistance that would involve heavy costs. At the same time, the Prussian II and III Corps advanced in order to concentrate in strength against the French invasion. In contrast, Wellington, still uncertain about the route of the main French advance, not least because he had assumed it would be farther west, via Mons, did not respond rapidly, a failure for which he was to be severely castigated by some later commentators.

Ziethen had informed Wellington's headquarters of the attack at once, sending letters to Wellington and to Major-General Karl von Müffling, the Prussian representative, but Wellington was essentially inactive, despite news of the French advance including the capture of Charleroi. Wellington's failure to respond strengthened Napoleon's command of the initiative, and also posed a particular problem for Blücher because, when the two generals met on 3 June, Wellington had agreed that, if Napoleon attacked, he would move his forces toward the Prussians in order to achieve a strong concentration able to defeat the French.

At the same time, Ney, who was in command of the French left advancing against Wellington, showed uncharacteristic caution on the fifteenth as he moved north from Charleroi on the Brussels road and failed to drive on against Wellington's forces. By dusk, French cavalry had encountered a unit of Wellington's army, Nassauers blocking the Brussels road at Frasnes. The French advance was not pressed home, depriving Ney of the opportunity of capturing the crossroads of Quatre Bras, two miles to the north. The contrast with Ney's conduct at Waterloo three days later suggests that he required battle to stir him up, but his experience of serving in the Peninsula from 1808 to 1811 had made him aware of Wellington's ability in defence. Moreover, it took Ney time to get his troops to Charleroi, across the Sambre, and then north.

By the evening of the fifteenth, Napoleon had achieved his objective of separating the two opposing Allied armies, a consequence of their forward location to the south of Brussels. The Prussian army offered Napoleon the prospect of a major battle, while Wellington's force, although beginning to concentrate, was still scattered. However, the French ability to exploit this situation was lessened by the congestion and poor staff-work that left about a third of the army still south of the River Sambre at 9:00 P.M. This delay did not promise well for the speedy moves necessary to exploit the central position and interior lines that Napoleon had opened up. He suffered from the absence of his long-term chief of staff, Marshal Berthier, who had remained loyal to Louis XVIII, indeed escorting him to safety in Ghent.

Late on the fifteenth, the night of the Duchess of Richmond's famous ball in Brussels, Wellington's scattered units were ordered to concentrate next day on the crossroads at Quatre Bras, where the Brussels–Charleroi road crossed that from Namur via Ligny to Nivelles. This position provided an opportunity to defend the route to Brussels and to march to Blücher's help, or, indeed, to receive Prussian assistance. However, Wellington's marching orders had been issued late, which meant that the French had the chance to gain and exploit the initiative next day.

Wellington, on the early afternoon of the sixteenth, rode over to meet Blücher, and he promised aid to the Prussians, in the shape of 20,000 troops, if he was not attacked himself. In practice, Wellington was in no position to provide help as he was to be engaged by the French left wing under Ney. The duke was to be criticised for misleading the Prussians as to his moves and capability, not least for indicating that his concentration was much more advanced than was in fact the case, and it is worth asking what would have happened if Wellington had not misled Blücher.[8] Whatever the case, the British presence at Quatre Bras certainly limited the French troops available to attack Blücher at Ligny.

Meanwhile, Blücher's concentration of three of his four corps provided Napoleon with an opportunity to defeat the Prussians, and he attacked at Ligny at about 2:30 P.M. on the sixteenth. On forward slopes, a choice that some have claimed Wellington criticised, the Prussians were exposed to French artillery and suffered heavily. However, they outnumbered the French, by 83,000 to 63,000 men, as Napoleon, who had not initially appreciated the strength of the Prussian deployment, had also failed to secure the necessary French concentration. Key French units were missing. Lobau's VI Corps did not arrive early enough on the battlefield, while a clash in instructions between demands for assistance from both Napoleon and Ney, a clash that owed much to poor staff-work and something to Ney's temper, ensured that d'Erlon's I Corps, a substantial force, marched between the two battlefields but without firing a shot in either.

The failure to use this force in battle that day constitutes one of the major might-have-beens of the battle. Correspondingly, a misunderstanding had led to a failure to concentrate the Prussian army; Friedrich von Bülow's large IV Corps was not present. It is not terribly helpful to consider, as is often done, one of the might-have-beens without the other or others.

Short of men – indeed, seriously outnumbered – Napoleon was not in a position on 16 June to outflank the Prussian right at Ligny as he had hoped. Instead, on what proved a very hot afternoon, he relied on costly frontal attacks round the village of Ligny, which changed hands several times as each side fed in fresh units. To the west, there was also bitter fighting in the villages of St. Amand, La Haye, Le Hameau and Wagnelée, with attacks succeeded by counterattacks. Using the Imperial Guard and General Édouard-Jean-Baptiste Milhaud's heavy cavalry corps against the Prussian centre at the climax, an attack at 7:30 P.M. preceded by a heavy artillery bombardment, helped Napoleon eventually to beat Blücher, but the Prussians had inflicted heavy casualties (19,000 Prussian and 13,700 French casualties), and they were able to retreat behind a rearguard line without being broken or crushed. Blücher himself was nearly captured and was badly bruised by the fighting.

The French losses ensured that Napoleon had a smaller margin of manpower for subsequent operations. On the other hand, despite having the larger army, a point Gneisenau denied in his biography of Blücher, the Prussians had been defeated, and their anger and shame about this defeat may be partly responsible for the subsequent determination to attribute blame to Wellington's inaccurate promises of an ability to send help.

Meanwhile, ten kilometres to the northwest, Ney had attacked Wellington's army at Quatre Bras at about 2:30 P.M. on the sixteenth. Initially, his force was far larger (28,000 men to 8,000), due to Wellington's delay in concentrating and moving, but the arrival of more units, especially Sir Thomas Picton's Fifth British Infantry Division, a mixed Anglo-Hanoverian formation, which were successfully rushed forward, eventually ensured that the Allies had 30,000 men. The battle was not on ground of Wellington's choosing, and the Allied units holding the crossroads, Prince Bernard of Saxe-Weimar's Nassau brigade reinforced by Major-General Willem Frederick von Bijlandt's Dutch-Belgian brigade, were under serious pressure by the time the reinforcements arrived. These reinforcements had to be deployed as they arrived, and the hasty deployment was reflected in the lack of adequate ammunition, but fortunately the French were not in a position to disrupt this deployment. The British were helped by the defensive possibilities of the vegetation, especially the hedges and the tall rye. Major-General Lord Edward Somerset, the commander of the First (Household) Cavalry Brigade, recorded in his diary:

> The troops that had first arrived had been attacked by the enemy near an extensive wood about a league in front of a small village called Quatre Bras on the road to Namur. The action was extremely sharp. The French brought a very

superior force into the field; notwithstanding which the British troops maintained their position with the greatest bravery and resisted the attacks of the enemy's cavalry; although unsupported by the British cavalry which had not yet come up. The action continued till night, but the enemy could gain no advantage. The loss was considerable on both sides, and on ours we had to regret that of the Duke of Brunswick, who was killed, gallantly leading on his troops.[9]

Prefiguring Waterloo, the British infantry at Quatre Bras formed lines against attacking French infantry and squares against their cavalry. Although General François-Étienne Kellermann's heavy cavalry briefly seized the Quatre Bras crossroads, they were driven back. French cavalry charges inflicted considerable losses on the British infantry, but unsupported, the French cavalry could not hold their ground and had to withdraw. The failure of the cavalry attacks should have given Ney pause when he launched the same at Waterloo. As at Waterloo, French cannon proved a serious problem for the British. *The Times* reported on 22 June:

> Many of the British officers present in the affair of the 16th declared that they never witnessed more severe fighting in the Peninsula [Portugal and Spain] than that which took place on the plains of Fleurus and its vicinity. The Duke of Wellington exposed himself as usual to imminent danger.

As a reminder of the risks to which commanders indeed exposed themselves, Frederick, Duke of Brunswick, who was acting as the commander of the Brunswick Corps, was mortally wounded.

Command was not simply a matter of bravery. Decisions on the allocation of troops were also crucial. Faced during the battle by strengthening British opposition and by Napoleon's new instructions to capture Quatre Bras and then operate against the Prussian right, Ney determined to press hard by deploying d'Erlon's I Corps, a force of about 20,000 troops, which would indeed have allowed the French to maintain the impetus. That this corps, instead, was moving, on Napoleon's orders, against Blücher's right, ensured that Ney lacked this follow-through at Quatre Bras.

The delay in issuing and communicating Napoleon's orders to Ney was also serious. Those to Ney to seize Quatre Bras and then turn against Blücher, a goal that gave urgency to the need for victory at Quatre Bras, were issued in late morning but only received in mid-afternoon. That Ney would not be able to react in time ensured that Napoleon had to rely at Ligny on the more costly method of frontal attacks, as indeed did the failure to use d'Erlon's corps in either battle.

As at Waterloo two days later, Ney misjudged the situation at Quatre Bras. A victim of Wellington's generalship in the Peninsula, he attacked late, launched piecemeal assaults, and failed to break or outmanoeuvre the defenders, although the buildup in Wellington's strength made French victory unlikely anyway. As a result, the battle ended in stalemate. Ney failed to defeat Wellington despite facing better odds than Napoleon confronted at Ligny. Indeed, as part of the busy process of postwar blame-shifting, Jérôme Bonaparte, Napoleon's youngest brother and a divisional commander at Quatre Bras, was to claim that 'the campaign was lost at Quatre Bras by Ney's unaccountable conduct.'[10]

At Quatre Bras, superior numbers enabled the British to push the French back at the close of the battle, recapturing most of the ground they had lost. Casualties, about 4,000 to 5,000 men on each side, were less than at Ligny, which was a far more serious battle. At the same time, indicating that numbers alone were not the key, Ligny was a battle where the outnumbered French won not least because they were better deployed than the Prussians. Against this background, Wellington lent Blücher vital assistance, even though he did not send troops to his aid, because he was responsible for distracting Ney's force and, indirectly, for d'Erlon's corps not joining Napoleon. As such, Quatre Bras was a success for both Wellington and Blücher, one that helped compensate for the failure of Blücher's army at Ligny. Looked at differently, the French had divided their opponents, and a detached French force had contained Wellington, enabling Napoleon to defeat Blücher and to have had the possibility of inflicting a heavier defeat.

The following morning, the seventeenth, Napoleon was still in the central position he had advanced into on the fifteenth and, despite his losses on the sixteenth, he had an opportunity to fulfill his original plans. Moreover, farther apart than on the sixteenth, due to Blücher's retreat after Ligny, Wellington and Blücher were not really in a state to provide mutual support on the seventeenth, not least because Blücher's army was seriously affected by demoralisation and desertion, especially by the Rhinelanders who had only recently come under Prussian rule. Over 10,000 Prussian troops deserted.

On the other hand, Wellington now understood the location of the main axis of French attack. For long, he had been 'humbugged', misled by Napoleon and by his own misplaced conviction that the French would advance on Brussels from the southwest, a conviction that was to lead to criticism from commentators. When initially informed by Blücher of French moves near Charleroi, to the south, Wellington was convinced that these were only part of Napoleon's army, and on that basis, Wellington's delay in concentrating troops on the Prussians and taking a strong position near Quatre Bras is understandable.

On the seventeenth, Napoleon could have chosen to press either of his opponents hard, but, with the benefit of hindsight, it was best to do so to both. To fail to press them hard risked either or both of them moving away, so lessening the chance for the grand strategy of the sequential defeat. Thus Napoleon needed to ensure a close pursuit of Blücher, and also that Wellington was held at Quatre Bras, or, if he retreated, that he was harried, made vulnerable, and prevented from taking up a new defensive position. Napoleon still had a long way to go even to make the odds comparable to those in 1814, let alone to make them more equal, but achieving these goals would have helped him narrow the odds.

The opportunity to press Wellington hard was enhanced on the seventeenth by d'Erlon's I Corps being back with Ney's army, which strengthened it and greatly lessened Wellington's advantage in numbers. Moreover, if Wellington could have been held by Ney at Quatre Bras, then Napoleon could have moved along the Namur-

Nivelles road to hit Wellington on his left flank, an operational coup that would more than counterweigh any British tactical success in defence. Indeed, 17 June was the great day of opportunity for the French, and, like many days of movement rather than conflict, the day that was crucial to the campaign, and yet it tends to receive insufficient attention.

Neither Ney nor Napoleon, however, understood, let alone grasped, their opportunities that day until too late. Ney did not hold Wellington, who, aware of the Prussian retreat, was able, instead, to withdraw north; while Napoleon passed the early part of the morning focusing on the aftermath of the battle at Ligny. Riding the battlefield, talking to troops, and ensuring medical assistance to the wounded were roles that endeared him to his troops, a part he liked to play and one that was crucial to his popularity with his men. But these roles were totally inappropriate in light of the situation, both as far as the Prussians were concerned and with reference to Wellington.

Napoleon needed to exploit victory but, instead, he displayed a lethargic going with the flow that accorded with his dozing as his troops marched past on the afternoon of the fifteenth and to the slow-motion character of his appearance at the great assembly of electors to which the new constitution had to be put at Paris on 1 June. Only in the late morning of the seventeenth did Napoleon, in response to information of his opponents' moves, understand the situation and try to fix Wellington, while Marshal Grouchy was ordered to maintain the pressure on the Prussians in order to prevent them from intervening on Wellington's behalf.

Napoleon, however, was to be thwarted on the seventeenth by Wellington's swifter response and by weather that turned very wet, unseasonably so, posing a particular problem for moving forward the French artillery. Wellington began to disengage at 10:00 A.M., which ensured that Napoleon's dispatch of the Imperial Guard to join Ney was of no value. Napoleon arrived at about 2:00 P.M. and criticised Ney for inaction, but Wellington by then had gone. Moreover, after a skillful disengagement of the bulk of Wellington's army, the well-organised and skillfully deployed British rear guard ably held off the French, preventing them from exploiting the British withdrawal. Somerset's lengthy account is valuable, as it provides a sense of respective fighting capability on the day before Waterloo and also shows the role of the cavalry in a mobile defence. In contrast, next day, the broken French cavalry was unable to provide such a defence after defeat at Waterloo:

> The infantry was first of all withdrawn, and effected their retreat towards Waterloo on the road to Brussels unmolested. The cavalry formed the Rear Guard, and commenced its movement between two and three o'clock, having been previously drawn up in three lines some distance in front of Genappe. Part of the Hussars and Light Dragoons passed on the flanks of the town, whilst the two heavy brigades of cavalry covered by the 7th Hussars and 23rd Lt. Drags. moved by the high road, which lead through the centre of it. As soon as the main body have moved off, a considerable force of the enemy's cavalry made a sudden attack on the rear, at the end of the village, and after some time drove them back on the Heavy Brigade which had retired up the hill beyond it. At this moment, Lord Uxbridge directed the 1st Regiment of Life Guards which had been placed on the road, to advance and charge, which order they executed with the greatest gallantry. Twice they attacked the French cuirassiers in the most brilliant manner, and with complete success, and thus checked the rapid advance of the enemy.

Somerset continued by referring to the combined arms operations of the French, a capability that was to be insufficiently in evidence at Waterloo:

> Soon afterwards the two squadrons of the Blues were ordered to form the Rear Guard, and covered the retreat with the utmost steadiness, notwithstanding they were exposed to a heavy cannonade from which they suffered some loss. The Enemy contented himself with following our

movements keeping up a fire from his skirmishers and guns but did not attempt to charge us. The cavalry having at length reached the position occupied by the infantry, retired behind them for the night.[11]

An officer of the Tenth Hussars was less sanguine. 'The retreat in rain . . . was against us – besides that our cavalry had suffered in the retreat as the Seventh Hussars had had the worst of it with the [French] Lancers on the chaussée [road], which is favourable to the lancers as they can only be attacked in front.'[12]

Wellington, nevertheless, held off the French on the seventeenth and had the opportunity to plan his moves. He wrote to Blücher on the morning of 17 June that he was retreating from Quatre Bras in order to avoid being outflanked by Napoleon, a realistic response that Blücher could be expected to accept, and also so as to keep contact with Blücher, which was a call for joint action. Wellington added that he would give battle on a ridge at Mont St. Jean (the Waterloo battlefield), if Blücher sent at least one corps to his assistance. Blücher, in turn, wrote at 6 P.M. that he would send his entire army, a promise Wellington received that evening. This promise enabled Wellington to plan his defensive position for a battle, rather than chart a continuing retreat. Indeed, the frequently posed question 'Could Wellington have won at Waterloo but for the Prussians?' needs to take note of the fact that, but for this promise, he would have made different moves on the seventeenth and eighteenth.

At the same time, because he was to rest on the defensive on the eighteenth rather than continuing to retreat, Wellington had to take care of his flanks in order to ensure that Napoleon would not outflank his new position. To that extent, Napoleon's operational potential helped influence the British response even if Napoleon did not exploit the potential. To protect the more westerly route to Brussels, that from the southwest, Wellington decided that 17,000 troops and twenty-eight cannon under Prince Frederick of Orange should adopt a defensive position to the south of Hal.

To the east, Wellington was greatly strengthened by the decision by Blücher's chief of staff, Gneisenau, to retreat north from Ligny rather than east toward Liège and, further to the rear, the Prussian Rhineland, and, in retreating north, to concentrate Blücher's IV Corps, that under Bülow, with the three others. Not only had Napoleon failed to execute a manoeuvre sur les derrières success-fully against Blücher on the sixteenth or Wellington on the seven-teenth, but he had also failed to direct the direction of the Prussian retreat. Blücher's injuries put the burden of command on Gneise-nau, who understood the operational and strategic importance of cooperation with Britain and was also the effective staff officer nec-essary to plan appropriate movements. In contrast, in 1792, after the battle of Jemappes, the Austrians had retreated east on Cologne, abandoning Belgium to the French and opening up the possibility that they would advance north on the Netherlands.

Grouchy, with his force of 32,000 troops and ninety-six cannon, failed to grasp the direction of retreat of the bulk of the Prussian army, so that, on the afternoon of the seventeenth, he was posi-tioned ready to advance to the east, the direction in which he believed the Prussians were retreating. Grouchy's failure owed much to his inability to maintain close contact with the Prussians. A slow start and the delay caused by heavy rain on the afternoon of the seventeenth were compounded by Grouchy's inability to under-stand, let alone control, the situation and by a slowness for which he was to be criticised.[13] As a result, Blücher, who retreated to Wavre on the seventeenth, was, by the end of the day, closer to Wellington than Grouchy was to Napoleon. It was only late on the afternoon of the seventeenth that Grouchy advanced north, and even then, he was not in contact with the main Prussian force. This Prussian proximity to Wellington posed a serious problem for Napoleon and reversed the situation that he had sought to achieve with his invasion and had indeed achieved in part on the sixteenth. But Napoleon was confident that the Prussians would not intervene when he attacked Wellington.

Napoleon's operational confidence that he could control the pieces matched that shown with his instructions to Ney on 16 June. In each case, it is possible to blame his subordinates, as well as poor staff-work, and each, indeed, bears a portion of the responsibility for failure. Yet the command and institutional faults of the army were in part Napoleon's fault, or he should at least have been aware of them and have known how to plan accordingly. These, in a sense, were lesser faults than Napoleon's confidence in his plan and his misplaced certainty that he could understand the options faced by his opponents and direct their responses accordingly.

In many respects, this mistaken confidence was to be matched by the German General Staff in 1914, as its planning of war with France and Russia was flawed by an assumption that it could dictate the responses of others and also because it had no Plan B in the event of the failure of its initial plan.[14] Napoleon lacked the resources of Germany in 1914, but the same attitudes that Helmuth von Moltke the Younger and his colleagues were to show in 1914 helped ensure that Napoleon would be unsuccessful with his plan.

Wellington drew up his forces on the evening of the seventeenth on the ridge of Mont St. Jean, a position that still blocked the road to Brussels from Charleroi and was about ten miles to the west of the Prussian positions near Wavre. Blücher's promise to march west next day and to attack Napoleon in the flank encouraged Wellington to decide to fight if Napoleon chose to attack on the eighteenth, a Sunday. The French, meanwhile, were strung out to the south of Wellington. They were to get the battle Napoleon wanted, but without his having the advantage of taking the British by surprise or depriving them of the prospect of Prussian assistance. French options had therefore closed in.

That night, Wellington's second in command and cavalry commander, Henry, Earl of Uxbridge, asked the duke what his plans were. Wellington replied by asking whether he or Napoleon would attack first and by pointing out that 'as my plans will depend upon his, how can you expect me to tell you what mine are? . . . There is one thing certain, Uxbridge, that is, that whatever happens, you and I will do our duty.'[15]

6.

THE BATTLE: EARLY STAGES

WELLINGTON'S POSITION WAS A strong one, because of the battlefield position he had chosen and the prospect of Prussian help – in other words for tactical and operational reasons. Riding the area in the weeks prior to Napoleon's invasion of Belgium, at a time when an invasion appeared a likely prospect, Wellington had seen the Mont St. Jean ridge as a suitable defensive position. Indeed, Henry, third Earl Bathurst, the secretary of state for war and the colonies, confidently told his colonial undersecretary, 'The Duke has long since fixed upon the position at Waterloo as that on which he meant to fight and I will not believe that in a position taken by himself he can be otherwise than victorious.'[1]

The inability to hold on at Quatre Bras made the Mont St. Jean ridge more suitable and underlined the need for a position that was strong not only in itself but also with reference to the Prussians. Nevertheless, other positions were considered between the one eventually adopted and the ground just north of Genappe, where the defender, on the higher ground, would benefit from the attackers' need to advance north across the River Dyle. Wellington instructed his quartermaster-general, Colonel Sir William De Lancey, to select a defensive position south of Waterloo, and De Lancey considered the ground later taken up by Napoleon, centring on La Belle Alliance. However, De Lancey thought this position too extended for defensive purposes. To hold it therefore would have lessened the density of the British defence, a density that was to be very important in the battle, while the position might also have been more readily flanked than the one eventually adopted on the ridge to the south of the Mont St. Jean farm.

The Waterloo Map that survives in the Royal Engineers Museum at Gillingham has pencil marks reputedly made by Wellington that reveal his plans for troop dispositions. The map also shows the way in which terrain was then recorded, with what this method of recording implies for the understanding of the situation. The modern system of contouring only developed later in the nineteenth century, but on the map, the summits of the hills around Waterloo carry numbers recording their relative height. This system, 'relative command', had been taught by a French émigré, François Jarry, who in 1799 became topographical instructor at the Royal Military College in High Wycombe.

'Relative command' was an apt description, as cannon on higher positions dominated those lower down. Wellington requested that the sketches, joined together as the Waterloo Map, be sent to him in order that he could plan his dispositions. Lost and recovered at Quatre Bras, the map was marked up by Wellington on 17 June and given by him to De Lancey with instructions to deploy the troops accordingly. De Lancey was carrying the map when he was mortally wounded by a French cannonball while in Wellington's entourage near the close of the battle.[2] De Lancey's fate serves as a reminder of the much-commented-upon danger to which the duke was exposed, one that Napoleon, who did not advance to the front, was not to match.

The position Wellington was to hold covered the roads from both Charleroi and Nivelles, which joined at Mont St. Jean village to the north of the Mont St. Jean farm, which, in turn, was to the north of the ridge along which the road ran from Braine l'Alleud to Ohain. The position was also linked by tracks to the area to the east where the Prussians were regrouping and was the last defensive position south of the Forest of Soignes. The battlefield was small and, even when the combat area expanded to include the area of

Prussian attack, it was only four kilometres by four kilometres, a marked contrast with the position at Leipzig. The fighting involving only Wellington's army took place in an even more concentrated space, one that had breadth but not depth. Ironically, no fighting took place at the actual village of Waterloo, which is to the north of the village of Mont St. Jean.

Wellington took advantage of the Mont St. Jean ridge to use his favoured deployment of a reverse slope that would protect his troops from view and from most artillery fire. This position had two strongpoints to the fore, the farms at Hougoumont and La Haie Sainte. The former, 400 metres in front of Wellington's right flank on the ridge, protected this flank and, unless the farm could be taken, channelled the direction of French attack on this part of the battlefield. Hougoumont was a formidable position, as, aside from the substantial farm buildings, it offered the defensive potential of a walled garden, an orchard, hedges and woods. Only 250 metres to the front of Wellington's centre, La Haie Sainte provided a bastion to protect the centre, which similarly threatened to disrupt any French advance. La Haie Sainte was smaller than Hougoumont, but its defensive value was strong, due to the cohesion of the farm buildings and its garden and orchard.

To the front of Wellington's left, there were two farms, Papelotte and La Haie; Frichermont, a château; and the small village of Smohain, all of which were garrisoned and could serve as strongpoints, but as significant in the protection of Wellington's left was the indented terrain, which owed much to the valley of the River Lasne. Steep slopes, sunken lanes and a vegetation of thick hedges offered a degree of protection against French advance, not least because these strengths were accentuated by the impact of the very wet weather. The rain had fallen in torrents the previous night. General Robert Manners of the Tenth Hussars noted:

> The ground here was very strong, having a ravine in its front, in which stand the hamlets of Smohain, La Haie and Papelotte . . . The enemy therefore here confined himself to

demonstrations, and made no serious attempt against this part of the position. It was subject, however, like the rest of our line, to his cannonade during the day.[3]

Aside from the prospect of Prussian arrival on Wellington's left, it is easy to appreciate why Wellington thought his right flank more vulnerable. Somerset noted:

> The position selected by the Duke of Wellington was on a high ridge a short distance in front of the village of Waterloo. Across the centre ran the high road to Brussels. The right flank, where Lord Hill's corps was posted, was thrown back – on the right of the centre there was a large building in a wood called Hougoumont, which formed a strong post, and was occupied by a detachment of the Guards. Beyond the left flank was the Prussian post at Wavre, and it was expected that if the British were attacked, the Prussians should move to their support.[4]

The strength of Wellington's position is often remarked, and it was the best on offer, but the position still had serious disadvantages. In particular, the approaches the French might take were not obstructed by a river and thus channelled by its crossing points. The Ligny brook had played such a role at Ligny, reducing the options on the Prussian left, but there was no equivalent at Waterloo. Napoleon was to criticise Wellington's choice of battlefield, but he was scarcely an impartial commentator, and the battlefield did provide Wellington with excellent defensive terrain, not least for the kind of battle he wished to fight.

Wellington's force, about 68,000 strong, was deployed on a frontage of three kilometres, with a 7,000-strong Dutch division located a kilometre farther to the west, a force that would protect against a flank attack round Hougoumont. To the same end, another 17,000 troops were twelve kilometres west at Hal. This was a disposition of troops, with 24,000 men held back from the battle, that would have looked very unwise had the French broken through Wellington's centre, and, in that event, Wellington had needed to feed in reserves in order to hold them off.

In some respects, the forces located at Hal reflected the strong concern for a western deployment that had reflected Wellington's view (but also led him to his conviction) that the French would advance on the Mons road, a conviction now transposed onto anxiety for his flank. Yet Wellington was not to know that Napoleon would focus so exclusively on frontal attacks, nor that he would not make more use of the troops he initially employed in the battle as a reserve in order to threaten Wellington's flanks. Moreover, the troops at Hal would have played a crucial role in covering the retreat to the North Sea at Ostend had Wellington been defeated. He would have had no wish to see his army suffer a punishing retreat comparable to that through the Netherlands in 1795.

The majority of Wellington's troops on the three-kilometre frontage he took on what became the battlefield was deployed west of the Brussels-Genappe road, and this compactness helped ensure that a lot of the infantry was formed up in a four-deep line. In contrast, the British left, to the east of this road, was less strongly protected, both in the main frontage and, even more, in flank units. This lack of strength was due to the position of the Prussians to the east and to Blücher's promise to march to Wellington's assistance. Indeed, fewer than a third of Wellington's infantry battalions and only five batteries of artillery were deployed east of the Brussels road. Thus the prospect of Prussian help not only determined Wellington's decision to fight but also the deployment he adopted.

In contrast, sixteen batteries were on the western half of the battlefield, which was also the section where Wellington spent most of the day. He correctly saw his presence as playing a key role in strengthening the defence. Moreover, instead of locating the cavalry on the flanks, as was conventional, seven of Wellington's nine cavalry brigades were deployed in support of the centre and right, contributing to an uncommonly compact deployment and an in-depth defence.[5] The cavalry brigades lost their cannon, which were joined to the other artillery batteries in the front of the infantry. Whereas the latter, like the cavalry, were on the reverse slope of the ridge, the cannon were on the forward slope, so as to be able to see the French in order to aim and fire at them.

Not everyone thought Wellington's position a good one, as a British visitor to Jérôme Bonaparte in 1823 noted:

> He [Jérôme] expressed his astonishment at Wellington taking up so bad a position at St. Jean, so had Grouchy come up instead of being humbugged by a weak body of Prussians near Wavre and had he [Grouchy] listened to the advice of his generals and marched on to the fire and if the English in that, or any other case, gave way, they could never have retreated, and must have surrendered.[6]

This view neglected Blücher's more advantageous position to Wellington's left, although a further delay in Blücher's arrival would certainly have found Wellington vulnerable.

Napoleon had intended to launch his attack at 9:00 A.M. on Sunday the eighteenth, but his troops were not ready. In part, the delay reflected the rain, the effects of which were particularly serious for moving the cannon forward. The weight of the gun-carriages was such that firm soil was necessary for their deployment and, in its absence, these carriages sunk into the mud. With his artillery background, this problem would have been a particularly important factor to Napoleon. Moreover, the combination of mud and wet crops made the advance far more arduous for the attacker, especially if having to advance uphill, which was the situation of the French. This combination reduced both the speed and the shock capacity of the attacking force. Indeed, Sir William Robert Clayton of the British Royal Horse Guards noted 'torrents of rain . . . the ground presented a surface of mud; and which, soon after the commencement of the action became so deep, on that part of the ground on which we moved, as to render it very difficult when advancing to the charge, to put our horses into a trot.'[7]

The softness of the wet soil also lessened the impact of the French bombardment. Instead of bouncing forward with deadly effect, cannonballs rested where they hit the ground, while howitzer shells were less effective than they would otherwise have been.

An officer of the Tenth Hussars noted:

> It was the ground that took off the effect of shot, much from its being deep mud, from the rain and trampling of horse and foot – so that often shot did not rise – and shells buried and exploded up and sending up the mud like a fountain. I had mud thrown over me in this way often.[8]

More serious than the rain as a cause of delay was the extent to which the French army had been spread over a large area the previous night, in part searching for the scanty shelter and firewood available. Logistics could scarcely meet such requirements, but the resulting problems compounded the difficulties created by poor staff-work. Bringing up and organising the French army for the assault led to serious delay, which progressively put back the time of attack. This delay in arranging his forces would have made a flank attack less plausible even had Napoleon sought it. He neither did so, nor attacked with the forces available while feeding in other units as they arrived, as the Prussians were to do.

Napoleon seems to have lacked urgency and energy on 18 June and was subsequently to claim that his fortune had abandoned him. He was not fit, and indeed, on 15 July, Captain Senhouse, who dined with him on H.M.S. *Bellerophon,* wrote of 'his body so corpulent as to project very considerably.'[9] At Waterloo, suffering from prolapsed haemorrhoids and cystitis and possibly from the after-effects of an epileptic fit, he was confident that he could beat Wellington and pleased that he had now fixed him. Thus, the issue of 17 June, that of ensuring contact, provided the context for Napoleon's views on the eighteenth, without his making the necessary transfer to the new circumstances.

Overconfidence probably played a role, and Napoleon's conduct of both campaign and battle suggests that he thought his opponents easy meat. Indeed, he was inclined to be dismissive of those who urged caution in the assessment of Wellington, such as Soult,

who had been defeated by the Duke at Oporto in 1809 and at
Toulouse in 1814. Napoleon was critical of Wellington and the
British troops in his remarks to his staff on the morning of Waterloo, although on other occasions, he had revealed more respect for
the Duke's generalship.[10]

Part of Napoleon's confidence reflected his knowledge that
Wellington's army contained many Dutch, Belgian and German
units, most of which had only limited experience.[11] Combined,
these troops were more numerous in Wellington's army than the
British. Moreover, Napoleon was sure that the Prussians would not
be a factor. He took this view because he exaggerated the impact of
Ligny, did not appreciate the nature and consequences of the Prussian moves on the seventeenth, and foolishly thought Grouchy equal
to any challenger.

The main French army, about 72,000 men strong – in other
words, only slightly larger than Wellington's army – was formed up
on either side of the Brussels road, with similar strength in each
part. In comparison with the British army, the French one was
markedly symmetrical in its dispositon. The plan was for a frontal
attack by massed forces along the axis of the road, an attack
designed to defeat Wellington, capture the Mont St. Jean crossroads, and move on to enter Brussels in triumph. Indeed, the
prospect of looting Brussels was believed to encourage the French
troops.

Wellington was to be reported as saying 'that Napoleon tried to
gain the victory at Waterloo in the same way he gained other victories, by moving upon the enemy immense bodies of cavalry at a
slow pace, and then following up advantages gained by furious
attacks of infantry.'[12] The front line was composed of Ney's 'left
wing' that had fought or failed to fight at Quatre Bras, with Reille's
II Corps to the left of the road and d'Erlon's I Corps to the right.
Behind was Lobau's VI Corps in the centre, a cavalry corps on either
side of it, and the Imperial Guard farther back in the centre. Thus,
with the crucial exception of a third of the army strength, including two corps, under Grouchy, the French army that had invaded
Belgium was now arrayed in three sections. The lengthy deployment

of this force was probably in part intended to intimidate Wellington's army. Ney was in tactical charge of the French forces, a surprising selection given his failures over the two previous days, but
Napoleon did not have a great choice and Ney, very much a fighting general, was believed able to inspire the troops.

Due to the delays of the morning, notably thanks to the weather,
and the problems of organising the French forces, many of these
troops were not yet in their designated positions when the battle
began. This delay was notably the case of the artillery that was to
comprise the Grand Battery, when, at about 11:30 A.M., the fighting started anyway with cannon fire against Hougoumont designed
to prepare for the advance on the wood to its south.

More information exists for the Battle of Waterloo than for most
in the French Revolutionary and Napoleonic Wars, and the battle
has received more attention, scholarly and nonscholarly, than the
other land battles. Yet, as for other battles, there is much that is
unclear, including, for Waterloo, the precise casualty figures. Writing on 22 June 1815, a British officer noted, 'Do not believe the
amount of loss in the first Gazette for numbers are coming up again
and I think the thing has been done cheaper than we imagined.'[13]

Moreover, there is a tendency to provide a clear narrative of the
battle, one essentially that follows the pattern set in nineteenth-
century accounts, of a sequence of French attacks, 'the five acts into
which that great drama was divided.'[14] This tendency is not without cause, but these accounts were, and are, very much an attempt
to explain what was in process a far less sequential and readily struc-
tured battle.

Wellington himself offered no such clarity. His dispatch written
next day, when, of course, he had other things on his mind, referred
to the French in terms of 'repeated attacks of cavalry and infantry,
occasionally mixed, but sometimes separate', which was correct but
not terribly helpful.[15] In August 1815, Wellington returned to the
theme with a comparison that would have been especially instructive to contemporaries:

The history of a battle is not unlike the history of a ball [dance].

> Some individuals may recollect all the little events of which
> the great result is the battle won or lost; but no individual
> can recollect the order in which, or the exact moment at
> which, they occurred, which makes all the difference as to
> their value or importance.[16]

The attack on Hougoumont was launched by the Sixth Division
under Prince Jérôme Bonaparte, Napoleon's youngest brother, who
had been made king of Westphalia in 1807, part of the party-bag
presents given to Napoleon's relatives after he conquered much of
Europe. The unimpressive Jérôme, who had done badly at Quatre Bras,
was to launch a series of attacks on Hougoumont during the day,
none of which succeeded. Moreover, this series had a seriously detri-
mental impact on II Corps. Although not all of this corps was
involved in the attacks, most of it was, especially the Sixth and Ninth
infantry divisions. Thus Hougoumont served to soak up a greatly
disproportionate number of French troops. Such a result was very
much against Napoleon's intention, because he seems to have intended
that a preliminary attack on Hougoumont would draw in some of
Wellington's reserves, easing the way for the main French attack on
the British centre, which was intended for soon after 1:00 P.M.

Wellington, who told the position commander, Lieutenant-
Colonel James Macdonnell, that Hougoumont had to be held at all
costs, did send in reinforcements, but not in numbers to match
those deployed by the French, a decision that left plenty of troops in
place to repel the French attacks elsewhere. Initially, the French
took most of the wood and Great Orchard near Hougoumont,
before British counterattacks after 12:15 P.M. retook the orchard
and held the French in the wood. A French attack by fresh troops at
12:30 led to a crisis when about thirty French troops forced the
entrance to the north gate at Hougoumont. However, the gates
were forced shut by the defenders and the French inside killed.
Moreover, at about 1:15 P.M., a counterattack drove the French back
from outside the gate and temporarily stabilised the situation,
enabling a reinforcement of the garrison, which sustained the problem it posed for the French.

Indeed, Colonel Stanhope was to report next day, 'The steadiness and inconquerable obstinacy with which the Second Brigade [of Guards] held a wood and house in the front of our right excited the admiration of all and saved us, for it was the angle from whence Lord Hill's corps was formed.'[17] Stanhope was suggesting that Hougoumont was the key to Wellington's right, and Jérôme himself claimed in 1823 that, without Hougoumont falling, Napoleon could not have won.[18] The battle for Hougoumont was to continue all day, and this serves as a reminder that events were taking place simultaneously across the battlefield. Although it was (and is) the general pattern of exposition, in practice there was no sequence of isolated grand French attacks staged while other units, both French and British, remained as spectators.

While the fighting raged round Hougoumont and, to the east, the Prussians advanced toward the battlefield, the main French attack on Wellington's army had been launched. The attack was preceded and prepared, from about 1:00 P.M., by the opening up of the French Grand Battery, orders for the assembly of which had been given at about 11:30 A.M. This battery consisted of eighty cannon, of which forty-two were six-pounders, eighteen twelve-pounders and twenty howitzers. The battery deployed for about a kilometre along the ridge south of the British position, a ridge that was slightly lower than the British ridge, which made it even harder for the French cannon to hit British positions on the reverse slope. The French artillery was deployed in front of the main French position, which reflected the extent to which there was no danger that Wellington would attack despite his number of troops being close to those of Napoleon.

The positioning of the French artillery ensured that the British forward slopes were exposed to fire from between 600 and 800 metres. However, due to the British deployment of their troops on the reverse slopes, which could only be readily hit by the howitzers (and then without the gun crews being able to see the target), the French target was essentially the British artillery on the forward slopes. These cannon were a difficult target, not at all that of massed troops, and, as a result, British casualties from the bombardment were relatively low. At Waterloo, the French artillery did not have the impact it achieved at such battles as Wagram and Ligny. This limited impact was a major failure for combined-arms operations, a failure resulting not from a lack of French effort but from Wellington's skillful exploitation of the topography. Like Montgomery in the Second World War, Wellington was very careful of the lives of his troops. His apparent views on Prussian folly in exposing their troops at Ligny would have driven home the value of using the reverse slopes.

The French crucially lacked information that would be of specific value for targeting and also for planning tactics. In the 1790s, the French had used balloons for artillery target spotting. One balloon played a reconnaissance role at the Battle of Fleurus in 1794 (a battle fought between Ligny and Charleroi) and, thereafter, about twenty more were sent to French armies.[19] Napoleon's decision to disband them can be seen as an instance of his inherent military conservatism, but the difficulties of transporting the gas-generating apparatus and the time required to inflate the balloons gravely limited their value.[20] Moreover, the amount of smoke on battlefields obscured the view: observation balloons became a practical instrument only when smokeless gunpowder was invented toward the end of the nineteenth century.

Thus there was nothing to help make the French artillery more effective at Waterloo. To have pushed the cannon closer to the British line would have been of scant use as a valley lay to the north of the Grand Battery, which would have increased the French difficulty in hitting their targets. Moreover, the British troops would have remained on the reverse slope. This position also rendered the French use of skirmishers of little value other than to fight their British counterparts. Without the presence of British skirmishers, French skirmishers could have caused problems for the British artillery.

The French frontal attack that was intended to settle the battle was launched at 1:30 P.M. by the four infantry divisions of d'Erlon's I Corps. They were expected to break into the centre of Wellington's position, a success that it was planned would be exploited by the French cavalry as well as the VI Corps and the Imperial Guard. This blow would shatter the British defence and the exploitation would destroy the army.

D'Erlon's troops, the First, Second, Third and Fourth Divisions, about 17,600 men in total, had to walk through the tall, wet crops and to tread their way through the Grand Battery, both of which delayed their progress. The French units then formed up in their assault formations across a frontage of over a kilometre. As with the British against the Americans at Bunker Hill in 1775, and, to a lesser extent, New Orleans in 1815, there was no element of surprise in this attack, and indeed, the French troops shouted 'Vive l'Empereur!' while their opponents remained silent. Moreover, the failure of the French attack at Hougoumont meant that the British units facing d'Erlon had not been weakened in order to seek to strengthen the front in that area or to cover for its collapse.

The French troops advanced in four dense columns. This density increased their vulnerability to the British cannon, which had not been silenced by the Grand Battery. Nevertheless, there were fewer British cannon than to the west of the road, which ensured that the British cannon fire could not inflict more damage on the French. However, as the French troops neared the crest of the ridge, they were exposed as well to heavy musket fire at close range, and this fire caused the advance to slacken. So also did the delay necessary while the columns deployed into lines. Nevertheless, despite the defensive fire and their heavy losses, at about 2:15 P.M., French units either crossed or nearly reached the hedge in front of the west–east road on the crest.

Some of the defenders on what was the weakest section of Wellington's front could not cope. Four out of the five battalions in Bijlandt's brigade, a Dutch-Belgian force that had engaged in a damaging and heavy firefight with the French, retreated in disorder, creating a serious gap in the defence. The officers tried to prevent the retreat but were unable to prevail and, although many of the Dutch-Belgian troops briefly returned to their posts, they soon fell back. The officers themselves took heavy casualties. Napoleon appeared to have won, far more rapidly than at Ligny two days earlier and without using his reserves.

Meanwhile, in the centre, and as part of the advance, French infantry of the First Division were drawn into a struggle for La Haie Sainte, capturing the orchard and cutting off the farm from the main British position. In response, Wellington, who was in the centre of his position, facing d'Erlon's advance, sent a battalion of Hanoverian infantry to help La Haie Sainte. This battalion, however, was surprised in an unprepared position and badly cut up in an attack by two French heavy cavalry regiments.

The retreat of Bijlandt's men was to be the high point of French success. D'Erlon's troops were inadequately prepared for the fighting that was to ensue, fighting that required both defensive strength, able to see off British counterattacks, and a capacity to sustain the advance. There were, for example, no light cannon with the advancing French units. To the east of the Brussels–Genappe road, the French attack found the British infantry behind the crest well able to respond. British battalions in reserve moved forward to join what was left of Bijlandt's brigade. Lieutenant-General Sir Thomas Picton, the divisional commander, was shot through the head, dying and falling from his horse. The fatalistic Picton had anticipated his death, and had already been wounded by a musket ball at Quatre Bras. Nevertheless, as with the navy at Trafalgar in 1805, British fire discipline ensured deadly volleys. Moreover, the infantry remained steady, counteracting the effect of the Dutch flight, and was able to advance against the French infantry. Indeed, Major-General Sir Denis Pack, the brigade commander, instructed the Gordon Highlanders to charge in order to save the situation, and, as they approached the French Third Division, the latter fell back.

The ability of the British infantry to hold back the French advance and thus thwart the first stage of Napoleon's plan was a key moment in both battle and campaign. Victory early in the battle, and at modest cost, would have left Napoleon in a very different situation from victory late in the day and at heavy cost. This moment tends to be underplayed in accounts of the battle and was certainly underplayed in the visual memorialisation offered by paintings and engravings. The comparisons with the repulse of the French cavalry and the defeat of the Imperial Guard later in the day are particularly instructive.

This contrast is significant for the way in which Waterloo was recalled and is understood. The general emphasis is on a long struggle, on British fortitude in the face of repeated attacks, and of eventual victory almost as a reward for this heroic defence. Such an approach necessarily moves away from any understanding of British victory primarily in terms of the defeat of d'Erlon's attack, let alone with reference to the earlier failure of Napoleon's attempt to drive his opponents apart. Other factors also play a part. The cavalry and Guard attacks seem more dramatic, the units involved were more prestigious, and the attacks were directed at the core of the British position. In the film *Waterloo* (1970), it is the French cavalry attack that is given the central place.

While these episodes were indeed very significant, there is, nevertheless, an underplaying of the British infantry's defeat of d'Erlon's attack, although this is less serious than the underrating of the eventually successful Prussian assaults on Plancenoit later in the day. The infantry clash as d'Erlon attacked was also to be overtaken in drama by the advance of the British cavalry against the French troops, but, while important, that advance overlooks the importance of the clash.

The likely effect of a protracted clash between the British and French infantry is unclear, not least because the two forces were not evenly balanced. The French, though superior in number and not affected, as the British were, by heavy casualties at Quatre Bras, were weakened by a lack of immediately available reserves, notably cavalry but also infantry, as well as by the serious confusion attendant on the smoke and noise of the battlefield. Moreover, the failure of the British to retreat in the face of the French advance posed a challenge for the French. More generally, the clash underlined the need for units to retain order and responsiveness in difficult circumstances.

These circumstances became far more difficult for the French, as this climax of the battle saw a decisive intervention by the British cavalry, which launched a surprise attack on the advanced French forces. To the west of the main road, in response to orders at about 2:20 P.M. from Henry, second Earl of Uxbridge, the commander of the British cavalry, the Household Cavalry Brigade under Major-General Lord Edward Somerset advanced against the French heavy cavalry that had routed the Hanoverians sent to help La Haie Sainte. The need to move up the reverse slope and to cross the road at the top of the crest ensured that they could not charge until shortly before they were on the French, but when they did so, they had the advantage of height on the slope, while their swords were also regarded as particularly deadly by the French. This was the sole major clash between heavy cavalry units during the battle, and it found the French with the advantage of longer swords and cuirasses (breastplates), while the British had surprise and the slope. Although the cuirasses provided some protection, they were heavy and impeded easy movement. In contrast, the British cavalry did not wear armour. As the French generally did not use their élite heavy cavalry in the Peninsula, this was its first major clash with British heavy cavalry.

After a bitter mêlée of individual clashes, which is what cavalry actions rapidly became, the French broke, being pursued by the British cavalry, some of whom crossed the main road and joined in the advance of the Union Brigade against the French infantry to the east of the road. That Brigade was composed of three regiments: the English Royals, the Irish Inniskillings and the Scots Greys, under Major-General Sir William Ponsonby. This advance also was launched by Uxbridge's order. The cavalry here had to advance up the reverse slope and pass through the British infantry before it could attack the French infantry in d'Erlon's divisions. Where the French had not yet crossed the hedges and road, they also had to be crossed by the British cavalry, but where the French had crossed, then the cavalry had to advance to clear the crest. The cavalry, over 1,300 strong, hit the French columns hard. The latter were not prepared for a cavalry attack, which provided the cavalry with their opportunity.

The French infantry were driven back, losing about 2,000 prisoners as well as two regimental Eagles, the symbol and rallying
point of a regiment. The First, Second and Third Divisions suffered
particularly heavily. The prisoners were escorted to Brussels.

The cavalry advance was famously to be recorded in Lady Butler's
painting *Scotland Forever,* but this depiction of the Scots Greys,
exhibited in 1881, apart from being criticised by experts because
some of the horses depicted would have collided with each other,
also showed the cavalry as charging, which was not the case. As,
however, with so many cavalry advances, for example that of the
Royalists under Prince Rupert in the English Civil War at the climactic battle of Naseby in 1645, the Union Brigade lost all discipline and cohesion. The troopers ignored efforts by the officers to
reform the Brigade so that it could respond to developments. Such
losses of control had happened sufficiently often in the Peninsular
War to make the failure at Waterloo reprehensible, but much of the
cavalry in Wellington's army at Waterloo had had no experience of
these attacks. At any rate, the Union Brigade charged on, attacking
the infantry, before advancing into the Grand Battery where they
inflicted considerable damage on the gunners and their horses. Not
a single cannon, however, was put out of action by spiking.

In this situation, without order and with their horses winded, so
that their riders lacked much mobility, the cavalry was hit by
French counterattacks from front and, more seriously, from the
lancers on the left of the British cavalry. Due to the vulnerability of
the disorganised and exhausted British cavalry, these lancers, who
could lack flexibility against prepared forces, proved particularly
deadly, their long lances unmatched by the British swords. The
lancers were also ready to stab repeatedly those who were unhorsed
and/or wounded. The British cavalry were driven back with heavy
casualties – including the commander of the Union Brigade, Ponsonby, who was killed – while the French regained the guns of the
Grand Battery.

To cover the retreat of what remained of the Union Brigade, the
British moved forward light cavalry and the rocket troops, which,
however, produced diversion rather than damage. At the same time,

some observers suggested that the rockets affected the French cavalry. Rockets were difficult to aim and direct, and they sometimes did as much damage to the force using them as to the enemy. Wellington was sceptical about the value of rockets because of the difficulty of controlling their flight. The rockets had been used during Wellington's retreat on the afternoon of the seventeenth, but on the eighteenth, only fifty-two rockets were fired, and the Royal Horse Artillery Rocket Troop fired far more round shot and case-shot than it did rockets. The extent to which Wellington's dislike for rockets was responsible for these figures is unclear.

To Wellington's exasperation, the Household and Union Brigades had lost much of their strength, and the survivors were disorganised. Indeed, in the battle as a whole, the brigades lost nearly half their members, mostly in these charges. Nevertheless, the cavalry had played a key role in destroying the French advance, not least by preventing d'Erlon's corps from exploiting their gain of the crest. The British infantry were already doing so, but the cavalry turned their success into a major trouncing of important French units. Somerset recorded:

> On the first advance of a large body of French cuirassiers to the ridge of the position occupied by the British infantry on the right of the high road, the Household Brigade immediately advanced to charge them; and drove them down the hill in the utmost confusion. The brigade pursuing its advantage, attacked and routed a large body of infantry that was posted further to the rear, but at length having suffered considerable loss, and having come upon the enemy's support it retired to rally and form.[21]

The British cavalry advance was not to be repeated, and the Union Brigade was the sole British unit to reach the main French positions prior to the final advance at the close of the battle. However, as the battle was one in which Wellington intended to remain on the defensive and Napoleon to break the British through attacking, it was the failure of d'Erlon's attack that was crucial. Thereafter, the battle was a matter of shifts and expedients for the French. That, itself, did not mean that the French could not win. Indeed, shifts and expedients had been important to Napoleon's successes, most obviously, but not only, at Marengo (1800) and Jena (1806), and arguably were an increasingly characteristic feature of battles as their scale increased.

Yet the balance of advantage had shifted against the French as a result of d'Erlon's failure. This shift was true not only because of their far greater losses in the battle so far, but also due to the extent to which both II Corps (at Hougoumont) and I Corps (to the east of the main road) had been seriously disrupted as far as their ability to contribute to victory was concerned. Each corps certainly continued to play an important role in the battle, important roles that are underplayed by the standard account of Waterloo in terms of sequential French grand attacks, with the attention shifting first to the cavalry and then to the Guard. Nevertheless, these roles were gravely compromised by the losses and disruption they had suffered. As a consequence of these losses, which Napoleon could not afford, the two corps thereafter played secondary parts in the battle.

As significant in the shifting balance of advantage was the French need to respond to the Prussian advance. At about the same time that the Grand Battery opened up (1:00 P.M.), Napoleon saw movement through his telescope on the hills to the east. This movement was probably the Prussian IV Corps moving near Chapelle St. Robert. In response, the two cavalry divisions of the French VI Corps, the Third and the Fifth, weak divisions with only 2,684 men in total, were ordered to advance and investigate. By about 1:15 P.M., a captured Prussian hussar confirmed the news of the Prussian advance and the remainder of VI Corps was sent to block Blücher, setting off at about 1:30 P.M.

The French VI Corps was a weak one, being particularly short of infantry. Whereas the Guard had twenty-two of the one hundred three French infantry battalions present, and the I and II Corps thirty-three each, the VI Corps had only fifteen battalions, divided between the Nineteenth and Twentieth Infantry Divisions. This weakness resulted when the Twenty-first Division was detached from the corps to join Grouchy, while the Forty-seventh Ligne of the Second Brigade of the Twentieth Infantry Division remained with the Army of the Loire controlling the Vendée. At Waterloo, the VI Corps deployed 7,433 infantrymen, a force insufficiently strong to hold the Prussian advance. Indeed, given its weakness, the corps' success in delaying the Prussian advance on Plancenoit was impressive. Numbers were clearly now a factor, both on the French right against the Prussians and insofar as reserves were available for use against Wellington. The formation of a new French line against the Prussians meant that Napoleon's sole infantry reserve was now the Imperial Guard.

The Prussian advance and Napoleon's response thus gave shape to the crucial issue of reserves. At this stage of the battle, Wellington still had reserves and, indeed, uncommitted forces to the west. Had he possessed the sort of knowledge of opposing moves in fact denied to commanders of the period, he could now have moved many of these forces toward the battle, providing a possible resource if the French attacks broke into the right of his position. Napoleon, in contrast, had to deploy many of his reserves against the Prussians, which removed the option of passing large numbers of fresh units through the earlier attackers in order to sustain attacks, maintain pressure and reinforce attacks. One of the most frequent 'what ifs' concerning the battle relates to earlier and more successful action by Grouchy based on a better understanding of Prussian moves. It is inappropriate to adopt such an approach unless also accepting the possibility that Wellington could have made more active use of his forces to the west.

The alternatives Napoleon faced were unpromising. As the speed of the Prussian advance was uncertain, it would be foolish not to cover his right flank. Facing this advance, Napoleon could have chosen to withdraw from the battle and seek to join with Grouchy, regroup and attack anew, but, even if the French forces had maintained the necessary cohesion, such a regrouping would have thwarted Napoleon's purpose, which was to defeat his opponents in detail (separately). The inability to do so took precedence over the tactical failures of the individual attacks at Waterloo and, indeed,

Ligny and Quatre Bras. Insofar as blame is a helpful concept at this point, Napoleon, not Ney, the battlefield commander at Quatre Bras and Waterloo, deserves the blame for French failure.

The movement of the VI Corps ensured that, apart from the Imperial Guard (a big exception), there could be no follow-up by French infantry to any gains by I or II Corps. They would have to provide any second wave themselves, which highlighted the problems created by their losses. Partly as a result, Ney was to rely on artillery and, even more, cavalry to try to break Wellington's right in midafternoon. Thus, the departure of Lobau's VI Corps meant that the French facing Wellington were outnumbered. This fact put a great premium on their ability to mount the necessary attack at the correct place, and thus gain momentum, using their advantage before their opponents could deploy. Thus, in many respects, the French were back in the situation their commanders faced when attacking in battles in the 1790s, for example at Jemappes in 1792.

The difference, however, was that Napoleon lacked the numerical superiority his predecessors had often enjoyed, as at Jemappes, while his opponents' fighting quality was high at Waterloo. The latter factor would have been even more important had the French been able to gain an advantage they then needed to exploit, but they were unable to create such a possibility. Moreover, the stripping out of a layer of reserves with the movement of VI Corps to face the Prussians ensured that the original French plan could not be relaunched against the same part of the British front or against a different part.

While the British Heavy and Union Brigades charged and the French countercharged, the leading Prussian units were struggling through the defile of the narrow and deep valley of the Lasne, a passage and crossing made more difficult by the results of heavy rain and the fact that there was only one bridge at this point. Fortunately for the Prussians, there were no French troops available to contest the passage, while Wellington, moreover, was holding his position and not planning to retreat, a move that would greatly have exposed the Prussians to French attack. Mutual trust, indeed, was necessary for such alliance operations.

A small French force could have achieved much in the Lasne valley, although there were other crossing points over the Lasne River, and indeed Lieutenant General Hans Ernst Graf von Zeithen's I Corps, which advanced later, was to cross farther north, near Genval. However, the crossing at Lasne, which was used by the Prussian units other than Zeithen's corps, was better placed for putting pressure on the French, as it exposed Napoleon's flank. In contrast, Zeithen's corps essentially protected Wellington, instead of exerting such pressure. Even allowing for the Prussian choice of axes of advance, the lack of French forces to the east of the main French formation and, more particularly, the fact that Lobau's VIth Corps did not move as far east as it might have done, lessened the depth of defence available to the French. This lack of depth was to cause major problems as the Prussians advanced, accentuating the pressure on Napoleon for action in what became a two-front battle, with the French being under attack on one of the fronts. Napoleon's confidence in Grouchy had led him to take no care of his flank, and, conspicuously, to establish nothing to match Wellington's dispositions for his own right flank. This failure was to have dire consequences.

7.

THE LATER STAGES

AT ABOUT 3:30 P.M., French cavalry supported by horse artillery contested the Prussian advance on the eastern end of the Bois de Paris. The commander of the Prussian First Cavalry Brigade, Colonel Count Wilhelm von Schwerin, was killed, one of the first Prussian casualties of the battle, but the French cavalry then retired, leaving the wood to the Prussians. Again, this was a less than firm defence, but it might have seemed that the French were about to defeat Wellington, which would have made the Prussian advance redundant, while the terrain was not suited to cavalry. Not that there is evidence that these considerations shaped the nature of the French resistance to the Prussian advance; indeed, the problems of interpreting evidence need to be set alongside the overready explanation of decisions.

Far from the Bois de Paris and the Prussian advance on what were still the margins of the battle, the French assaulted the centre of Wellington's army with a renewed infantry attack launched at about 3:00 P.M. against La Haie Sainte. The position was nearly surrounded by the French, but they could not break through into the farm buildings – scarcely surprising given the lack of any ready point of access. The compactness of the position also aided the defence and, as yet, the shortage of ammunition facing the defenders was not acute. The role played by the defence of La Haie Sainte in the battle captured the general difficulty of the French situation.

It was proving very hard for the French to use their resources effectively, a product of the earlier, key decision for frontal attack rather than manoeuvre. Indeed, it is easy to understand Wellington's response, in 1842, to Clausewitz's critique, when the duke, having been critical of those who try to rewrite the past with false perspectives, added a reflection:

> It might be a nice question for military discussion whether Buonaparte was right in endeavouring to force the position at Waterloo, or the Duke of Wellington right in thinking that, from the evening of the 16th, Buonaparte would have taken a wiser course if he had moved to his left, have reached the high road leading from Mons to Brussels, and have turned to the right of the position of the Allies by Hal.[1]

Returning to the afternoon of Waterloo, Ney moved forward to observe the situation and, as have many other generals in the confusion and smoke of battle, appears to have misunderstood developments. He saw Wellington moving some of his units, as well as wounded and prisoners, back to reverse-slope positions, where they were protected from the French cannon, and wrongly concluded from this withdrawal that the British were tottering. To exploit this perceived opportunity, and to prevent the British from recovering and creating a new front line, Ney called on his cavalry, although it has also been suggested that the attack initially owed much to the forward movement of some of the cavalry sensing the possibility for action. This explanation was certainly asserted after the battle by a French participant who claimed responsibility.

The motivation of commanders in the battle is difficult to establish beyond doubt, not least, in this case, because Napoleon devoted much of his subsequent career to asserting his rectitude, while Ney, shot by a firing squad in December 1815, was not in a position to challenge and explain. Given that Ney did make mistakes in both campaign and battle and was certainly highly overwrought on the day of Waterloo, it is all too easy to argue that he was responsible for even more mistakes. Nevertheless, Napoleon might have done better had he had the services of Murat.

Cavalry certainly offered a force able to break a weak defence and to catch up with retreating troops, and Waterloo, following Quatre Bras, demonstrated that it was important not to allow the British to retire and regroup. Instead, any rear guard would have to be over-come. At Waterloo, the British, however, were not retreating. Instead, in defensive positions, they resolutely faced the first of a series of cavalry attacks that continued until nearly 6:00 P.M. These attacks were very different from those successfully launched by the French at the overextended British cavalry earlier in the afternoon, not least in their methodical and sustained character. Indeed, during the period from 4:00 P.M. until nearly 6:00 P.M., the French deployed a total of about 9,000 to 10,000 cavalry, supported by about seventy-six cannon. At about 4:00 P.M. on 18 June, over 4,800 French cavalry from Milhaud's IV Reserve Cavalry Corps, which was composed of two divisions of cuirassiers, and General Charles Lefèbvre-Desnoëttes's Guard Light Cavalry Division, attacked, and, soon after 5:00 P.M., they were joined by about another 4,500 men, as Keller-mann's III Reserve Cavalry Corps and General Claude-Étienne Guyot's Guard Heavy Cavalry Division were, at Ney's insistence, fed into the attack.

The French force was formidable, but it faced several major hur-dles. First, there were the serious disadvantages of cavalry attacks on unbroken and prepared infantry. Secondly, the French were out-numbered, and indeed heavily so in the contact zone. Although there were ancillary French infantry assaults on Hougoumont and La Haie Sainte, the cavalry attacked without infantry support and faced a formidable force: about 14,000 infantry supported by sixty-five cannon, and with nearly 8,000 cavalry available in support. In a very different context, this situation prefigured the German tank attack on the well-entrenched and -prepared Soviets at Kursk in 1943, an attack that also failed and, indeed, was seen as a turning point of the war on the eastern front.[2]

Throughout the series of French cavalry attacks, none of the British squares broke. As a result, the defeat of the initial French assault directs attention to the serious command failure, also seen with Jérôme's attacks at Hougoumont, that of repeating defeat and reinforcing failure. This practice is a characteristic military mistake, one that draws on the disinclination to admit failure, the confidence that one more attack or surge will guarantee success, as indeed it sometimes does, and the belief that conflict is primarily a struggle of will. The French attacks can be related to this pattern. Moreover, as another instance of command failure, about 6,500 French infantry were available on the left and not committed to Hougoumont, but they were not used to support the cavalry attack until 5:30 P.M., which was too late to affect the battle in this quarter. By then, the French cavalry had suffered heavy casualties and was exhausted and probably, at least in part, demoralised.

Instead of an earlier commitment of infantry to support the cavalry, cannon were employed, but, although they inflicted serious casualties, such that the British squares preferred to be under cavalry attack (masking the French cannon, which were therefore unable to employ plunging shot), and although some of the French horse batteries were moved forward, most of the French artillery could not get close to the squares.[3] There was no space for the cannon on the slope, which was occupied by the French cavalry, who remained close between attacks, while the frontline British infantry squares were on the reverse slope for the initial attack and thus not exposed to French fire. Only French infantry could have supported the cavalry with sufficient close firepower, and it was not available, a situation that repeated that at Quatre Bras.

The French cavalry themselves lacked drive. Instead of trying to force their reluctant horses to make a breach, the cavalry trotted forward and gesticulated with their sabres or fired their carbines, which did little damage. The failure to charge home against unbroken squares was understandable and accorded with the difficulties of urging horses to this task, but this failure helped ensure that the squares remained unbroken. The cavalry, of course, faced a difficult task, moving uphill, across ground made soft by rain, and having to cope with the confusion created by British artillery and infantry fire.

Confusion and chaos became worse with successive attacks, not least as the difficulties created by noise, smoke and casualties were accentuated by the breakdown of unit cohesion as squadrons split and cavalrymen sought to respond to the problems posed by the unbroken squares. Officers urged their men on, but many troops seem to have been reluctant to close with the British squares, and understandably so. The problem for the cavalry was compounded by the fact that they were fired on not only from the front of the British formations but also, as they moved out of the range of the men at the front, from the flanks and rear.

The slaughter of the French horses, on which many of the British infantry concentrated their fire because they offered larger targets than the troopers and were not protected as the latter were by their breastplates, added to the confusion. Many cavalrymen were injured or trapped by the collapse of their dying mounts, while dead and injured horses created a formidable obstacle to fresh attacks, not least because injured horses became unmanageable and careered off. The noise of shot hitting the breastplates of the French cuirassiers was one of the distinctive sounds of this stage of the battle.

The French cavalry also failed to spike a single British cannon, nor even to damage one. This failure ensured that the cannon, having been overrun, could be used anew against new French attacks once the French had fallen back. The gunners found shelter in the British squares, running out again after the cavalry pulled back, or took shelter under the cannon, where they were difficult for cavalrymen to reach. The French troopers did succeed in catching some gunners as they ran toward the squares. The unwillingness of the French cavalry to dismount in order to spike the cannon reflected in large part the sense of vulnerability that all cavalrymen had when dismounted, as well as the point that the French cavalry really was vulnerable to British infantry and cavalry attack when dismounted. Moreover, spiking guns (driving a spike into the vent through which the powder was ignited) required equipment and time, and, however simple and limited these were, there was a reluctance, in the height of battle, to ensure either.

British artillery posed a serious problem for the French cavalry, which seems to have taken more damage from the British cannon than from the musketry. Muskets were not particularly effective against the armoured breastplates of the cuirassiers. Moreover, the issue of infantry effectiveness was exacerbated because the speed of loading ensured that some British soldiers failed to ram their musket balls sufficiently down the barrel to take the full force of the exploding gunpowder. The survival of the British artillery in the face of the French cavalry repeated that of the French Grand Battery in the face of British attack. This shared failure indicated the psychological context within which cavalry operated.

Wellington's defence was far more effective than the French attack. This defence was multilayered, with the British cannon in advance; the infantry squares providing mutually supportive fire, such that the French were not attacking vulnerable individual squares in a series of distinct battles; and the British cavalry in reserve ready to counterattack should the French penetrate past the frontline squares. This was both a coordinated defence and a defence in depth. Neither might have stood up so well had the French been able to bring up effective supporting infantry and cannon fire, but if the British defensive system would then have had to match like with like, there is every sign that they could have done so. Indeed, British cavalry counterattacks proved effective. The presence of a strong British defence in depth begs the question of whether the French cavalry attack would have had much point even if better supported. The second line of squares would have been a formidable problem for the cavalry even if one of the squares in the first line had collapsed.

Numerous cavalry attacks were launched by the French during the afternoon, generally, but not invariably, in a sequence as waves of horsemen advanced. In the front line, the French cavalry faced thirteen squares, one for about every 100 metres of front, a relatively high density of defence. Five squares were British and eight German: KGL, Hanoverian and Brunswick. The second line of nine squares was all German. The shape of the squares varied, but these formations are referred to as squares.

Wellington and his staff were present, controlling this crucial stage of the battle, with the duke needing to take shelter inside squares. His doing so reflected Wellington's personal stamina on what was a very long day and his preference for direct presence in the key zone of conflict, as well as the fact that he spent much of the battle on the right of his position where the conflict was fiercest. Wellington indeed wrote next day to Lady Frances Webster, 'The finger of Providence was upon me, and I escaped unhurt.'[4] Such a remark was at once a commonplace, a testimony to the extent to which soldiers were religious and fatalistic, and an indication of the sense that a great struggle, one with pronounced religious and moral worth, was taking place.[5]

Wellington's presence certainly had an impact. Lord Apsley claimed, 'The victory was entirely won by the Duke's own personal courage and conduct. He stood in the squares as the French cavalry charged them, and led them on when the cavalry retreated.' Colonel Stanhope reported, 'The Duke of Wellington exposed himself in the hottest fire the whole day and has lost a number of his staff.' A cavalry officer noted, 'The Duke was in the hottest fire as usual – and a Hanoverian regiment giving way he headed and cheered them back himself.' Castlereagh was to comment on the 'extraordinary way in which Wellington exposed his own person.'[6]

In addition to the major French cavalry assaults, individual cavalry units launched attacks as their commanders rallied them. The latter pattern of advances was easier to maintain than the mass attacks, which were difficult to arrange once initial corps' cohesion was lost. As a result, the overall impression became that of disjointed French moves, with a breakdown of cohesion making coordination impossible and complicating the situation for any later description, whether by participants or historians. Ney could not really respond to this confusion, and, indeed, he in part surrendered operational command responsibilities by choosing to lead the first massed cavalry attack at about 4:00 P.M. Thereafter, Ney rushed round the battlefield seeking to rally his men for fresh attacks.

Ney's background was very much that of the cavalry and, as a result, he took a direct part in the cavalry attack, in contrast to his earlier actions. Born, like Napoleon, in 1769, he had joined the cavalry in 1787 and held subsequent cavalry commands, including in General André Masséna's Army of the Danube and Switzerland in 1799, and been inspector-general of cavalry in 1802. In battle, Ney distinguished himself by bravery and leadership in combat, as with the charge across the bridge at Ulm in 1805 and in the seizure of the bridges during the battle of Friedland in 1807, but was also frequently wounded.

At Waterloo, Ney was not shot during the cavalry attacks, and also avoided capture, as the British cavalry did not launch a major counterattack, but the danger to which he exposed himself was indicated by his having three horses shot under him during the cavalry attacks. Ney was determined to keep the pace of the attack up and angrily countermanded Kellermann's orders that Baron Blancard keep his carabiniers in reserve to the southeast of Hougoumont. Instead, Ney had them join the attack after 5:00 P.M. The degree to which Napoleon was responsible for Ney's feeding of failure is unclear. Ney clearly insisted on the first attack, but the addition of General Claude Michaud's Reserve Cavalry Corps (Kellermann and Guyot) was a different matter, not least because this was a key reserve force, and one that could readily have been used elsewhere on the battlefield, for example against the Prussian advance, in support of the Young Guard counterattack on Placenoit, or indeed as a reserve affecting British dispositions and moves. The control of reserves was the key attribute of overall command, as Napoleon showed with his insistence that he retain control of the Imperial Guard. He failed to display an equivalent control of the Reserve Cavalry Corps, possibly because he was focusing on the Prussian threat. Count Henri Bertrand, Napoleon's grand master of the palace, who served Napoleon as an aide at Waterloo, insisted that Ney had been instructed to use the line cavalry and not that of the Guard, but that Ney was able to ignore this after Marshal Edouard Mortier, the Guard's cavalry commander, had to relinquish command due to a severe attack of sciatica.[7] Bertrand also insisted that Napoleon told Ney that he was only to use the cavalry if the British were broken and that they should be supported by the infantry.[8]

At any event, Ney was convinced that this was a moment of destiny, one in which will and opportunity combined. Faced, for example, with reluctance by Baron Jacques-Antoine Delort, the commander of the Fourteenth (Cuirassier) Division, part of Milhaud's corps, who pressed Ney on the danger of attacking unbroken infantry enjoying the advantage of height, Ney insisted, 'in the name of the Emperor', that the cavalry advance to attack, and shouted, 'Forward, the salvation of France is at stake!'

This approach was to subordinate operational considerations to tactical issues, a classic problem in conflict, and, moreover, with the tactical opportunities anyway highly unpropitious. Ney can be faulted for his failure to understand the tactical and operational disadvantages of these attacks, a failure arising from his personality, his concept of command, and the exhausting pressures of a campaign and battle that appeared to be slipping away from France. Yet this can be seen as an aspect of a French campaign that throughout had 'something fortuitous about it, an air of improvisation, a succession of miscalculations.'[9] If Napoleon can also be faulted for failing to control the situation, it was scarcely easy to direct or restrain a general like Ney who led from the front.

More generally, this issue of control was a problem with cavalry operations, as the British experience showed. Moreover, this feature was accentuated by the leadership culture in the cavalry, notably the necessity to accompany a charge and, frequently, to lead from the front. Honour was seen to lie in this role, and honour was a key concept among officers, indeed one that was frequently mistaken for competence. Thus Ponsonby had died in the Union Brigade's advance, trying to retire on a blown horse in the face of the French counterattack, while three-quarters of the French generals in the French cavalry attack on the British squares were killed or wounded.

These casualties contributed directly to the tactical and operational failure of the French cavalry attacks. The French cavalry itself became mixed, and the breakdown in unit cohesion, as units merged in a confused mass, made it difficult to rally the troops, either in order to mount fresh attacks or to withdraw. This difficulty contributed directly to the extent to which, having reached the British positions, the cavalry, already at a serious disadvantage, were not able to make the most of their situation. This failure was dramatised by French cavalrymen who stood off from the British squares and gestured at them, for example by waving their swords.

Moreover, the loss of commanders lessened the possibility of any reconsideration of the use of the cavalry, not least had Ney been a casualty. That his longevity and stubborn determination ensured that the option for such reconsideration was absent made this factor less serious in practice, but, had Ney died, the command situation would have been serious: at best, disrupted and, at worse, with a serious gap between Napoleon and the battlefield command. Guyot was wounded twice in the charges and lost two horses, although Kellermann was not wounded.

The British cavalry counterattacks on the French cavalry benefited from the lack of any comparable exposure to infantry and cannon fire. As a result, the British cavalry was not chewed up. Moreover, the fire to which the French cavalry was exposed disorganised them, and this gave the British cavalry a major advantage. On occasion, however, the French cavalry was able to win encounters with its British rivals.

A stress on French failures should not diminish the strain placed on the British defence, especially by the French artillery, and therefore the impressive resolve of the defence, especially after the initial hesitation of the inexperienced was ended by the failure of the first attack.[10] Colonel James Stanhope of the First Foot Guards reported next day:

> When the French cavalry attacked us in our squares (which
> they did with the most persevering gallantry, never retiring
> above 100 or 150 paces and charging again) our men
> behaved as if they were at a field day, firing by ranks and
> with the best possible aim. Under a most destructive can-
> nonade and having several shells burst in the middle of us,
> not a man moved from his place. . . . At last we became
> exposed to the united efforts of all their arms and changed

from line to squares and from squares to lines, as the circumstances of the case required. . . . There was a moment
peculiarly critical and where nothing but the extraordinary
steadiness of the troops saved the day.[11]

Captain Howard of the Thirtieth Regiment thought 'the most
critical point of the day . . . about four or half past four. The attacks
we have to sustain were principally from cavalry aided by artillery
which were frequent and desperate driving in our light troops and
artillery men who took shelter in the different squares on hands and
knees to avoid the fire opened by them on the enemy. Their cavalry
often passed to our rear without making the slightest impression
upon any body of infantry.'[12]

The squares took heavy casualties, who remained lying alongside
those who fought on, while the physical and psychological strains of
repelling and awaiting attack were considerable.[13] The smoke and
smell of the British muskets were also significant. The heat was also
strong, in part due to the smoke, which lay thick in the heavy, hot
afternoon air, and was accentuated by the sweat of horses and men
who thronged the small battlefield. This sweat contributed to a
potent mix of smells that included copious quantities of human and
animal urine and feces from the densely packed forces, as well as the
sulfur in the gunpowder that exploded as muskets and cannon were
fired.

The noise also pressed hard, not least on nerves, especially the
steady sounds of muskets being prepared and fired, as well as the
explosions of artillery fire, and the sounds of munitions hitting
home. Edward Neville Macready of the Thirtieth Foot found that
the roaring of the cannon and the shouting together produced the
impression 'of a labouring volcano'. An aspect of the disorientation
of battle was given by the novelist Stendahl in the account of
Waterloo in his novel *La Chartreuse de Parme* (1839). Stendhal, the
pseudonym of Henri Beyle, had served in the French army from
1800 to 1814, but he did not fight at Waterloo. He noted the contrast between the sight and sound of battle:

> Our hero realised that it was shot from the guns that was
> making the earth fly up all around him. He looked in vain
> in the direction from which the shots were coming. He saw
> the white smoke of the battery an enormous distance away,
> and, in the midst of the steady and continuous rumble pro-
> duced by the firing of the guns, he seemed to hear volleys of
> shot much closer at hand. He could not make head or tail of
> what was happening.[14]

At the same time, despite the pressure of anticipation affecting
the British infantry squares, the French cavalry attack was not continuous. And this episodic quality provided the infantry with
opportunities to vary their position, for example by lying down in
the face of French cannon fire and also by rapidly forming into lines
in order to fire on the retiring French cavalry, and then returning to
square formations when the latter turned back.

As at the Battle of Trafalgar, where there was wide variation in
British command competence, method and bravery, there were
weaknesses in the Allied response.[15] Indeed, Lord Apsley, who was
present, reported to his father the next day, 'Do not mention this.
Some of our German and *also English* cavalry gave way.'[16] Stanhope
noted, 'Our cavalry could not be brought on,' and, later, wrote that
Uxbridge 'was most furious against the cavalry – in whose defence
it is however to be said that they were outnumbered nearly two to
one.'[17]

Besides the fact that at least one Allied cavalry brigade, Major-
General A. D. Trip's Dutch and Belgian heavy cavalry, refused to
charge, the Brunswick infantry seemed shaky to at least one British
observer, Captain Alexander Mercer of the British Horse Artillery.
However, the Brunswick infantry did not break as Bijlandt's
Netherlands brigade had done in the face of the first major French
advance, that on Wellington's left on the ridge. The retreat of Bijlandt's brigade, nevertheless, served as a warning to Wellington
about the reliability of units under pressure, and it is noteworthy
that the Brunswick squares were strengthened by deploying British
battalions on either side of them. Moreover, under French cannon

fire, the three squares comprised of the inexperienced troops of the First Nassau Regiment had to be rallied by Major-General Jean-Victor de Constant Rebecque, the Prince of Orange's chief of staff. Possibly a firm French cavalry attack on these or the Brunswick squares would have led to their breaking, creating a serious problem for the defence.

As a response to these pressures, Wellington ordered two brigades to advance. Du Platt's KGL brigade was moved through the British front line in order to assist the defence of Hougoumont. This deployment had the effect of narrowing the possible front of the French advance, as well as increasing British firepower in the area and affecting the angle of possible French attack. Moreover, also at about 5:00 P.M., Wellington ordered Major-General Frederick Adam's brigade to move through the Brunswick squares, creating a new front line that screened them. This move formed a new front line northeast of Hougoumont's Great Orchard, a front line intended to resist French cavalry attacks, as well as to oppose French infantry moving forward east of Hougoumont to support the cavalry attacks and to put pressure on the garrison at Hougoumont. Captain James Shaw Kennedy recorded being told by Adam that 'some time before that brigade was moved across the road, the Duke said to Adam, in a very brisk and animated manner, "By G – , Adam, I think we shall beat them yet!"' This assessment was well grounded.[18]

The new, farther forward front line gave Wellington even greater defence in depth but was more vulnerable than the previous one, as it was more exposed to French artillery fire. Moreover, the now more spread-out squares were less able to provide sustained mutual support. Nevertheless, by then, the French attack had been greatly weakened by heavy casualties, as well as by mounting exhaustion.

In the event, these squares were attacked at about 5:30 P.M. by French infantry – Bachelu's division and Foy's brigade – but the attacking infantry were not provided with necessary support from artillery or cavalry, and, partly as a consequence, were heavily exposed to British defensive fire from both cannon and muskets. The clash turned into one between squares and French columns. General Gilbert Bachelu's division broke first in response to the heavy British fire, and this fire, in turn, led to the flight of General Maximilien Foy's brigade. The British did not mount a pursuit, a move that would have meant abandoning their defensive formations, but these French units were now broken, and only some of the troops could be rallied by the commanders. A useful French force had been squandered to little purpose.

The French had greater success farther east, where the defence of La Haie Sainte, which had first come under direct attack from 1:30 P.M., finally fell. The garrison had been reinforced after the initial attack, with the British benefiting from the retreat of d'Erlon's corps in order to reoccupy positions between the farm and the ridge of Mont St. Jean, especially a sandpit and a hedge line, each of which formed defensive sites. The French infantry renewed their attacks at about 3:00 P.M., and La Haie Sainte was largely surrounded. Nevertheless, the French were unable to break into the farm buildings. There was bitter fighting in the gateway to the barn, a position that was weakened because the door had been burned for firewood the previous night. The severity of the struggle can be glimpsed from the efforts of the French to seize the rifles from the defending troops as they pointed out through the loopholes in the walls.

The determined and able defenders (all Germans) were also able to inflict heavy casualties on the French cavalry launching their repeated attacks on Wellington's right. These casualties reflected the extent to which the cavalry riding past to the west of the farm offered clear targets to the defenders and were unable to return fire. By 5:00 P.M., however, the defenders of La Haie Sainte, commanded by Major George Baring of the KGL, were very short of ammunition despite repeated requests that it be sent. Nevertheless, French attempts to set fire to the barn roof were thwarted by soaking it in water, carried in large camp kettles.

The French assaults on La Haie Sainte from 5:00 P.M. to 6:00 P.M. were held off, with much fighting at the entrance to the barn, an entrance blocked with bodies. This fighting underlined the importance of the potential offered by local features to the course of conflict. After a lull, the French, nevertheless, launched fresh attacks, benefiting from fresh troops and from the weak and exhausted state of the defence. Very short of ammunition, the defenders held the initial attacks using rifle butts and bayonets, but the French increased the pressure, climbing onto the roof of the stables, from which they fired down into the yard, and finally forcing an entrance into the barn. French engineers also broke through the farm's main gate, which was on the Genappe road.

Baring issued orders to retreat, a withdrawal that was carried out in fierce circumstances with hand-to-hand fighting in the passageway through the farmhouse. The French bayoneted wounded soldiers whom they captured. Baring's men fell back into the garden to the north of the farm, but this position was judged untenable now that the farm buildings were under French control and able to command the garden. At about 6:15 P.M., Baring ordered his men to retreat north to the main British position.

Gaining the farm was a major achievement for the French, as it covered the direct approach to the Mont St. Jean crossroads and Wellington's centre. Thus La Haie Sainte was far more important as a position than Hougoumont, both with regard to the flow of the battle, and also in terms of the symbolism of success. What happened at La Haie Sainte was much more obvious to the combatants on both sides than developments at Hougoumont.

Wellington, however, had failed to provide sufficient strength to hold the position. This failure was in part a matter of manpower. Only about 400 men were available at the outset, and only about 400 reinforcements from the KGL and the Second battalion of the First Nassau Regiment were sent during the battle. More significantly, the failure to ensure the necessary ammunition supply indicated a lack of preparedness, an issue that was to cause serious recriminations after the battle. This lack of preparedness was also seen in the dispatch of Baring's pioneers and tools to Hougoumont, which lessened the possibility of reinforcing La Haie Sainte, a position left much weakened by the failure to prevent the burning of the barn door and the absence of farm carts that might have served as barricades. As a result, moreover, of the lack of pioneers and tools, it proved impossible to build platforms behind the walls, while the number of loopholes was few. This rarity had the result of greatly reducing the number of British firing positions, which, ironically, helped much in the conservation of ammunition, a classic instance of unintended consequences. James Shaw Kennedy was scathing, subsequently, about the failure to prepare the site, arguing that this endangered the Allied centre:

> The garrison was insufficient, the workmen were taken away, the place was declared to be sufficiently strong for all that was wanted of it, and nothing whatever was done during the night towards its defence; in place of which, the works of scaffolding, loopholing, building up gates and doors, partial unroofing, throwing out the hay and securing a supply of ammunition, should have been in progress all the night and during the morning.

Maybe so, but the nature of the army staff that night scarcely made it possible to ensure that this occurred.[19]

The French themselves deployed up to 7,000 troops against La Haie Sainte, although, given the physical constraints of the restricted site, only 2,000 men could be used for each assault. This factor underlined the problems created by the compression of the battlefield and, in particular, by the French failure to manoeuvre against the British flanks; although, looked at differently, this compression provided an opportunity for massing troops for particular assaults. The troops for the attacks on La Haie Sainte came from d'Erlon's corps and were ordered forward by Ney, although the final assault benefited from the availability of the First Brigade under General Guillaume Pégot of the Fourth Infantry Division, a relatively fresh brigade brought from the French right in order to increase the pressure on the British centre. This troop movement was an important instance of the extent to which the Prussian advance, while very important, could not stop a degree of French consolidation, as critical final attacks on the British centre were launched.

As with the earlier French cavalry attacks, Ney very much took a hands-on command role, pressing forward the assault on La Haie Sainte by bullying the commanders and seeking to motivate the troops. Yet again, this activity raises questions about his ability to distinguish operational command effectiveness from the pursuit of tactical goals. The defenders suffered between 350 and 400 casualties (43 to 50 per cent of their force), but, as at Hougoumont, the French lost far more and also suffered in operational terms from having committed large numbers of men in nearly five hours of fighting.

In the aftermath of the fall of La Haie Sainte, opportunities opened up for French pressure on the British centre, which was a more defined pressure point than the British right against which the French cavalry had been launched. Cannon could now be brought up to within 300 yards of the British position. Ney, however, no longer had the cavalry that he might have launched in an effort to exploit the success. If the terrain in the centre was not well-suited to cavalry, not least due to the steep banks on the sides of the roads, nevertheless, the earlier British cavalry attacks in this area had shown what could be achieved against unprepared infantry.

Seeking to use combined arms, and to increase the pressure on the British defence, Ney brought up a battery of horse artillery, a move to which he had hitherto not devoted sufficient attention. These cannon used canister shot, which was particularly effective at the expense of infantry, against General Sir James Kempt's brigade, drawn up on the ridge. However, the battery fell back when exposed to accurate rifle fire from the sharpshooters of the 1/95 Rifles, who had retreated from the sandpit north of La Haie Sainte.

This episode at once showed how the French artillery could have been more effective, and yet that it could only have been so had it been covered by support from significant numbers of troops. This point suggests a different way of looking at the battle. The French prepared a demonstration victory: artillery at the Grand Battery shredding the British in readiness for the great assault; rather than a move forward of combined arms, in a methodical attempt to increase French firepower and general capability in the prime area of combat. To have pursued with the latter approach would have

forced attack (or retreat) on the British, as it would have been necessary to protect their exposed troops from closer French artillery
fire, but such an attempt would have required on the part of the
French not only a different command style but also a better ability
to grasp the flow of the battle.

Ney's weaknesses as a commander have already been noted, but
they were aspects of a more general problem with French command.
There were twenty-three French marshals alive, but only eight were
willing to serve Napoleon in 1815. It would possibly have been
preferable to have Davout or Soult serve as the commander at the
front, but Davout was in Paris as minister for war, while Soult was
chief of staff. Each, however, was better than Ney at combining
bravery and tactical skill with an understanding of the flow of the
battle.

In an attempt to exploit the fall of La Haie Sainte, French
infantry, including Pégot's brigade, were also launched forward.
These infantry units mounted an attack on the British centre, but
although the French made some headway, putting pressure on the
British, they were unable to drive their opponents back: the British
infantry still benefited from the good defensive positions on the
ridge that they had taken at the outset when repelling d'Erlon's
corps. The French bombardment led Colonel Colin Halkett to press
Wellington for permission to withdraw his troops, but, fearing the
effect on the foreign contingents, Wellington insisted that the units
maintain their position despite their losses.[20] Indeed, rather than
advance from its reserve position, the Cumberland Hussars fled the
battlefield.

Ney sent his aide-de-camp, Colonel Hemyns, to Napoleon to
seek more troops, but the emperor refused, claiming that he had no
more. This claim was an exaggeration, as the Middle and Old
Guard were still uncommitted. On Napoleon's behalf, it could be
argued that Prussian pressure made it unwise to commit these
units, his sole remaining reserve, against the British, as they might
be needed to help the Young Guard who had already been fed into
the struggle for the battle for the village of Plancenoit, which had
become the key point in blocking the Prussian advance. Moreover,

Ney had not used the troops he already had well. However, there was also a reluctance on Napoleon's part to commit his reserves, a reluctance that rested on his sense that he understood the flow of the battle, as well as on his determination to retain and demonstrate control.

Given that much of the final reserve of the remaining Guard units was anyway to be launched later at the British centre, it might have been as well to do so at 6:30 P.M., when pressure was already being brought on these positions, and before some of the available French strength had been lost. Such a remark is not a 'what if' intended for idle amusement but a product of the extent to which any discussion of both battle and campaign entails an evaluation of command decisions, an evaluation that necessarily entails a consideration of the alternatives.[21] By delaying the attack by the Guard, Napoleon provided an opportunity for Wellington to strengthen his line.

Reserves were also an issue for Wellington throughout the battle, but not so much their availability as their deployment, with La Haie Sainte being a key location where and near where more men and supplies were needed. James Shaw Kennedy noted a conversation he had with Wellington on 20 June, with the Duke asking about 'the gap . . . in the line of battle behind La Haye Sainte', and Kennedy, who was then a captain in charge of the quartermaster-general's department of the Third Division, replying:

> The moment that the opening occurred I galloped straight to your Grace, and informed you of the circumstances . . . and you answered by saying that you would order the Brunswick troops to the point, and more troops; and you ordered me to get to the spot as many of the German troops as I could, and as much artillery as I could.

Kennedy noted that Wellington 'perfectly recollected the circumstance.'[22] Wellington's command was very 'hands-on'. John Garland of the Seventy-third Regiment recalled being in a square with the Thirtieth:

About half past 6 or 7 o'clock the Duke of Wellington rode
up and spoke, 'Who commanded the square?' I replied
Colonel, now Lord Harris, who happened at that moment
not to be so near his Grace as myself. He then desired me to
tell Colonel Harris to form line, but should we be attacked
by the cuirassiers to reform square.[23]

Meanwhile, the Prussian advance on Napoleon's right continued.
In its route stood Lobau's 10,000-strong VI Corps, the Nineteenth
and Twentieth Infantry Divisions, with supporting cavalry and at
least twenty-eight cannon, which blocked the road from the Bois de
Paris to the village of Placenoit. Lobau had had the time to advance
into the wood and contest the Prussian advance there, a choice that
would have given the French opportunities to benefit considerably
from the defensive cover, to confuse the Prussians, and probably to
have delayed them greatly. In particular, forcing a fighting advance
in the wood onto the Prussian IV Corps under Bülow would have
obliged it to advance on a broader front; and needing to advance on
such a front would certainly have caused delay for the Prussians,
providing fresh opportunities for the French attacks on Wellington.
Nevertheless, although Lobau, instead, had rested on the defensive
to the southwest of the wood, his corps, which took up its position
at about 2:30 P.M., was well deployed. It had the advantage of
higher terrain and benefited from woods on either flank.

Prussian cannon were in action by 4:00 pm, a welcome sound to
the British. The fighting began at about 4:30 P.M., with the two
foremost Prussian brigades advancing against the French behind a
cavalry screen and skirmishers. Lobau, an effective and highly
experienced general, mounted a good resistance, but the Prussians
steadily increased the pressure. Initially, they attacked with about
10,000 troops and twenty-four cannon, but Bülow was able to feed
in more men from his 30,000-strong corps, a very powerful force,
containing four infantry brigades (or divisions), as well as three of
cavalry and eighty-six cannon. The French were more heavily outnumbered than they had been at Ligny.

The Prussians displayed an impressive capability. They

advanced to contact and deployed from the line of march in the face of the enemy. Their role was the stuff of textbooks, while they also deserved credit for fighting with great determination at the end of a long and tiring day. By 5:00 P.M., Bülow had taken the key terrain, the high ground formerly occupied by Lobau. While this terrain did not match the significance of the ridge that Wellington used for his position, winning it, nevertheless, was crucial for the movement of the tempo toward the Prussians. Gaining this high ground cleared the way toward Plancenoit and also provided the Prussians with clear visibility, which was important for their artillery.

Soon before 6:00 P.M., these cannon provided the prelude to the start of the first Prussian attack on Plancenoit itself. About 6,500 men attacked, only to be resisted by the French in fierce house-to-house fighting that serves as a reminder of the variety of terrains used for Napoleonic conflict. Such urban conflict was not new. Indeed, Colonel Hudson Lowe (later Napoleon's jailer on St. Helena and a cause of much irritation to the former emperor), who was present with Blücher's forces at the Battle of Leipzig in 1813, wrote of the attack on the French in that city on 19 October:

> Under cover of a most formidable fire from about fifty pieces of artillery [the infantry] made their attack, the foremost battalions dispersing in small parties, and pushing the enemy at every point where the ground best admitted . . . the enemy firing from the houses (and streets which had been barricaded and filled with obstructions of every kind) and making at every corner and at every house a most obstinate resistance . . . the dead and the dying absolutely obstructed the passage in the gates and streets.[24]

Plancenoit, two years later, was a smaller version of this type of fighting.

Cannon were deployed in the streets of Plancenoit, which was damaged greatly by the fighting, but it was not a battle decided by firepower. Instead, weight of numbers helped the Prussians capture the church and most of the town in the first assault. This success was a serious threat to Napoleon's rear, a threat demonstrated when the main Genappe road, less than a kilometre from Plancenoit, came under the fire of Prussian cannon.

Napoleon's failure to keep his opponents apart was therefore visited upon him. Moreover, the pressure from the two armies on the French army now became simultaneous, because, to have neglected Wellington in order to turn on the Prussians, even had it been possible, would have invited a British advance, although such an advance also would have proved difficult. Concentrating against Napoleon on the battlefield, the Prussians had therefore fulfilled Blücher's promise to send aid, and this advance vindicated Wellington's decision, taken in the light of this promise, that the battle be fought at Mont St. Jean, although the late arrival of the Prussians on the battlefield posed a major problem for him.

Napoleon had no illusions about the threat this Prussian advance posed. However successful Ney might be against the British, the French position risked dissolution if the Prussians maintained the pace of their advance. In contrast, the British were in no position to mount any attack other than a counterattack. As a result of the threat, Napoleon, at about 6:45 P.M., ordered forward the Young Guard, a force about 4,750 strong, under Count Guillaume Philibert Duhesme, an effective commander who had been dismissed in 1810 for corruption and brutality. Duhesme's men recaptured Plancenoit but, in turn, were attacked by a fresh Prussian assault on the village.

In hard fighting, with the deadliness of the shot increased by the close quarters of the conflict, the Prussian assault was initially checked; but availability of reserves again proved crucial. The fresh Prussian Fourteenth Brigade was fed into the fight shortly before 7:00 P.M. and within twenty minutes had overrun most of the village. Duhesme was mortally wounded in the head by a musket ball but was kept in the saddle with the help of Guardsmen. In response to the crisis, Napoleon, in turn, dispatched two battalions of the Old Guard under Maréchal de Camp Jean-Jacques Pelet. They arrived to find some of the Young Guard fleeing from the Prussians. The situation was rescued by the Old Guard, who mounted a bayonet charge in the village, an advance backed by elements of the Young Guard.

By 7:30 P.M., the French were again in control of Plancenoit, which not only protected Napoleon's rear but also anchored the position immediately to the north, where Lobau's VI Corps was under heavy pressure from Bülow's Thirteenth and Fifteenth Brigades. Lobau's men were outnumbered and in the open, and thus vulnerable to Prussian cannon. This success at Plancenoit provided Napoleon with the opportunity to launch the remainder of the Guard against Wellington. Only after this stratagem had failed did the Prussians finally break through. Equally, Prussian pressure ensured that fewer Guard units were available to mount the attack on Wellington, and the Prussian advance hit the last French attack on Wellington by discrediting the report Napoleon had spread that Grouchy was on the way to provide help.

Meanwhile, more Prussian units were arriving on the battlefield. Bülow's IV Corps alone was about 30,000 strong, but its exhausted units were now being supplemented by General Georg Pirch's II Corps, the 5,000-strong Fifth Brigade, which arrived about 6:30 P.M. Shortly before 8:00 P.M., by which time the attack of the Middle Guard on Wellington's forces had been repulsed, these fresh Prussian troops led the final attack on Plancenoit. A half hour of intensive street fighting defeated the outnumbered Guard, many of whom died in the village. The brutality of the struggle extended to the treatment of the wounded, who were killed by both sides.

As the village fell, so Lobau's troops to the north, who had already suffered heavily in four hours of bitter conflict with the Prussians, gave way, greatly increasing the overall impression of French collapse. The surviving Guard units actually retreated from the Prussians in a disciplined fashion, but, as later, in the face of Wellington's advance, this ability to maintain cohesion made little difference to the fact of defeat: Napoleon's right flank had collapsed, and, with the loss of most of the Young Guard, his reserve had shrunk as well as failed.

On the other hand, the strength of the defence on the right provided an opportunity for much of the French army to flee south.

There was to be no surrounding of the defeated French force. In some respects, the situation at Waterloo therefore prefigured the Austrian defeat by the Prussians at Sadowa in 1866: the Austrians held off Prussian attacks on their front, although their counter-attacks failed, but the Austrian right collapsed in the face of an unexpected Prussian attack. Austrian counterattacks, however, served to cover their retreat.

On 18 June 1815, meanwhile, the Prussian III Corps, under Lieutenant-General Johann von Thielmann (with Carl von Clause-witz as chief of staff), was under pressure to the east at Wavre from Grouchy's far stronger force. Napoleon had instructed Grouchy to advance on Wavre, an instruction underlined in a message received by the marshal at about 4:00 P.M. Fighting began there about 10:30 A.M. on the eighteenth, an interesting comment on the start-ing time at Waterloo, and the Prussians were driven out of the sec-tion of the town south of the River Dyle. Thielmann feared defeat and pressed Blücher for reinforcements, but Gneisenau, Blücher's chief of staff, refused, arguing that Waterloo was the key battle and Wavre a sideshow. This was an important decision, as Wavre lay on the route of any Prussian retreat. The decision not to reinforce Thielmann also serves as a reminder of the multiple choices facing the Prussians and the extent to which the choices they made greatly affected the situation confronting Napoleon, and thus Wellington.

In the event, the Dyle proved a good defensive position for Thielmann, although, benefiting from his superior numbers, Grouchy was eventually able to fight his way across the river. As with Napoleon's success over Blücher at Ligny, Grouchy did not crush Thielmann, but even had he done so, the lack of any immedi-ate link between the two battlefields on 18 June ensured that Wavre was an inconsequential sideshow. Conversely, had Napoleon succeeded, then a victory for Grouchy at Wavre would have placed Blücher between two victorious French forces. Blücher was a deter-mined commander, but he would have been hard-pressed to extri-cate himself without heavy casualties and, following on from his serious losses at Ligny, such losses would greatly have lessened his effectiveness and underlined Napoleon's triumph.

Grouchy not only did not crush Thielmann, he also failed to march to Napoleon's assistance. There was no heroic advance to the sound of the guns, which Grouchy, twelve miles to the east, had heard at about noon. One of his corps commanders, General Maurice-Étienne Gérard, suggested that Grouchy respond, but the marshal assumed that this sound was of an engagement arising from Wellington's retreat, and he felt that he could not disobey Napoleon's orders to pursue and engage the Prussians. Such an engagement was intended both to prevent them from going to Wellington's assistance and to maintain the tempo of French success seen at Ligny.

Even had Grouchy turned west, he was farther from the battlefield than the Prussians and would therefore have been unable to arrive in time. Moreover, there were serious hindrances posed by the terrain and the exhaustion of his men. Not only would Grouchy have had to face muddy tracks and narrow bridges similar to those that had already delayed the Prussians but, on the left bank of the Dyle, he would have had a longer route to the Waterloo battlefield, possibly taking fifteen to eighteen hours, compared to the Prussians, who had more direct roads. This is the context necessary when considering Jérôme Bonaparte's claim that Grouchy's arrival could only have made a difference had he arrived at what Jérôme presented as the critical moment, 3:00 P.M., 'at which time the English lost ground and in such a case the battle *might have* been fully gained before Blücher's arrival.'[25] Aside from distance, the Prussians, moreover, would have been able to obstruct any advance by Grouchy, not least at the crossing places over the rivers. Certainly the terrain would have made it very difficult for Grouchy to bring up his artillery.

Grouchy anyway believed that the whole of the Prussian army was north of the River Dyle and that he would expose himself to Prussian attack if he sought to disengage from the fighting at Wavre. Moreover, if he had followed Gérard's suggestion of letting the latter take his corps to Waterloo, while the rest of Grouchy's army was engaged at Wavre, then Grouchy would have been under greater pressure. Not knowing that much of the Prussian army was in fact already marching to Waterloo, Grouchy appears to have thought that, by fixing the Prussians at Wavre, he was fulfilling Napoleon's goals and letting him defeat Wellington, thus finishing the job planned in the aftermath of Ligny for 17 June. Jérôme accepted the criticism 'that the communication between the Emperor's army and Grouchy's corps ought to have been carefully kept up.'[26]

Yet Grouchy's failure was consequent on the more serious failure by Napoleon at Ligny. By failing to ensure appropriate planning and staff-work, he left d'Erlon's corps without direct orders from him to take precedence over those from Ney. This mistake ensured that d'Erlon was not available to help Napoleon press Blücher hard after the battle. There was no firm pursuit and no attempt to deny Blücher the cover of nightfall. As a result, Ligny was not exploitable, nor exploited, as Waterloo was to be by the British and Prussians. Napoleon left Ligny at about 10:00 P.M. on 16 June in order to sleep, and Grouchy, who sought orders at about 11:00 P.M., was told to return in the morning. Early that morning, Napoleon was still asleep. When Grouchy was finally received, at 8:00 A.M. on the seventeenth, the emperor took him to tour the battlefield. Thus, opportunities to review the situation and to order a pursuit were not taken.

This failure was crucial given the Prussian decision to withdraw north, as they were therefore able to get closer to Wellington. Napoleon, however, was sure that Blücher would conform to Napoleon's plan and retreat on his line of communications – in other words, eastward toward Liège and the River Rhine. This view was typical of the overdetermined nature of his assumptions, specifically his confidence that he could fix his opponents. The capture, by French cavalry, earlier on the seventeenth, of several Prussian cannon to the east, toward Namur, seemed to confirm this assumption, but, in fact, these cannon came from a detached Prussian unit. Moreover, from a different perspective, as Grouchy pointed out to Napoleon when, at about 11:30 A.M. on the seventeenth, he was instructed to pursue and fight the Prussians, they had a head start of about fifteen to sixteen hours.

On the eighteenth, the Prussian advance on Plancenoit had soaked

up twenty-five of the thirty-six infantry battalions that had been in
Napoleon's reserve at the start of the day. Partly as a result, there is a
sense of aftermath about the last French attack, that by the remaining
Guards units on Wellington's position between Hougoumont and La
Haie Sainte. This attack involved five battalions from the Middle
Guard in the first wave, and a second wave of three battalions from
the Old Guard, which, in the event, did not close toward the British
but, instead, remained in the valley southwest of La Haie Sainte to
which they had advanced as the second wave. Of the remaining three
Guard battalions, one was deployed east of Hougoumont, as a reserve
for the attack, and two, the most senior Grenadier battalions,
remained in reserve south of La Belle Alliance.

Supporting the attack was the Guard Horse Artillery, as well as
other guns, what Guard cavalry was left, other cavalry and infantry
units from the corps of d'Erlon and Reille. Thus, the final assault
included the movement of non-Guard units north of La Haie Sainte
and to the right of the Guard advance, while the British in and near
Hougoumont were also put under fresh pressure from the ever-
ineffective Jérôme. This was an assault along the French line but
with a particular emphasis, that of the fresh Guard units. The inde-
cisive nature of much of the French advance was captured in the
account of a French officer in d'Erlon's corps:

> We again descended into the hollow to renew our attack on
> the plateau where we had been already so roughly handled.
> We there found our old antagonists as much weakened as
> ourselves, so ere long the attack resolved itself into a desul-
> tory skirmishing fight.

Such conflict was more common than the focus on grand advances
might suggest.[27]

Nevertheless, this wide assault ensured that, had the Guard succeeded, it would have been more difficult for Wellington to move
troops from elsewhere along his line. A stronger attack north of La
Haie Sainte might have increased the chance of success, although
the terrain posed problems.

Napoleon led the advancing Imperial Guard units to their start-
ing line and, as they advanced, he rode forward up the road to the
orchard south of La Haie Sainte, where he handed over command to
Ney. Although British participants in the defence were to report
that the Guard advanced in columns, due to the widespread smoke
over the battlefield, the British would not have found it easy to see
the early deployment of the Guard. But as they were used to being
attacked by columns, it is not surprising that that was what they
claimed to have seen. In contrast, General Jean-Martin Petit, the
commander of the First Regiment of Foot Grenadiers, claimed that
they advanced in squares.

An advance in squares might seem to be the logical formation in
light of the strong danger of attack by British cavalry, a danger
already seen earlier in the day, but troops moving in close column
were pretty much invulnerable to cavalry as long as they did not
panic in the face of a surprise attack, as d'Erlon's men had done and
the Guard should not have. Furthermore, the idea of an advance in
square is not plausible; such manoeuvres are difficult, certainly
insofar as the circumstances at Waterloo are concerned. There was a
need there for advancing with speed over undulating fields that
were knee-deep in mud and covered with bodies. Squares would
also have had less chance than columns when they actually reached
the defenders' lines. Petit's story may be explained as an attempt to
take the edge off the French defeat by making the advance seem
more dramatic.

The Imperial Guard marched at about 7:30 P.M., their muskets
shouldered and the officers with drawn swords. Ney and other generals rode in front. French morale was boosted with the false report,
deliberately disseminated, that the heavy firing from Plancenoit that
could be heard marked the arrival of Grouchy, and thus that the battle was going France's way. The importance of this misinformation is
unclear, but it has been suggested, for example by military historian
David Chandler, that, when it was understood that they had been
misled, this greatly affected the morale of many of the French troops.
A belief in Grouchy's advance was also held on the Allied side, with
Saxe-Weimar thinking, when Prussian troops attacked the Nassauers

by accident, that he was being attacked by Grouchy.

Wellington, meanwhile, strengthened his defences, in particular by moving cavalry from the flanks to provide a stronger reserve. He was able to do so because the Prussian advance had strengthened the position on his left. More specifically, the movement of Zeithen's I Corps, of which the First Infantry Brigade (division-strength) advance guard reached Ohain at about 6:00 P.M., enabled Wellington to call in the Fourth and Sixth Cavalry Brigades, as well as some horse artillery. Had the Guard broken through the British infantry, they would therefore have been exposed to a strong cavalry counter-attack, which might have had an impact comparable to that inflicted by the British heavy cavalry on d'Erlon's corps earlier in the afternoon.

If the potential damage that could have been done by such a cavalry attack was weakened by the losses among the British cavalry earlier in the day, that was even truer of the French. Their cavalry was weak and not in a position to drive off its British opponents. Instead, it was the artillery that was the principal supporting arm for the Guard advance. The potential of this artillery was shown by a battery of horse artillery under Lieutenant-Colonel Jean-Baptiste Duchand, the commander of the Old Guard Horse Artillery. This battery advanced with the first line of the Guard infantry, its cannon between the formations, and came into action less than 100 metres from the ridge, hitting the British infantry hard.

Irrespective of the particular combination of arms involved, the Imperial Guard attack as a whole suffered from the extent to which Wellington's relatively narrow front enabled him to ensure a heavy defensive concentration. There was nothing at Waterloo to match many of the extended fronts of the period, such as that at Leipzig or the battlefield at Vitoria, which extended for over eight miles. Instead, Waterloo was a slogging match more like Borodino, which was similarly fought on a limited front. This comparison probably helped explain Napoleon's eagerness, on the morning of Waterloo, to discover whether the British had erected field fortifications, as such fortifications had proved a major obstacle to his forces at Borodino. The British had not done so, in part because they did not have the time, in part because such fortifications were not generally part of the tactics of British infantry defence, although they had been used in Portugal in 1810, and in part because Hougoumont and La Haie Sainte acted as substitutes.

The British had been warned by a French cavalry colonel less than thirty minutes before the advance of the Imperial Guard that they were coming. He was a keen royalist who approached the British infantry shouting 'Vive le Roi!' The importance of this information is unclear, but what is notable is that so few French troops defected during the battle. Royalism clearly had few backers in the army, or, if it did, they were deterred by serious issues of practicality and prudence, as well as by unit cohesion and, possibly, a degree of nationalism. Certainly there was no comparison on the battlefield to the financially induced disloyalty shown to Siraj-ud-Daula, the nawab of Bengal, when fighting Robert Clive at Plassey in India in 1757. Nevertheless, however few, the betrayals that did occur encouraged a paranoid suspicion among at least some of the French troops, one that was directed in particular at the officers.

By the time the Guard advanced at Waterloo, British artillery was already much damaged by the strains of combat, including French fire, and many of the gun crews were exhausted. As a result, the British fire was less heavy than earlier in the day, leading to complaints from the infantry. Nevertheless, the cannon fire was strong enough, and the advancing French took many losses from the British cannon. The dispersed nature of the British artillery, which reflected Wellington's general lack of interest in the idea of a grand battery, enabled it to provide direct fire support for the British defenders. The French yet again suffered from the nature of the British position, not only the height and slope provided by the ridge (which was higher than it is today as a result of subsequent earth-moving to create the commemorative hill of the Butte du Lion), but also the forward line of the British right, which allowed fire on the advancing French from front and flank. Indeed, the French had to seek to escape the obtuse angle that the British position forced upon them. By the time of the Guard attack, the strength of the British concentration was such that this desperate last French throw was highly unlikely to succeed.

Despite the British fire, the French still came on, moving up the slope. The Second Infantry Division (a non-Guard unit), under Baron François Donzelot, advancing just to the left of the Genappe-Brussels road, was directed against Brunswick and Nassau units. The former seemed unsteady, but Wellington personally held them firm, and the Nassau troops halted the French. They began to drive them back, but some of the Nassau men in the Second Battalion panicked and retreated, although they then rallied behind the ridge. Robert Manners of the Tenth Hussars reported:

> At one time the Brunswickers gave way, and victory seemed almost within the grasp of the enemy. . . . The Brunswickers being rallied, advanced again in their turn, with loud shouts, and drums beating, supported by our brigade, and drove the French back.[28]

To the left of Donzelot, the Imperial Guard attacked. The 1/3 and Fourth Grenadiers encountered British infantry in line. The French stopped and fired, but badly. Their strength had been affected by the sound shooting of a Belgian battery of six six-pounders and two howitzers under Captain C. F. Krahmer. The British infantry, Halkett's brigade, returned the volley with their steady shooting and then charged, only to find the Guard retreat rather than stand the charge. Halkett's men were then instructed to pull back in order to preserve their defensive position. However, under heavy fire from Duchand's gunners, this movement became a chaos, and it took a while to restore grip and order. Luckily, the French were unaware of the opportunity and unable to exploit it. This was the moment for the French to launch a charge by their cavalry, but none was available.

The Guard units advanced in echelon from the front, so that the next units to advance up the ridge were to the left of those just described. These were the 1/3 and 2/3 Châsseurs à Pied, each of which had taken heavy losses from the British cannon. They could not see the British Guards to their front because the latter were lying down behind the crest. From the French perspective, they were advancing into open terrain, which must have been surprising and disconcerting. As the French, under heavy cannon fire, neared the British position, Wellington, who was to its rear, shouted to the commander of the British Guards, 'Now, Maitland! Now's your time!'

The rising of these troops from the ground led to the sudden appearance of a four-deep line of more than 1,400 soldiers who fired at the close range of about forty yards. This volley hit the French hard, and they lost more than a fifth of their surviving troops and, crucially, their senior officers. The moment was re-created in Sir William Allen's painting *Before the British Fire the Old Guard Recoils*.

The French force stopped and began to move back down the slope, pursued by the British Guards charging with their bayonets. This pursuit, however, had to be stopped because the Fourth Châsseurs, who constituted the remaining unit of the advance by the Imperial Guards, appeared on Major-General Peregrine Maitland's right flank. Maitland's order to reform led to confusion among his troops, with one battalion mistakenly forming a square, but the French were unable to exploit the confusion.

A lieutenant in Bolton's battery that was on the right of Maitland's Guards recorded:

> The Duke of Wellington rode up to our battery and hastily asked me who commanded it; I replied . . . that it was then under Napier. His Grace then said 'Tell him to keep a look to his left for the French will soon be with him' and then he rode off. I had scarcely communicated the Duke's message when we saw the French bonnets just above the high corn and within forty or fifty yards of our guns. I believe they were in close columns of grand divisions, and upon reaching the crest of our position they attempted to deploy into line; but the destructive fire of our guns loaded with canister shot, and the well directed volleys from the infantry prevented their regular formation. They remained under this fire about ten minutes advancing a little, but finding it

impossible to force our position they gave way and went to the right about: upon which the Duke ordered a general charge to be made and in a moment our infantry and the French were so mixed together that an end was put to our firing for the day.[29]

The Fourth Châsseurs was, in turn, attacked from its left by the Fifty-second Light Infantry, a strong battalion, whose commander, Sir John Colborne, on his own initiative, had wheeled it forward so that it was deployed in line on the left of the Fourth Châsseurs. Its devastating volley hit the French hard. The French returned fire, but under pressure and affected by the retreat of other units, the Fourth Châsseurs fell back: '. . . the French column appeared to be in great confusion, and the Brigade rushing forward, they immediately gave way, without retaining any order or discipline.' Lieutenant George Gawler, who commanded the right company of the Fifty-second, was to cause controversy by emphasising the role of Adam's brigade in the defeat of the French Guards. He informed William Siborne that Colborne

> gave the word 'Charge, Charge'. It was answered from the regiment by a loud steady cheer and a hurried dash to the front. In the next ten seconds the Imperial Guard, broken into the wildest confusion, and scarcely firing a shot to cover its retreat, was rushing towards the hollow road in their rear.[30]

The role of the Fifty-second, which was supported by the second battalion of the Ninth, like that of Halkett's and Major-General Count Kielmannsegge's brigades to the left of Maitland's, serves as a reminder that the French Guards were not only defeated by their British counterparts but by other units as well.

As the five battalions of the Middle Guard fell back with Donzelot's men, the French position unravelled, which throws some light on the claim that Napoleon would have won but for the Prussians. The retreat of the Guard greatly hit the morale of the other French units, leading to a collapse of determination: 'La Garde recule' was followed by 'Sauve qui peut'. This collapse of determination was accentuated by the realisation of the Prussian advance to their right. What were supposed to be Grouchy's troops were, in fact, firing on the French, a step that led to fear of betrayal on the part of some of the French and to the awareness of the Prussian advance by most.

La Haie Sainte, the capture of which had cost so much effort, was now swiftly abandoned by the French, while Hougoumont was no longer under pressure. In contrast, British units advanced, with Wellington encouraging the Fifty-second to do so after it was disconcerted by firing on the Twenty-third Light Dragoons, which it had mistaken for French cavalry. Such accidents were common in the battle, not least due to the combination of confusion and smoke, stress and twilight.

The infantry was not alone. British light cavalry was prominent in harrying the retreating French, and without the danger of a counterattack by fresh French cavalry that had greeted the advance of the Union Brigade, although, as yet, the second line of the Imperial Guard, with its three battalions, had not retreated. As the situation deteriorated, the second line staged a controlled slow retreat under heavy attack, especially from Adam's brigade. During this retreat, the second line units suffered many casualties. An officer in the Tenth Hussars, a regiment of 452 men in the Sixth Cavalry Brigade under Major-General Sir Hussey Vivian, recorded:

> We were coming up, down went a party of [French] lancers on a party of the 23rd on our right, checked them, then came our right squadron on the lancers, drove them back – then came a body of heavy dragoons on our right squadron – then our centre squadron on them – and away they went – then we soon came on the [infantry] square which the right squadron charged – and I hear broke completely – I went with mine to the left of the square . . . we were among infantry – Imperial Guard, blue [uniforms] with large fur caps – who were throwing down their arms and themselves

roaring *pardon,* on their knees many of them – on top of the
hill a party of infantry formed, and with cavalry behind them,
commenced a sharp fire – we checked . . . about 35 paces
from them – then Lord Robert gave a hurrah – and at them
we went – they turned directly horse and foot in most complete flight – infantry throwing themselves down, cavalry off
their horses. Soon we came to a deep hollow – on the opposite side a steep knoll – with a square of infantry very well
formed – a party of the 18th [Hussars] rushed down the hollow, up the hill and at the square in most gallant style – but
as I foresaw were checked and turned by their fire. . . .
I decline the honour of charging squares unnecessarily –
though one could not but admire the gallantry of the thing.[31]

Robert Clayton of the Royal Horse Guards recalled, 'Towards the
close of the day . . . we charged the squares of infantry, from whose
fire we also suffered considerably.'[32]

One of the apocryphal remarks that is attached to the battle
stems from the Guard's retreat. General Pierre Cambronne, the
commander of the 2/1 Châsseurs, one of the Guard battalions, a
hard-bitten veteran who had risen from being a private soldier, in
response to a call for surrender, allegedly shouted either 'Merde!'
(shit) or, less plausibly under the circumstances, 'La Garde meurt,
elle ne se rend pas!' (The Guard dies, but does not surrender), the
words inscribed on his tomb. In any event, Cambronne was
wounded and captured, while his regiment was destroyed. Of the
Old Guard in reserve, Major Belcourt's 2/3 Grenadiers, the battalion east of Hougoumont, was surrounded and exposed to heavy fire,
including canister shot. Having lost many of his men, Belcourt
ordered the survivors to break formation in order to present less of
a target and to retreat more successfully.

By now the French were under pressure from the general advance
that Wellington had ordered and encouraged when he rode east
along the British line, receiving the cheers of his troops. Many of the
French units disintegrated under the pressure and a large number of
troops rushed to surrender, further increasing the collapse of the

French army and the chaos on the battlefield.[33] The paranoid suspicion of at least part of the French army played a role in the collapse of morale across much of the army that accompanied the checking of the Guard and the realisation that the troops advancing on the right were Prussian and not Grouchy's men. On the British far left, General Pierre François Joseph Durutte's Fourth Infantry Division had captured Papelotte from Nassau forces, but it was driven back and attacked by both the British Fourth Cavalry Brigade and the Fifth Dragoons from the Prussian I Corps. Durutte had his right hand cut off and his head split open, but he survived.

In his 'Memorandum upon the plan of the Battle of Waterloo', written in October 1836, Wellington placed considerable weight on his general advance:

> That attack was ordered possibly at half-past seven, when I saw the confusion in their position upon the repulse of the last attack of their infantry, and when I rallied and brought up again into the first line the Brunswick infantry. The whole of the British and Allied cavalry of our army was then in the rear of our infantry. I desired that it might be collected in rear of our centre; that is, between Hougoumont and La Haye Sainte. The infantry was advanced in line. I halted them for a moment in the bottom, that they might be in order to attack some battalions of the enemy still on the heights. The cavalry halted likewise. The whole moved forward again in very few moments. The enemy did not stand the attack. Some had fled before we halted. The whole abandoned their position. The cavalry was then ordered to charge, and moved round the flanks of the battalions of infantry. The infantry was formed into columns, and moved in pursuit in columns of battalions.[34]

This British advance was a major triumph, and not some automatic consequence of French failure, because to secure success at Waterloo, it was necessary to rout the French. To have permitted them to withdraw under Prussian pressure risked leaving the French army as a potent force in being, not least if it preserved its cannon and could subsequently join Grouchy. Indeed, in a letter sent to his brother Joseph on the nineteenth, Napoleon hoped for such an outcome from the campaign.

Moreover, an advance indicated that the British had not been ground down and, instead, that they retained the ability to fight. Casualties had been heavy, and Wellington pressed Bathurst next day for reinforcements, 'in good British infantry particularly, and cavalry.'[35] Yet for Wellington's battered army to advance in good order at the close of the day, retaining the capability to attack successfully at what became the close of the battle, demonstrated its strength and was an aspect of the psychological victory over the French. Moreover, this attack enabled them to defeat, rather than just check, the French. Before he advanced, Wellington did not know that all the French would abandon their positions. Now victory was assured.

Further to the French rear, the 1/1 and 2/1 Grenadiers south of La Belle Alliance maintained their squares and, sheltering Napoleon as well as the Imperial Grenadiers' Eagle, slowly retreated south toward Rossomme. Napoleon, however, now sought the greater safety of a rapid return to Paris, which would enable him to salvage something from the wreck, the expedient he had followed when abandoning the army he had led into Russia in 1812, and indeed from Egypt in 1799. Riding to Le Caillou, with the remains of the duty squadron of Châsseurs à Cheval, he was then escorted by the 1/1 Châsseurs to Genappe. At 2:00 A.M. on 19 June, Napoleon recrossed the River Sambre at Charleroi, which, as on the advance, was not the site of a battle.

The British forces had taken heavy casualties at Waterloo, were mostly exhausted, physically and mentally, and lacked the large number of fresh or relatively fresh troops that Blücher was deploying on the battlefield. For example, of the Prussians, Ziethen's I Corps had only arrived on the battlefield at 7:00 P.M., and only its two leading regiments saw action. As a result of their exhaustion, the British were ordered to halt while the Prussians took over the pursuit, a bloody affair in which the Prussian cavalry, including the First Cavalry Brigade of I Corps and the Second Cavalry Brigade of

II Corps, proved particularly devastating. Nevertheless, the French right near Plancenoit held on against the Prussians for long enough, before breaking, to permit much of the French army to escape. Colonel Stanhope noted:

> The arrival of the Prussian cavalry sweeping round the right flank of the enemy, in masses with columns as far as the eye could reach, was a magnificent spectacle. The French were beat before but this was a very pretty finale. The Prussians pursued all night and gave no quarter and took most of the artillery which had not fallen into our hands before.[36]

Many of the wounded French troops were killed by the Prussians, usually bayoneted to death, while a large number of those who were not wounded were killed in the retreat, not least by being lanced in the back. The British cavalry was also deadly to the French wounded, although less so than the Prussians. Indeed, the French sought to surrender to the British and to gain their protection from the Prussians.[37] Both British and Prussian troops looted the dead and wounded of both sides, sometimes killing the latter of their own side. Local peasants also took part in this pillage, a time-honoured sequence to the heroism and savagery of battle. Others, however, acted far more honourably. At any rate, the dead and wounded, both men and horses, packed the battlefield. Little was done for them that night. During the night and on the nineteenth, many of the wounded died, some, at least in part, as a result of medical attention in the form of heavy bleeding. For days after, the wounded continued to be found on the battlefield.

Both battle and campaign led to a hardening of attitudes toward opponents. The anonymous officer in the Tenth Hussars was angered by the conduct of the French Lancers in their pursuit of the British on 17 June and at Waterloo:

> It was there [on 17 June] that Hodges was taken and left for dead by them (beasts!) after he surrendered. . . . They [the French] are brutes. Brave certainly and too clever but

insulting when successful – and treacherous – and, as far as I saw, abject in defeat – The Lancers piked off Hodges in cold blood and the prisoners of the Life Guards – because they said we used rockets in the pursuit. Men [the French at Waterloo] threw down their arms, appeared to surrender – then took them up again and fired at those who spared them. I saw one of them sabred for this act and rejoiced at it. You will think I am getting savage – but you know how often I have said I thought mercy absurd at the beginning of a rout . . . though I do, I could not help saving some – had I known what was happening at the time to [Major] Howard [of the Tenth Hussars] my feelings might have been different – in charging the infantry he was shot in the mouth and perhaps in the head even brain – for he fell senseless to the ground – a brute stepped out and beat his head with the butt end of a musket. I declare it casts a cloud over our success whenever I think of his loss and of his sweet young wife and child.[38]

Wellington met Blücher near La Belle Alliance between 9:00 and 10:00 P.M. on the evening of the battle. They agreed that the Prussian cavalry should pursue the French. The Prussian is claimed to have greeted Wellington with the phrase 'Mein lieber Kamerad, quelle affaire!' which the duke claimed included the only two French words Blücher knew. According to his son, who served on his staff, Blücher embraced the duke on meeting. He probably said that he hoped that the battle would be called after La Belle Alliance. If so, he was to be disappointed, while General Vivian was proved wrong in his expectation that Mont St. Jean would be the name chosen. Wellington preferred Waterloo, a name that would prove easier for the British.

8.

WATERLOO: A DEFENSIVE TRIUMPH

At length our day of tumultuous exultation is ended, the bells have ceased their clattering peals, the ringers have reeled to their heated beds and our rustic politicians, wearied with their own huzzas, dream of peace and plenty for years to come, or plan, for years of deprivation that are past, schemes of punishment and revenge to be inflicted on that reptile [Napoleon] now fangless, who lately 'made a world turn pale'. Our towns and villages have been walking groves of laurel, and our atmosphere is still glowing with the embers of many a bonfire.[1]

AS THIS ANONYMOUS CORRESPONDENT reported from Devon, the news of victory at Waterloo was greeted with rapturous joy across Britain. For all Napoleon's failings, and the maladroit conduct of several of his generals, the French at Waterloo were a formidable army and their defeat a major achievement for Wellington and his force. Yet it is unclear that Napoleon's grand strategy was sustainable anyway. Aside from his precarious political position within France, which was a key constituent of the strategic situation, Napoleon faced an international political prospect that made any victories in battle of limited value. After all, he had triumphed already in battles in 1813 and 1814, but without winning the campaigns of those years, still less the war. Moreover, in 1815, aside from the armies in Belgium, large Allied forces, especially Austrians and Russians, were approaching France from the east, and were due to invade in July. An Austro-Piedmontese army of 80,000 troops was moving on Grenoble by the end of June, an Austro-German army of 180,000 was assembling in south Germany, and the Russians were organising an army of 150,000. Alexander I of Russia was keen to fight and to lead his troops into Paris.

Despite the tensions at the Congress of Vienna, of which he was well aware, the chance of Napoleon dividing the hostile alliance, as the French Revolutionaries had done in 1795 and Napoleon in 1807, was scant, not least because the Vienna settlement gave all the major powers strong stakes in the new order. Indeed, an Allied defeat at Waterloo would simply have galvanised the Seventh Coalition formed at Vienna to greater efforts.[2] The consequences of 1795 had seen to that. Confidence in the eventual outcome was displayed by Metternich, the Austrian chancellor, even as he digested the news of Prussian defeat at Ligny.[3]

More generally, like Hitler's from December 1941, Napoleon's inherent weaknesses had become more apparent from mid-1813, once he faced united opposition in the Sixth Coalition, and the formation of the Seventh Coalition in 1815 was part of this process. Indeed, war followed politics. Once Austria, Prussia, Russia and Britain cooperated effectively, as they did from 1813, Napoleon was rapidly defeated, although his own inappropriate and indifferently executed strategy in 1813 contributed greatly to the defeat. The Waterloo campaign was a reprise of the situation in 1813–14. Napoleon's assumption that military victory could translate into political success was seriously flawed. It reflected a failure to understand the general European context as well as the limitations of French resources and will.

Yet, if not as one novelist has recently written, 'a battle which decided the fate of the Western world,' Waterloo was also not a strategic irrelevance.[4] Napoleon was crushed, with the war ended beyond any hopes that events or Allied divisions would provide him with opportunities. Wellington, his army and the Prussians were responsible for this crushing. Each was important, but their respective shares were different. Without his troops, Wellington's qualities would have been of scant value. In the Peninsular War, as at Waterloo, the British stood up well in very difficult circumstances, resting still under fire and firing on when the situation seemed dire. Their skill with the bayonet was such that British victories were not solely triumphs for defensive firepower. Wellington demonstrated, not least at Assaye (1803), Argaum (1803), Salamanca (1812) and Vitoria (1813), his success in attack; but it is appropriate that the dominant image is of Waterloo, of lines and squares of infantry bravely fighting off larger numbers of attacking French.

The defensive nature of Wellington's tactics at Waterloo was eloquently captured in the diary of Edmund Wheatley, an ensign in the King's German Legion. He wrote of the squares formed that afternoon to resist the French cavalry, 'We dashed them back as coolly as the sturdy rock repels the ocean's foam . . . we presented our bristly points like the peevish porcupines assailed by clamorous dogs.'[5] In many respects, Waterloo was a repetition of Wellington's encounter with the French at Vimeiro in 1808, and the result was the same. Although Napoleon did not fight the British in the Peninsula, he was informed of events there, but he did not grasp the challenge posed by Wellington, while the French did not display any learning curve in dealing with the British.

Heroism in defence was also the image that was most acceptable to those who came after. It spoke of victory in fortitude, and of triumph against the odds. Thus, the dominant British image of the Anglo-Zulu war of 1879 was of the successful defence of the heavily outnumbered garrison at Rorke's Drift, and not the subsequent decisive victory by a larger British force at Ulundi. Similarly, although the British had attacked the Franco-Spanish fleet at Trafalgar in 1805, it was the extent to which this was a victory against the odds that commanded respect, and the dominant visual impression was of Nelson exposed to French fire and of the British ships and crews under pressure.

With more men and more time, Napoleon might have won at

Waterloo, possibly by the repeated use of his costly frontal attacks against the British centre, which was in a dreadful state by late afternoon, but also possibly by threatening Wellington's flanks. Yet Wellington had reserves to his right. Moreover, to have threatened Wellington's right might simply have driven him back on the Prussians, achieving the concentration that Napoleon wished to avoid, although such a process of withdrawal would also have disordered the British and provided fresh opportunities for Napoleon to exploit their problems. Anyway, given that Wellington had occupied a strong position, it would have been very useful to out-manoeuvre the British out of it.

Napoleon, however, had no more time nor troops, and could not therefore have put much pressure on Wellington's flanks; but, allowing for the problems he faced, he did not fight well with the troops he had. Having moved slowly on the morning of 17 June, Napoleon had simply followed Wellington north and had made little attempt to take control of the situation; although the spread-out nature of his forces, the time taken to advance, and the heavy rain and mud, were none of them conducive to boldness nor speed, and, in combination, were particularly deleterious. Napoleon's subsequent lack of tactical imagination in the battle on 18 June was in keeping with his earlier failure on 15–17 June to obtain a decisive success while his opponents were divided.

It was no longer good enough to rely on the fighting quality of his troops and his responsiveness on the battlefield. Napoleon, indeed, now offered boldness without merit. As Wellington noted on 2 July, 'Napoleon did not manoeuvre at all. He just moved forward in the old style, in columns, and was driven off in the old style.'[6] Fighting through to glory would not work for the French at Waterloo, not only as Napoleon had not kept the British and Prussians apart, but because he had totally failed to appreciate that he had failed to do so.

To use an ugly phrase, Napoleon's situational awareness was very poor. This weakness not only was due to poor intelligence but was a product of a more serious failure in his understanding, namely his inability to appreciate the strengths of both the British and the

Prussians. This failure was crucial because it meant that reliance on contingencies, a reliance that matched the poor French staff-work, was less likely to work to Napoleon's benefit.

Yet French command at Waterloo was more than a personal failure. There were also developments in the nature of war, particularly its greater scale, that made Napoleon's task more difficult, not least by widening the gap between means and end. In the Waterloo campaign, Napoleon suffered much from poor staff-work, not least in the confusion over d'Erlon's orders on 16 June (see pp. 82–83). In part, this confusion reflected the difficulty of grounding a new system in a hurry, without the continuities present prior to Napoleon's abdication in 1814.[7] Yet there was also a contrast between Napoleon's methods and the new Prussian general staff system, which provided both coherent central direction and an effective system of links between the centre and individual units, a system designed to ensure unity in command. Each Prussian corps and division contained a group of staff officers headed by a chief who was responsible both for advising the commander and for maintaining links with the centre. This was a corporate system unlike the essentially personal command one used by Napoleon. The latter, anyway, was placed under greater strain because, throughout the campaign, Napoleon's orders were not always as clear as they might be, and notably so given the nature of his staff and commanders.

Other difficulties were posed by the major increase in the resources (including manpower) used for war in the period from 1792 to 1815. This increase helped to accentuate long-term logistical and command-and-control problems, and these problems encouraged an emphasis on attack, to obtain a quick decision, an emphasis that contributed to the high-tempo warfare of the period. This tempo posed major difficulties for the coordination of forces. Periods of intensified warfare, as in northern Italy in 1796, Germany in 1813, France in 1814, or even the battles of Quatre Bras, Ligny and Waterloo on just three days in June 1815, placed major strains on operational and logistical capability and organisation, as issues of prioritisation and coordination came to the fore.

A reasonable assessment of Waterloo was offered by the distinguished French military historian André Corvisier: 'The tactical
errors of Napoleon, who no longer had the vigour of youth, and the
lack of initiative of his subordinates, in conjunction with the
numerical inferiority of the French forces, explain this defeat
which, sooner or later, was inevitable.'[8] Indeed, the arrival of the
Prussian forces represented a major decline in French operational
quality. Yet Corvisier's account fails to give due weight to the
Allied success. The French were outfought and outmanoeuvred,
and the British troops were aware of this achievement. Claiming
that 'there has not been such a hard contested battle since the
Great Roman War,' Private John Abbott wrote that 'we fixed our
bayonets and gave the proud messieurs such a dressing as they will
ever think of.'[9]

This pride was expressed by veterans of the battle, leading others
to regret they had not been there. An unidentified Peninsular veteran who landed at Ostend on 22 June noted:

> I have ever since regretted that I was not present with my
> regiment at the glorious battle of Waterloo. After serving in
> the Peninsula during the whole of that eventful war,
> encountering every obstacle and hardship that is liable to
> fall in the way of a British soldier whilst on active service,
> had fortune favoured me to be present on that memorable
> field where laurels were gathered in plenty by the army of
> Great Britain, it would have for ever crowned my san-
> guinary wishes.[10]

It is appropriate, however, to end this section by recalling the
heavy losses suffered by the three armies, losses the impact of which
was magnified by the immediacy and unpredictability of death and
by the close proximity of the combatants. In light of the casualties,
it was scarcely surprising that Wellington, the authoritative figure
for national military assessment, expressed a clear sense of the grim-
ness of the battle. Indeed, he made the pithy remark that, next to a
battle lost, the greatest misery was a battle gained. In July 1815,

Wellington told Frances, Lady Shelley that he hoped he had fought his last battle: 'I never wish for any more fighting.'[11] Thomas Sydenham, a friend of the duke, recorded that when Wellington discussed the battle, he 'mentioned it with some expression of horror, such as "it was a tremendous affair", "it was a terrible battle", or "it was a dreadful day".'[12]

9.

THE AFTERMATH

'NEVER WAS A VICTORY more complete or rout more irrevocable than that of the French army.'[1] The verdict of an English cavalry officer was more to the point than Napoleon's determination to fight on after his defeat on 18 June, a choice that was as much psychological and habitual as a response to his actual circumstances, which were very bleak. After the battle, the French army retreated in disorder and under heavy pressure from the Allies, especially the Prussians, pressure that led to continuing losses. The French troops were numerous enough to mount a resistance, but they had been routed, rather than defeated, and this conditioned their response. Captain Jean-Roch Coignet of the Imperial Guard recorded:

> It was worse when we arrived at Jemappes. The Emperor tried to re-establish some kind of order among the retreating troops, but his efforts were in vain. Men of all units from every corps struggled and fought their way through the streets of the little town. . . . The one thought uppermost in the minds of all was to get across the little bridge which had been thrown over the river Dyle. Nothing could stand in the way of them.[2]

Some units maintained formation, but most did not. The French troops who crossed the Sambre at Charleroi at noon on the nineteenth arrived as a 'mob', and many threw away their arms. The Prussians arrived there the following morning.[3] Ironically, it was Grouchy's well-managed retreat to France that was most successful, but then Wavre was scarcely a battle to match Waterloo.

Having recrossed the River Sambre at 5:00 A.M. on 19 June and decided that it was not possible to organise resistance there, Napoleon fled back to Paris, arriving at 5:30 A.M. on 21 June, nine days after he had left. On the day after Waterloo, the fleeing Napoleon had written from Philippeville to his brother Joseph, his regent in Paris, that he could still collect 150,000 troops to continue the war, a number that could be supplemented to 300,000 men from the national guards, fédérés (revolutionary volunteers) and dépôt troops, and then by another 100,000 conscripts. Napoleon ordered a concentration of forces at Laon and Rheims, a concentration designed to hold off the Anglo-Prussian invaders until Grouchy arrived with his army to strengthen it, and thus to allow France to prepare for a new struggle. Moreover, General Jean Rapp's Army of the Rhine and General Jean-Maximilien Lamarque's Army of La Vendée were ordered to march to Paris so as to be ready to help this defence, while instructions were given to hold the frontier fortresses.

The conscripts of the class of 1815 were indeed starting to appear at the dépôts: about 46,000 men out of the 120,000 eligible were already in motion. But for this process to have continued, Napoleon would have had to enjoy the aura of success. He urged his troops to fight on, but he knew that he had failed. The Allies were clearly going to exploit their victory.

Wellington and Blücher advanced into France, although the British army had been much weakened by the losses involved in its victory and large numbers of bodies were thrown into the mass graves on the battlefield. Resistance, however, was minimal. Napoleon's army was broken. The chief role in the 'Hundred Days' had been taken by the army, and it was now defeated. The main 'civilian' component in Napoleon's return to power had been provided by the large number of jobless and hungry demobilised veterans. The social basis for a lasting resistance was absent.

As his regime collapsed and the Allied forces advanced, Napoleon was urged by some advisors, including his brother Lucien and Davout, the minister of war, to fight on. They wanted him to dissolve the hostile Chamber of Deputies and to rule as a dictator, thus bringing to an end the constitutional government of Louis XVIII that Napoleon had continued in an attempt to curry popularity. To this end, he could have called on the Parisian workers to rally to him, but such a call would have caused civil war, and the tired and defeated Napoleon was no longer the general of 1795, ready to order cannon fired on opponents in the streets of Paris. Nor was he willing to lead the forces that Davout wished to regroup and build up, eventually beyond the River Loire. This course again threatened civil war. Instead, Lafayette acted promptly to thwart Napoleon, persuading the Chamber of Deputies on 21 June to vote to make itself permanent.

With the Chambers unwilling to back him and support dissolving, Napoleon abdicated in favour of his son on 22 June, but the legislature did not take up his idea for the successor. Moreover, Ney told the Chamber of Peers that Waterloo had been a disaster and that Paris would fall soon. By then, Napoleon's presence or absence was of limited consequence. Indeed, he left the Elysée Palace in Paris on 25 June. Only 27,000 troops had assembled at Laon on 24 June, and serious resistance could not be mounted against the advance on Paris, although Grouchy, after the sharp action at Wavre on 18 June, had successfully withdrawn into France via Namur and Dinant, a route to the east of the British and Prussian advances. When Grouchy's troops reached Laon on 26 June, about 60,000 French troops in total were there.

British and Prussian forces had entered France on 21 June, by Baray and Beaumont, respectively. In a step taken in part to lessen resistance, Wellington proclaimed that he entered France to bring liberation from a usurper, and he also benefited from the prospect of fresh military support from Britain. Castlereagh noted on 22 June, 'We hope to reinforce the Duke with nearly 10,000 men now, and nearly as many more when the troops from Canada arrive,' in other words, the troops that had been fighting the Americans in the War of 1812.[4]

The pace of Allied advance was rapid, with the town of Cambrai falling to the British on 24 June. The privilege of conquering the town had been given to Sir Charles Colville, who held the local rank of lieutenant general and was commander of the Fourth Division. This division had been posted at Hal to protect Wellington from flank attack, and it had therefore missed out on the fame of victory at Waterloo. Colville had been a favoured commander of Wellington in the Peninsula, and, in order to provide him with honours and to take advantage of his fresh troops, Cambrai, one of the few French positions that did not immediately surrender, was designated his target. Colville also had valuable experience of such assaults in Spain.[5] There was neither the time nor the heavy artillery for a siege, so Colville attacked by escalade, his columns, covered by artillery, advancing under fire to scale the walls. This operation succeeded with light casualties. It serves as a reminder of the skills required of the British troops: They had an offensive as well as a defensive capability. The citadel held out, but surrendered the next day, and Louis XVIII arrived at Cambrai on the twenty-sixth.

On the afternoon of that day, Wellington attacked Peronne with the First Brigade of Guards under Major-General Maitland. After a key defensive hornwork was stormed in the face of light resistance, the garrison promptly surrendered. It was permitted to go home and Dutch troops were installed as a new garrison. Meanwhile, on 24 July, St. Quentin had been abandoned by the French and the castle of Guise had surrendered to the Prussians. Blücher and Wellington, however, had agreed that they must focus on Paris and ignore both the border fortresses and the French army, a repetition of the strategy eventually followed in 1814.

Due to the Prussians' advantage in the initial pursuit, as well as the delays for Wellington's forces caused by the captures of Cambrai and Péronne, and the need to wait for supplies, Blücher's army was farther advanced than that of Wellington, but this absence of Allied concentration was no threat. Instead, this lack of concentration facilitated operational flexibility, and Blücher was able to get between Grouchy, now at Soissons, and Paris. Moreover, the political dimension worked in favour of the Allied forces. There was a willingness to surrender on the part of the provisional French government, which was a commission of five, including Lazare Carnot, Armand Caulaincourt and Joseph Fouché, chosen by the Chambers, a commission dominated by Fouché. Yet, despite this willingness, the Allies were keen to occupy Paris and to be seen to do so.

Far from solely fighting off the French at Waterloo, Wellington and Blücher had overthrown Napoleon. As a result, they were able to turn their defeat of the French invasion of Belgium into a strategic triumph. At the same time, particularly for the Prussians, there was a desire to take revenge on the French for the exactions suffered from conquering French forces in 1806–07 and in the subsequent occupation of 1807–08. Major William Turner wrote from near Paris, 'Every town and village is completely ransacked and pillaged by the Prussians and neither wines, spirits or bread are to be found. The whole country from the frontier to Paris . . . laid waste.' Turner linked this devastation to a desire for revenge. 'That infernal city Paris will be attacked and no doubt pillaged for it is a debt we owe to the whole of Europe.'[6]

On 28 June 1815, the overextended and vulnerable Prussian advance guard was attacked by French forces at Villers-Cotterêts, but they were driven off when the main Prussian force arrived, took about 1,000 of the troops prisoner, and captured six cannon. On the twenty-ninth, while Napoleon, then in the palace of his first wife, Josephine, at Malmaison to the west of Paris, contemplated trying to use the forces of Grouchy and Davout to defeat first Blücher and then Wellington, Quesnoy surrendered to Prince Frederick of the Netherlands, and Wellington's advance guard crossed the River Oise; the remainder of the army followed the next day.

Blücher crossed the River Seine at St. Germain on the thirtieth. The right bank and the northern approach to Paris were strongly defended around Montmartre, and Blücher, in response, decided to advance on the left bank, where Paris was less well defended. Blücher was strongly opposed, notably in a cavalry charge mounted by General Rémy Exelmans, but, on 2 July, established himself on the heights of Meudon and at the village of Issy. Paris was now open on its vulnerable side, and Davout was no longer interested in mounting a firm resistance.

The resistance of Paris collapsed on 3 July, after a French dawn attack on the Prussians at Issy was repulsed, while the advancing British forces were building a bridge across the Seine at nearby Argenteuil in order to link the two armies. Later that day, a convention was negotiated at St. Cloud by Wellington, Blücher and Davout, stipulating that the French army should evacuate Paris and retire behind the River Loire. Anglo-Prussian forces occupied Paris without resistance on 7 July, and Louis XVIII returned the following day, a return that was greeted with singularly little popular joy.

Wellington played a key role in the political transition within France, in part because he had the relevant skills from his years of managing Spanish politics and Blücher had no interest in such activities. In Paris, the leading player was Fouché, the minister for police, who claimed to control the 25,000 fédérés in the city who had pledged to fight the return of Louis XVIII. Fouché sought a peaceful settlement that would not be dominated by royalist ultras and persuaded Wellington that he could deliver an orderly transition, not least by blocking the idea of a regency in the name of Napoleon's son by Marie Louise of Austria, the never-crowned Napoleon II. Wellington pressed successfully for a ministry with which he could deal, with Talleyrand, with whom he had negotiated at Vienna, as its head and also foreign minister, and Fouché as minister of police. Fouché, in turn, helped ensure the surrender of French forces.

France fell as Prussia had done to Napoleon in 1806, without a lengthy struggle. The situation would have been different in 1815 had Napoleon won, for the Allies, most of whose armies were not yet engaged, would have kept on fighting. Napoleon's regime, however, was dependent on his main battle army and on his prestige. Resting on these fragile, and now weak, foundations, the regime rapidly collapsed. Dismayed by the heavy casualties, Wellington said, 'I hope to God that I have fought my last battle.' That would not have been the case had Napoleon proved successful. As William, Lord Cathcart, the British representative at the Austrian headquarters, then in Heidelberg, noted, 'It seemed to be the received opinion that Bonaparte's hopes and expectations depended greatly on the result of his first battle.'[7]

While attention focused on the northern front, there had also been conflict elsewhere in France in 1815. The British were particularly concerned about the ports, both French and others. Indeed, the protection of Antwerp from French conquest was one of Wellington's key goals in Belgium, and one that would have been compromised had he been obliged to fall back on the Ostend axis. The ports were a strategic issue, as any revival of French naval activity posed a problem for the Royal Navy. In turn, the strength of this navy provided opportunities for Britain, with George Keith Elphinstone, Viscount Keith, the commander-in-chief of the Channel fleet, ordering a blockade of France. Moreover, Britain could make a major effort against France's ports, offsetting her numerical inferiority on land as a member of the anti-Napoleonic Coalition.

The Mediterranean was an area of especial British concern and, closing a cycle, British forces, which had been driven from Toulon, the great naval dockyard, in 1793 by French troops including Napoleon, returned to the port there at the close of the campaign. Earlier in July 1815, under the command of Major-General Hudson Lowe, later Napoleon's unwelcome custodian on St. Helena, British forces at Genoa cooperated with a squadron under Edward, Lord Exmouth, the commander-in-chief in the Mediterranean, to occupy Marseille. In conjunction with local royalists, they then advanced on Toulon and, on 24 July, restored it to Bourbon control.

The threat to Toulon from the British fleet had led Marshal Guillaume Brune, the commander of the Armée du Var, to fall back from the Piedmontese frontier, that with Italy. Victor over the Duke of York in Holland in 1799, Brune eventually surrendered at Toulon when he heard news of the collapse of the Army of the Loire, an instance of the manner in which the surrender of one army led to that of other forces. Having surrendered, Brune set off for Paris. At Avignon, however, on 2 August, he was seized by a crowd who claimed he had been guilty of murders during the Terror of 1793, claims for which there is no evidence. Allegedly saying 'Good God! To survive a hundred fields and die like this,' Brune was torn to pieces, which were thrown into the River Rhône.

Elsewhere, the French put up a credible resistance to the invading forces. Farther north than Brune, Marshal Louis-Gabriel Suchet, in command of the Army of the Alps, marched into Savoy on 14 June in an effort to seize Alpine passes through which Austrian forces could advance. Initially successful, Suchet was soon put under pressure by Austrian numbers and by Austrian troops appearing at Lake Geneva. News of Waterloo was followed by instructions from the provisional French government to negotiate an armistice with the Austrians. An armistice was signed on 28 June and Suchet abandoned Savoy, but the Austrians continued their advance, seizing Geneva and then Lyon.

The articles of capitulation for Lyon signed by Suchet were similar to those for Paris and allowed his troops to join Davout's force. Davout, who had been placed in command in Paris but been forced to evacuate the city and retire to the Loire Valley, successfully held the line of the Loire before submitting on 16 July. He was then replaced by Marshal Jacques-Étienne Macdonald, who, in March, had not backed Napoleon's return, instead escorting Louis XVIII to Ghent. Macdonald was given the task of disbanding Davout's army.

General Jean Rapp and the Army of the Rhine initially put up a strong performance in Alsace, driving back the Austrians on 28 June and 8 July. The Austrians, under Prince Schwarzenberg, who had commanded the Austrian contingent in the invasion of Russia in 1812, were supported by the Bavarians under Prince Wrede, who had, as a Bavarian general, fought for France in 1805–13. Meanwhile, major fortresses, such as Verdun and Strasbourg, remained in French hands. Either Suchet or Rapp would possibly have done better than Ney and Grouchy in the Waterloo campaign. Indeed, on St. Helena, endlessly sloughing off his own responsibility, Napoleon was to claim that he would have won had he had Suchet in place of Grouchy.

Waterloo, however, had truly been a decisive battle. For example, Rapp's victory on the River Souffel, north of Strasbourg, on

28 June could not be exploited, not only as Rapp was heavily out-numbered, but also because Napoleon had already been defeated. On 22 July, a truce was concluded for Alsace. The same day, Marshal Bertrand Clausel, the commander of the Armée des Pyrénées Occidentales, surrendered Bordeaux. A British squadron under Captain F. W. Aylmer had anchored in the estuary of the River Gironde near Bordeaux on 13 July 1815, and the coastal batteries there had abandoned Napoleon.

Waterloo also determined the struggle between Napoleon and counterrevolutionaries in the South. The battle led to the revival of royalist militias, with the Duke of Angoulême, initially based in Spain, nominally in charge. Their targets, in a White Terror, were people identified as opponents of the royalists, but the violence also had a religious complexion, with Catholics attacking Protestants who were portrayed as disloyal. Meanwhile, a few garrisons continued to hold out against Louis XVIII during the summer of 1815, but the last, Montmédy, a frontier position over against Luxembourg, surrendered on 13 September.

The ready collapse of Napoleon's regime can be seen to vindicate earlier claims about its weakness, such as that in the House of Commons by Nicholas Vansittart, the chancellor of the exchequer, on 14 June 1815: 'Hearing as he did, in many parts of France, murmurs half suppressed, and seeing in others open hostilities against the ruling power, he could not but cherish a belief that the real supporters of Buonaparte were very few indeed, beyond the limits of the army.'[8]

Napoleon's defeat encouraged other powers to join the attack on France. The Portuguese regency had refused to send help, much to the anger of the British government mindful of past support for Portuguese independence. Short of funds and the ruler of an exhausted state confronting opposition and insurrections in Spanish America, Ferdinand VII of Spain had joined the Seventh Coalition only in May. The British made the payment of their subsidy conditional on Spanish troops crossing the frontier, and they invaded France, at each end of the Pyrenees, in late August when they were not needed. The Spanish forces were then persuaded to turn back by the French government.

There was scant fighting on behalf of Napoleon outside France, but Joachim Murat, who had become Napoleon's brother-in-law in 1800 and been made a marshal in 1804, tried to raise Italy, underlining Allied fears about the impact of Napoleon's return to power. Murat had been made King of Naples by Napoleon in 1808, and, by abandoning Napoleon, kept his kingdom in 1814. Napoleon, once returned, pressed Murat to support him, but to wait before acting. Instead, aware that the Austrians were now willing to see him deposed, the naturally ambitious Murat decided to drive them from Italy.

Moving into the Papal States on 19 March, Murat invaded central Italy in order to attack the Austrians further north. Rome was seized. At Cesena to the north of the Apennines on 30 March, Murat successfully attacked Austrian forces trying to block his advance on Bologna. Murat benefited from the extent to which many Austrian units were north of the Alps, and, at Rimini on 31 March, he issued a proclamation to all Italians. This called for a new order, a 'war of independence' for Italy, but, in fact, very few Italians responded. Murat had little chance, not least because Napoleonic rule had proved unpopular in Italy, in part because of the burdensome conscription it had entailed and in part due to the Napoleonic assault on Italian religious life.[9]

Murat defeated an Austrian force at Sant'Ambrogio on 4 April, and a subsidiary Neapolitan force entered Florence on 7 April. However, the balance of advantage now moved toward the Austrians, whose forces were concentrated to produce a large army. They captured Bologna on 16 April and drove the Neapolitans from Cesena five days later. The successful Austrian offensive put pressure on Murat, who sought to secure his retreat to Naples by attacking the Austrians at Tolentino southwest of Ancona on 2–3 May. Murat, however, was defeated, and this defeat led to the dissolution of his army through desertion. This news reached Brussels before Napoleon's invasion of Belgium and also enabled the Allies to invade southern France.

As with Napoleon at Waterloo, Murat's defeat in the field proved crucial. Protracted resistance to the advancing Austrian army could not be mounted, while the British played a major role with their naval power. They were already present off Ancona and Gaeta, as well as protecting Sicily. H.M.S. *Tremendous* under Captain Campbell, supported by a frigate and a sloop, arrived off Naples, and Campbell declared that he would bombard the city unless the Neapolitan navy surrendered within forty-eight hours. This surrender duly happened, and the arsenal was also brought under control. Murat's position collapsed. A military convention of 20 May led to an armistice, the departure of Murat that day, and the arrival of King Ferdinand IV of Sicily, a Bourbon, to take back the Neapolitan throne for his family. On 23 May, Naples and its forts were occupied: Lord Exmouth, the commander of the British fleet in the Mediterranean, landed British marines, and Austrian troops also arrived.[10]

Fleeing Naples, Murat was, as a result of earlier betrayals, unwelcome to Napoleon. Instead, he fled first to Toulon, and then, as royal control was reestablished in France, to Corsica, where he raised a few followers and took shelter in the inaccessible terrain of the interior. The role of bandit-leader was unattractive, however, and Murat sought to return to his former kingdom. He duly invaded Calabria on 8 October, but was speedily defeated, captured, and, after a court-martial, executed on 15 October by a firing squad of troops of the Bourbon king. Also in Italy, Tuscan forces had landed on Elba on 30 July, and its garrison had surrendered, bringing Napoleonic rule there to an end. In Belgium that June, there had been even less support for Napoleon in 1815 than there was for Murat in central Italy.

Another former Napoleonic marshal, Jean Bernadotte, who had been elected crown prince and regent of Sweden in 1810, had played a prominent role against Napoleon in 1813 and a minor one in 1814. Yet in 1815 he refused to join the Seventh Coalition. Instead, in June 1815, he overcame Norway's resistance to its transfer from Denmark to Sweden. Unlike Murat's campaigning, however, this activity did not disrupt the international system or even potentially help Napoleon. Instead, a diplomatic solution to disputes in northern Europe was negotiated, with Russia taking the leading role. As part of the settlement, Prussia purchased Swedish Pomerania and Denmark received the Duchy of Lauenburg.

There were also hostilities in the French empire. This was now far smaller than in 1792, and the key positions were the profitable Caribbean sugar islands of Guadeloupe and Martinique, newly returned to French control as part of the peace settlement in 1814, having been seized by British amphibious forces in 1810 and 1809, respectively. At Martinique, Lieutenant-General Sir James Leith, the governor of the British-ruled Leeward Islands, as well as the commander-in-chief in the West Indies, a veteran of the Peninsular War, moved rapidly, sending troops from nearby St. Lucia. They landed on 5 June and occupied all the strong positions, helping to stop a revolution in favour of Napoleon. Similar success was achieved on the nearby island of Marie-Galante.

In Guadeloupe, the situation was more difficult for the British. An insurrection, mounted, ironically, on 18 June, succeeded with the support of the local authorities, and Napoleon was proclaimed emperor the next day. In response, Leith, covered by Rear-Admiral Sir Philip Charles Durham, the commander-in-chief of the Leeward Islands station, landed his men on 8 August. The British forces advanced rapidly in columns the next day, preventing the French from concentrating, and on the tenth the French surrendered. The last French flag was struck to Durham, as the first of the war also had been on 13 February 1793 when, in command of H.M.S. *Spitfire,* he had captured the French privateer *Afrique.*

Leith had been helped in his task by bringing the news of Waterloo to Guadeloupe. Some French soldiers, however, deserted, refused to surrender, and took refuge in the woods on the island. Low-level guerrilla opposition continued on Guadeloupe, but the crisis was over. Relief at victory was indicated by the subsequent awards: Leith received a sword worth 2,000 guineas from the British government and the Grand Cordon of Military Merit from Louis XVIII, while Durham was created a Knight Grand Cross of the Order.

The rapid restoration of Bourbon control contrasted with the major British effort required to capture Martinique in 1809. Ten thousand troops had been required then, alongside a very heavy bombardment of Fort Desaix. The British were fortunate that such an effort was not necessary in 1815, as the necessary troops were not available in the West Indies. British naval superiority in the Caribbean was clear in 1815, but the same had been the case in 1809–10. The impact of the French defeat at Waterloo was a key distinguishing feature, helping to explain the more rapid British success.

After leaving Malmaison outside Paris at 5:30 P.M. on 29 June 1815, Napoleon sought a port from which he could flee abroad. He reached Poitiers on 30 June and Niort on 1 July, arriving in the Atlantic port of Rochefort on the afternoon of 3 July. Napoleon planned to go to America, but the British naval blockade, which had been reestablished with the resumption of conflict, made it impossible for him to leave France by sea. The British government was concerned to prevent Napoleon from taking refuge in America, and Rear-Admiral Sir Henry Hotham was instructed to 'keep the most vigilant lookout for the purpose of intercepting him.'[11]

In the event, Napoleon was thwarted. The British fleet denied him the final strategic option, his own freedom. Unlike the Spanish American revolutionary Simón Bolívar, Napoleon found no foreign bolt-hole. Bolívar, in contrast, was able to escape after unsuccessful attempts to overthrow Spanish power in South America, fleeing, for example, to British-ruled Jamaica in 1815 and returning anew to Venezuela in 1816 to raise the flag for revolution.

Napoleon felt he would meet with better treatment from Britain than from his other foes, and that despite his marriage into the Austrian ruling family. Meanwhile, Louis XVIII had ordered his arrest. To thwart this, Napoleon, after discussions between Grand-Marshal Henri Bertrand and Captain Frederick Maitland of the seventy-four-gun warship H.M.S. *Bellerophon* on 14 July, boarded the ship between 4 A.M. and 5 A.M. the following morning in order to throw himself on the 'generosity' of the prince regent. Napoleon took over Maitland's cabin and sent him an invitation to breakfast at his own table. Captain Humphrey Senhouse, the commander of the *Superb,* Hotham's flagship, wrote to his wife, Elizabeth, later that day, 'I have just returned from dining with Napoleon Bonaparte. Can it be possible?'[12] The fate of the former emperor, however, was unclear. Napoleon claimed that Maitland agreed that he be allowed to retire to Britain, but Maitland stated at that time that he had explained that he had no authority to grant terms and solely said that he would take him to Britain, where his future would be decided.[13]

Napoleon appealed to the prince regent, the future George IV, 'as the most powerful, the most constant, and the most generous of my foes,' a description at once flattering and accurate. He was taken to Torbay (arriving on 24 July), and later Plymouth, but was kept on the *Bellerophon* and not permitted to land. Many locals rowed out to the ship in an attempt to get a glimpse of Napoleon, and his stay led to a sermon by Luke Booker, *The Parallel: Nebuchadnezzar and N. Buonaparte.*

Sir Francis Burdett, a radical MP, considered moving a writ of habeas corpus in an attempt to secure Napoleon's release, but the government's determination to detain him matched the national mood. There was no chance of a trial akin to that held in Nuremburg after the Second World War, as neither France nor the Allies wanted Napoleon to stand trial, which left him as a problem for the British.

On 31 July, Admiral Lord Keith and Sir Henry Bunbury, the undersecretary for the colonies, informed Napoleon that he would be held as a prisoner for the remainder of his life and detained on St. Helena. Napoleon sent protests to the British government on 31 July and 4 August, but, on 7 August, he was transferred to H.M.S. *Northumberland* for the voyage to St. Helena, an island in the distant South Atlantic. Napoleon, now styled General Buonaparte, arrived on St. Helena on 17 August and was imprisoned by the British until his death, probably by poisoning, on 5 May 1821. This imprisonment was a consequence and sign of British power, and one made secure by British naval dominance. His successive residences on the island are now 'the shrines of a cult.'[14]

The legal basis of the detention of Napoleon was a cause of some embarrassment to the British government and led to complaints by the imprisoned dictator. Indeed, the prime minister, the Earl of

Liverpool, would have preferred that Napoleon suffer the fate of
Ney, as long as it was at the hands of the French. Blücher also
wanted Napoleon shot, an idea opposed, however, by Wellington,
who, moreover, thwarted Blücher's plan to demolish the Pont
d'Iéna (de Jena) which had been built in Paris in 1806–13 to commemorate the victory of 1806 over Prussia. In 1815, Napoleon was
presented by the British government as an enemy of the human race
in order to justify his detention, and in 1816 an act of Parliament
was passed so as to regularise his position.

The prince regent himself was with his brother Frederick, Duke
of York, the commander-in-chief, at a society ball at Mrs. Boehm's
house in St. James Square, London, when the official news of victory
at Waterloo was brought by Major Henry Percy, grandson of the
Duke of Northumberland and one of Wellington's aides-de-camp,
who had been wounded in the foot at Waterloo. A later account
recalled:

> The first quadrille [a type of dance] was in the act of form-
> ing, and the Prince was walking to the dais on which his
> seat was placed, when I saw every one without the slightest
> sense of decorum rushing to the windows, which had been
> left wide open because of the extreme sultriness of the
> weather. The music ceased and the dance stopped; for we
> heard nothing but the vociferous shouts of an enormous
> mob who had just entered the square, and were running by
> the side of a post-chaise and four, out of whose windows
> were hanging three [in fact two] nasty French eagles. In a
> second the door of the carriage was flung open and, without
> waiting for the steps to be let down, out sprang Henry Percy
> – such a dusty figure – with a flag in each hand – pushing
> aside everyone who happened to be in his way, darting
> upstairs, into the ballroom, stepping hastily up to the
> Regent, dropping on one knee, laying the flags at his feet,
> and pronouncing the words 'Victory, Sir! Victory!'[15]

Percy was immediately promoted to colonel by the prince. The opposition Whigs were far less pleased by the victory, while radicals such as William Hazlitt were thrown into despair. Percy's confirmation of the victory, in the form of the delivery of the dispatch Wellington wrote on 19 June, was important, as some of the early reports were alarmist, especially from those who had fled Brussels fearing Napoleon's advance. Similarly, there had been false reports of victory in Paris.

Advance knowledge of Napoleon's defeat is often attributed to the banker Nathan Rothschild, who had moved to London in 1808 and had played a key role in providing Wellington's forces in the Peninsula with the specie they required. Rothschild was also very important in helping to finance the Seventh Coalition in 1815. An oft-repeated story claims that advance knowledge enabled Rothschild to make a financial killing by selling holdings in order to create an impression of defeat and then buying them back more cheaply. However, the evidence for this account is lacking.[16]

Victory for Wellington confirmed the decisions of the international peace congress of Vienna, a congress that both set the seal on Britain's triumph over France and marked the beginning of a period in which the British empire was faced with no effective threats. The impact of Napoleon's defeat would probably have been different had it been achieved by Austrian and Russian forces, not least in terms of their subsequent role in western Europe. Instead, Napoleon's return and defeat ensured the British a more satisfactory result. In the peace settlement, British control of a host of wartime gains, mostly from France and its allies, including Cape Colony, the Seychelles, Mauritius, Trinidad, Tobago, St. Lucia, Malta, the Ionian Islands, Sri Lanka, Essequibo and Demerara (the last two the basis of British Guiana, now Guyana), were all recognised.

As a result of its gains, Britain ruled far more than just the waves, and this empire was a far more widely flung congeries of possessions than any other empire in the world, either then or previously. This empire was also very much one that had been tested in war, and that, if necessary, was ready for further conflict, as its fleet was the largest in the world and its public finances the strongest. There were benefits at the level of individual careers. Peregrine Maitland of the

Guards went on successively to be lieutenant governor of Upper Canada, lieutenant governor of Nova Scotia, commander-in-chief of the Madras army, and governor and commander-in-chief at the Cape of Good Hope.

Britain's territorial gains ensured that she had a system of bases to protect her trade while denying others positions, such as Cape Colony, that would potentially be a threat in hostile hands. British naval interests have also been seen as playing a role in the European territorial settlement, with shipbuilding ports that would be a threat in French hands put into those of British allies: Trieste and Venice with Austria, Genoa with the Kingdom of Sardinia (Piedmont), and, crucially, Antwerp with the new Kingdom of the United Provinces.

The British royal family also gained great prestige as royal status for their possession of Hanover (hitherto an electorate), proclaimed by the prince regent in October 1814, was swiftly recognised by the Congress. Thus, the status of the Hanoverian ruling family in Germany now matched those of Prussia, Bavaria, Saxony and Württemberg. Moreover, Hanover gained territory, notably East Friesland, Hildesheim and Osnabrück, as well as part of the former prince-bishopric of Münster, so that in 1815 it was the fourth largest state in Germany, after Austria, Prussia and Bavaria. These gains were agreed to at Vienna before Waterloo, but the effort made by the KGL and Hanoverians during the battle made them appear justified. The gains reflected not just dynastic ambition and the extent to which there was a general sharing out of German territories, one in which Prussia particularly benefited. There was also credit 'for Hanoverians who had upheld personal union [of the dynasty with Britain] during its darkest days in 1803.'[17] The major role of Hanoverian units, notably of the KGL, at Waterloo testified to this, although there was a significant contrast in ability and, possibly, enthusiasm in the battle between the KGL and the new Hanoverian levies.

Napoleon's return and subsequent defeat also ensured that France received worse terms than those initially imposed by the Congress. The Second Treaty of Paris, signed on 20 November

1815, stipulated an occupation of northern France of five years (it ended in 1818), a large indemnity of 700 million francs, and the cession of the towns of Beaumont, Bouillon (both to the Netherlands), Landau (to Bavaria) and Saarlouis (to Prussia). Moreover, by the Quadruple Alliance of 20 November 1815, the four great powers – Austria, Britain, Prussia and Russia – renewed their anti-French alliance for twenty years, a step designed to limit the chances of France disrupting the peace.

Napoleon had failed, totally. His legacy was a weaker France, with Russia, the power frequently seen by French politicians over the previous century as a barbarian threat, now dominant in Eastern Europe. Indeed, in September 1815, on the third anniversary of Borodino, in a dramatic display of power, Tsar Alexander I reviewed a parade of 150,000 Russian troops east of Paris, in the Russian occupation zone, alongside Francis I of Austria and Frederick William III of Prussia, each of whom was also dressed in Russian uniform. Earlier, on 10 July, the three monarchs had reached Paris. The Allies maintained control of France with an occupation force commanded by Wellington, their unanimous choice. From 1815 to 1817, this was 150,000 strong and thereafter until 1818 contained 120,000 troops. The major contingents were from Britain, Austria, Russia and Prussia, with smaller ones from Bavaria, Denmark, Hanover, Saxony and Württemberg.[18] In Europe, in place of Napoleon, came an attempt to develop a practice of collective security through a congress system and Tsar Alexander's Holy Alliance of Christian Monarchs (or at least those of Russia, Austria and Prussia), designed to maintain the new order.

Within France, the new political order very much matched the ideas of the Holy Alliance. After elections by a propertied electorate in August 1815, the Talleyrand-Fouché ministry was replaced by a new Chamber of Deputies that included a large number of ultra-royalists. The new ministry was led by Louis-Antoine du Plessis, the Duke of Richelieu, a former émigré who had served Alexander I, and Ney was tried for treason in November 1815. He was the man held responsible for Napoleon's success in regaining power, and his fate was a warning to others of the consequences of such treason. Ney was convicted, sentenced to death, and shot by a firing squad in the Luxembourg Gardens in Paris on 7 December. Maréchal de Camp Charles-Angelique de la Bédoyère had already been tried for going over to Napoleon at Grenoble on 7 March as he advanced on Paris. He was executed by firing squad on 26 August. D'Erlon fled and was sentenced to death in his absence. Those who had voted for the execution of Louis XVI were exiled, as were some of the Bonapartist generals, while the army was disbanded in order to be reconstituted. Symbolic links were broken with the removal of eagles and tricolours from the regiments.

Unlike Louis XIV after his defeats in the War of the Spanish Succession (1701–14), Napoleon left a smaller France, and one with fewer opportunities for further expansion. Moreover, France's relative decline owed much to French politics, specifically the heavy loss of life in the French Revolutionary and Napoleonic Wars, in which over a million Frenchmen died. The Revolution itself was less bloody, but a combination of civil war and emigration led to heavy losses and disrupted family life and peacetime reproduction strategies. Partly as a consequence, France's population grew by less than 50 per cent between 1750 and 1850, while that of England nearly tripled. This contrast can in part be attributed to a fall in the French birthrate arising from the spread of birth control in the late eighteenth century, but repeated choices for war were also important.

Across Europe, divine sanction was seen in victory over France. Indeed, Prussian troops at Waterloo had sung the Lutheran psalm 'A Mighty Fortress Is Our God'. In his 'Ode for the Day of General Thanksgiving' for victory, held on 18 January 1816, William Wordsworth urged 'this favoured Nation' to 'be conscious of thy moving spirit . . . thy protecting care' (lines 189–200). Such writing did not contribute greatly to poetry, but it did help Wordsworth, now, with his support for the French Revolution long set aside, very much an establishment poet, to gain the Poet Laureateship in 1842. The clergy were also active giving and, in some cases, publishing commemorative sermons. A Privy Council order relating to thanksgiving for Waterloo was issued on 29 June, to be implemented around the country as soon as possible. The minimum requirement was the reading of the authorised State Prayer, which was done in the mainstream dissenting churches as well as the Church of England. The Thanksgiving appears to have been held mostly on 2, 9, or 16 July, but sometimes as late as 13 and 20 August, as well as on 18 January 1816 (thanksgiving for the end of the war), and on the first anniversary of the battle.

Sermons published in 1815 included those by William Howley, the future Archbishop of Canterbury, Thomas Chalmers, the leading Scottish Presbyterian minister, Thomas Bowerback, Henry Cotes, Daniel Mathias, Edward Patterson, Peter Roe, John Sergrove and John Vickers. In 1815 there were probably published about 100,000 words in sermon form about the battle, more words indeed than in any other genre, apart from journalism. A common theme was the need to support those who had suffered in the battle, in particular by giving generously to support the Waterloo subscription. The national fund-raising committee was preempted by spontaneous local collections, and these were driven from below and their organisation improvised by the church wardens. Most of the Waterloo sermons were demonstrably connected with local fund-raising, and some even printed the names of the donors. On the military side, the sermons all emphasise that the Allied armies withstood an assault for a long time and give credit to Blücher.

This commemorative effort was not restricted to the British Isles. The energy of the empire was brought into play as when George Mountain, the Rector of Fredericton, New Brunswick, in modern Canada, published the sermon he preached in 1816. Later published Waterloo sermons included John Somerville's *National Gratitude,* preached on the fourth anniversary of the battle, and Richard Glover's *Esdraelon and Waterloo,* a sermon given on Wellington's death in 1852. The principal Waterloo sermon, and the first to be subsequently published, was Robert Morehead's 'On the Good Name of the Dead', first preached on 2 July 1815, and included in Thomas Frognall Dibdin's *The Sunday Library; Or, The Protestant's Manual for the Sabbath-day* (1831). This sermon by the Scottish Episcopalian minister closed:

And now, may that Almighty God, who strengthened the
arms of our warriors on the day of battle, and crowned
their efforts with glorious victory, grant that the memory
of their 'good name' may fire, as incense from the altar, the
hearts of our children in every succeeding age; and may he
speedily close the wounds of private affection, by the ani-
mating spectacle of national security and dignity won by
their blood, and by all the triumphant hopes and consola-
tions of Religion.

Some Waterloo sermons were preached on commemorative days
well into the nineteenth century. Providence was also seen at play
by the participants, one cavalry officer writing after the battle,
'Altogether it is a glorious thing and I cannot help hoping that all
is to end well after it – and that it has been ordered by Providence
to humble the military pride and break the ferocious spirit of that
nation.'[19]

All, meanwhile, wanted to claim the credit of victory at Waterloo, for which both houses of Parliament voted thanks on 23 June
1815. George, Prince of Wales, the prince regent, had made himself
field marshal in 1811, and in 1814 Sir Thomas Lawrence depicted
him on canvas as a general. In 1821, en route to Hanover, his sole
visit there as king, George was shown the battlefield by Wellington, the king being interested to see where Uxbridge, now Marquess of Anglesey, had lost his leg near the close of the battle. Later
in life, George used to tell people that he had been at the Battle of
Waterloo and would seek confirmation from Wellington, winning
the tactful reply 'So you have told me, Sir.' For George, Lawrence
also painted the portraits of those who had secured the defeat of
Napoleon that line the Waterloo Gallery at Windsor Castle.
Lawrence was well rewarded for this work, while, as a sign of favour
and prestige, he also became president of the Royal Academy in
1820. George was a keen patron of the Academy.

London, the capital of the world empire, had not only Nelson
resplendent on his column in Trafalgar Square, but also Waterloo
Bridge (built from 1811 as the Strand Bridge, opened in 1817, and

replaced by a new bridge in 1944), Waterloo Road (1823), and
Waterloo Station, where the London and Southampton Railway ter-
minated from 1848. Waterloo Station remains the largest railway
station in the world. As a more prominent rebuilding of London in
the early nineteenth century, Waterloo Place was the southern end
of John Nash's new triumphant Regent's Street, the most radical
change in London's topography since the Great Fire of 1666.
Waterloo Place was designed to be the central node of London,
where the new Regent Street reached the prince regent's palace at
Carlton House. However, in the late 1820s, the prince regent, now
George IV, transformed the situation by deciding to demolish Carlton House when he moved to Buckingham Palace.

At a more mundane and humorous level, a much revered pater-
nal boot that had served at Waterloo played a role in Elizabeth
Gaskell's novel *Cranford* (1851–53). 'Waterloos' were the name
given to sets of false teeth made from the teeth of soldiers who had
died in the battle. Moreover, 'meeting one's Waterloo' became a
phrase evocative of failure, one that owed its popularity to a remark
in a speech of 1859 by Wendell Phillips (1811–84), an American
writer, namely, 'Every man meets his Waterloo at last.'[20] In turn,
Arthur Conan Doyle had Sherlock Holmes remark, in *The Return of
Sherlock Holmes* (1905), 'We have not yet met our Waterloo, Watson,
but this is our Marengo.'

Yet there was a far more difficult social dimension to the after-
effects of Waterloo. Victory made the demobilisation sought by the
government possible, and the release into the labour market of large
numbers of ex-soldiers and -sailors helped to exacerbate the serious
economic problems of the period, problems that led to high levels
of unemployment and social discontent. This situation offered few
prospects for demobilised veterans, and their position was exacerbated by the lack of adequate state provision for veterans. The difficulties were accentuated by poor harvests. The government itself
faced serious fiscal problems, problems greatly eased, but not
ended, by the peace.

Meanwhile, dominated by the landed interest, Parliament passed
the protectionist Corn Law of 1815, which prohibited the import of

grain unless the price of British grain reached 80 shillings a quarter. This measure kept the price of supplies artificially high, leading to food riots among hungry agricultural labourers, with attacks on farmers and corn mills and demands for higher wages. The conflicting social politics of the period and the very different resonances of Waterloo were such that many of the new brick-built farms that reflected the subsequent prosperity of tenant farmers were known as 'Waterloo Farms'. In light of this agricultural aftermath, it is instructive to note the poem 'Grass' by the American Carl Sandburg (1878–1967):

> *Pile the bodies high at Austerlitz and Waterloo.*
> *Shovel them under and let me work –*
> *I am the grass; I cover all.*

Alongside the 'Waterloo Farms', popular agitation contributed to what was presented as a deliberate counterpoint to Waterloo, 'Peterloo'. On 16 August 1819, about 60,000 people turned out in St. Peter's Field, Manchester, to hear 'Orator' Henry Hunt demand parliamentary reform. The excited Manchester magistrates read the Riot Act in order to disperse the crowd and ordered the Manchester and Salford Yeoman Cavalry to seize the speakers, but the untrained, amateur cavalry also attacked the crowd, leading to eleven deaths and many injuries. The arguably inherent violence of the horseman toward those on foot, a violence seen in a different context in Waterloo, also came into play. There was public outrage at what was termed, by analogy with Waterloo, the Peterloo Massacre. *The Times* deplored 'the dreadful fact that nearly a hundred of the King's unarmed subjects have been sabred by a body of cavalry in the streets of a town of which most of them were inhabitants.'

Unlike destitute former soldiers, Wellington himself emerged from the war with £200,000 (an enormous sum for the period) voted by Parliament, which he spent on the estate of Stratfield Saye in Hampshire (which remains in the family), the title Prince of Waterloo and a large estate from the king of the Netherlands, and the Order of Saint-Esprit set in diamonds from Louis XVIII.

Wellington, moreover, was a key figure in the conservative ascendancy in Britain, and indeed was prime minister from 1828 to 1830 and briefly in 1834. Wellington's position might seem a clear demonstration that 'Waterloo made the world safe for gentlemen again.'[21] The police force in County Durham, established in 1839, was commanded by Major James Wemyss, a Waterloo veteran.

Far from being rigidly conservative, however, this was not a world unwilling or unable to respond to developments. Instead, the British political order sought to mould developments. Although much criticised for his conservatism, Wellington himself was willing, when necessary, to accept change, forcing an unwilling George IV to agree to Catholic emancipation in 1829 (a step that divided the Tories and shattered the cohesion of the conservative press), and himself giving way in the House of Lords to pressure for parliamentary reform in 1832.[22]

At the same time as political divisions played a role in Britain, the memory of the battle served to offer an inclusive nationalism, as with David Wilkie's painting *Chelsea Pensioners Reading the Gazette of the Battle of Waterloo*. A response to Wellington's unpopularity as a conservative, and an attempt to underline his association with patriotism, this was a masterpiece that made a great public impact when it was exhibited at the Royal Academy in 1822.[23] The scene depicted was one of public joy, not the joy of stage-managed official celebration but a carefully constructed vision of a popular celebration in which men and women, old and young, military and civilians, Scots, English, Welsh and Irish, joined without differences of rank.[24]

This vision of the response to the battle was the one that was to prevail as political and social differences receded. Wellington himself had encouraged such an approach by having the Waterloo Medal awarded not only to the senior officers but to all ranks who had fought at Waterloo and Quatre Bras. It thus became the British army's first campaign medal. As another instance of inclusion, the Waterloo sermons were not politically conservative. They came from a variety of positions but tended to share a view that Wellington was the harbinger of new global liberty, that Napoleon stood for atheism, and that a restoration of the ancien régime was unwelcome. It is instructive to note that the Church of England established a structure in western Europe, Palestine and Turkey shortly after the war.

As far as the fighting itself was concerned, a heroic note was repeatedly struck, as in Lady Elizabeth Butler's painting *Scotland Forever,* a depiction of the advance of the Scots Greys, for which Lady Butler prepared by having the regiment twice advance on her. Lady Butler, who married into the army, was a specialist military painter who saw her figures as Homeric. She had already painted *The 28th at Quatre Bras* (1874), and she visited the Royal Horse Guards, where the riding master helped her make studies of floundering horses. Colonel James Brame, the deputy adjutant general, had a Waterloo uniform made up for her. In 1874 or 1875, Lady Butler made a study of the Scots Greys in *A Quiet Canter in the Long Valley, Aldershot.* After *Scotland Forever* (1881), her works included *Dawn of Waterloo* (c. 1893). She said she wanted to show a range of emotions in *Scotland Forever,* as she believed that war called forth the range of human impulses, but the public saw the work as simply patriotic. The painting was used by advertisers, such as a brand of safety razors, and was also inspirational enough to be copied by the Germans in 1915, exchanging Greys for Uhlans (German cavalry).[25]

Fascination with Waterloo led to numerous publications, including William Siborne's successful *History of the War in France and Belgium in 1815, Containing Minute Details of the Battles of Quatre Bras, Ligny, Wavre, and Waterloo* (1844), which was read by Lady Butler. In 1830, Siborne had been instructed by Wellington to undertake the construction of a diorama or model of the battlefield at Waterloo. He did so on the basis of thorough and lengthy research, living for eight months at the farmhouse of La Haie Sainte, a key point in the battle, and produced a detailed survey of the battlefield as the basis for his model. He also consulted those who had taken part. In 1833, however, the Whig government refused to allot funds for the work, and Siborne, who had only the time that he did not need to be at work as assistant military secretary in Ireland, did not finish the model until 1838. It was publicly exhibited, but Siborne did not recoup the £3,000 the model had cost. Siborne's dioramas, one now displayed at the National Army Museum and the other (smaller) one at Dover Castle, were controversial, as they differed from Wellington's official account of Waterloo, notably by presenting the Prussian troops as arriving before the duke reported they had and thereby playing a major role in the battle. Aside from the success of Siborne's two-volume 1844 book, with its accompanying atlas, this was not, however, the end of the family's engagement with the battle. In 1891, Siborne's second son, Major-General Herbert Siborne, edited a selection from the letters his father had accumulated, under the title *Waterloo Letters*.

Such accumulated memories helped explain the frequency of Waterloo references in the correspondence of those involved in later wars, for example the Crimean War (1854–56). More specifically, there was a strong concern not to let down regimental forebears. Indeed the Russian attack on the British lines on Inkerman Ridge on 5 November 1854, was regarded by some as akin in part to a second Waterloo, although, ironically, Britain's French ally helped save the day. This echo still resonated in 1914 with cavalry officers referring to Waterloo when they wrote of their hope for clashes with German Uhlans.

The battle was also celebrated by panoramas, theatrical entertainments, and the 1816 competition launched by the British Institution for Promoting the Fine Arts. The 360-degree panorama painting of Waterloo exhibited in a rotunda by Henry Aston Barker toured throughout Britain and went as far as Boston, returning to London in 1842. Barker made a profit of £10,000 from his Waterloo panorama at the Leicester Square Panorama in 1826. Philip Astley staged *The Battle of Waterloo* in his hippodrome with 144 consecutive performances on its first run in 1824. The show was revived annually for several decades. Wellington visited a performance and approved of it, as he also did of Barker's panorama.

The British Institution for Promoting the Fine Arts offered a prize of 1,000 guineas for the best painting to commemorate British victories in the war, and thirteen of the sixteen submitted

were of Waterloo. Waterloo was to be standard fare for painters into
the 1840s. George Jones, who received the second prize from the
Institution, became known as 'Waterloo Jones'.

The reflected fame of Waterloo helped ensure that Wellington's
funeral in 1852 was far grander than those of George III (1820),
George IV (1830) and William IV (1837). This state funeral, carefully arranged by Queen Victoria's husband, Prince Albert, and the
prime minister, Edward, fourteenth Earl of Derby, celebrated
national greatness and provided an opportunity to link people, state
and church in an exuberant patriotism.[26] *The Illustrated London News*
of 20 November 1852, declared:

> The grave has now closed over the mortal remains of the
> greatest man of our age, and one of the purest-minded men
> recorded in history. Wellington and Nelson sleep side by
> side under the dome of St Paul's, and the national mau-
> soleum of our isles has received the most illustrious of its
> dead. With a pomp and circumstance, a fervour of popular
> respect, a solemnity and a grandeur never to be surpassed in
> the obsequies of any other hero hereafter to be born to
> become the benefactor of this country, the sacred relics of
> Arthur Duke of Wellington have been deposited in the
> place long since set apart for them by the unanimous deci-
> sion of his countrymen. All that ingenuity could suggest in
> the funeral trappings, and that imagination and fancy could
> devise to surround the ceremonial with the accessories that
> most forcibly impress the minds of a multitude, all the
> grace that royalty could lend, all the aid that the state could
> afford in every one of its departments, all the imposing cir-
> cumstances derivable from the assemblage of great masses of
> men arrayed with military splendour and in military
> mourning, together with the less dramatic but even more
> affecting grief expressed by the sober trappings of respectful
> and sympathetic crowds, all the dignity that could be con-
> ferred by the presence of the civil and legislative power of
> the great and ancient kingdom; and lastly, all the sanctity

and awe inspired by the grandest of religious services performed in the grandest Protestant temple in the world, were
combined to render the scene, inside and outside of St Paul's
cathedral on Thursday last, the most memorable in our
annals. . . . To the mind of the people, and to the superstition of thousands who would be loath to confess, although
they would find it impossible to deny, the hold of such feelings upon their imagination, 'the signs and portents of
nature' were added to the commemorative deeds of men, to
render the last scene in the history of the hero more awe-
inspiring than it might otherwise have been!

Tennyson, then the poet laureate, wrote, in his 'Ode on the Death
of the Duke of Wellington' (1852), of 'that world-earthquake
Waterloo!'[27]

A less heroic account was provided by the details of what happened with reference to the Wellington Monument in Somerset.
Because his family had been from Somerset before it moved to
Ireland, Wellesley took the title Viscount Wellington in 1809. He
also purchased an estate near the town of Wellington, although he
only visited it once, in 1819, when the townspeople bodily towed his
carriage to the edge of his estate. After Waterloo, the local gentry
planned to build an obelisk in honour of the duke, and the highest
point on the Blackdown Hills was chosen as a site, a spot on the
duke's own land. The original idea was to have a cast-iron statue of
the duke at the top, sculpted figures of an English, an Irish and a
Scottish soldier on the plinth, and Waterloo guns at the base. In
1817, the foundation stone was laid, but the plans proved too
elaborate for the money available and the project remained incom-
plete. Meanwhile, an obelisk was erected in Phoenix Park in Dublin
in 1821. The duke's death led to renewed interest in the Somerset
monument, with a new design by H. E. Goodridge replacing the
1817 Thomas Lee design, but the 175-foot obelisk, to Goodridge's
design, was not finished until 1892. The monument is based on an
Egyptian obelisk, but was adapted to resemble a bayonet of the 1815
period.

This delay was not the sole mishap with the Somerset monument. Twenty-four cannon had been promised to form a foreground, but in 1819, when fifteen arrived at Exeter, it was discovered that they had not been at Waterloo and were indeed naval cannon. As a result, it did not seem worth meeting the heavy expense of moving them. One was sold to meet the dock dues, and the others were sunk as bollards or buried. In 1890, the issue was raised afresh, but it was decided that the cannon, if they could be recovered, were not worth transporting to the site. Finally, in 1910, four were dug up and reached the monument. During the Second World War, these cannon were removed to be transformed into scrap to help the war effort, although it appears that they were not used for this purpose but, instead, were eventually buried. After the war, one of the cannon still at Exeter was eventually acquired by the Rotarians and brought, in 1985, to the monument, where it stands at the base. The monument itself had been given to the National Trust in 1933.[28]

Local neglect thus vied with local interest. Either can be stressed, just as the scaffolding that covered the Monument in 2008 can be seen as evidence of neglect or of a determination to preserve it. Whatever the situation, four of the nearby youths in the pub The Waterloo Cross, when asked on 3 September 2008, what the pub was named after, were not very forthcoming. One thought the name was something to do with Napoleon. Wellington did not feature, an ironic commentary on the claim in the comic operetta *Iolanthe* (1882) that 'every child can tell' that Wellington had thrashed Napoleon. A more unusual pub reference was to Blücher, after whom a pub in Tiverton, The Prince Blucher, was, and still is, named. Elsewhere in Devon, there is a Waterloo monument in Great Torrington, along the impressive walk above the indented River Torridge. This monument takes the form of a stone pyramid with two Gothic arched recesses on each face, 'Erected in 1818 to commemorate the battle of Waterloo. Peace to the souls of the Heroes.' If Waterloo cannon did not end up at the Wellington Monument, some did outside part of the old College of the Royal Military Academy at Sandhurst, which is the home of Waterloo

Company. Liverpool has an entire district called Waterloo, complete with a Hougoumont Avenue.

As a parallel to the Wellington Monument, the loyal citizens of Leeds decided to commission a statue of the duke to stand outside the new town hall. It was placed there in 1855 but left, boarded up for three years, until Queen Victoria herself came to unveil it and open the town hall in 1858. The statue was moved in 1937 to parkland adjacent to the University of Leeds. In 2008, the statue's boots were painted bright red.

The end result of Napoleon's efforts in 1815 had been to enhance British maritime and Russian land power. Both states were on the edge of Europe and thus more able to protect their home bases than other European countries, and yet were also capable of playing major roles in European politics. The tactical and operational proficiency of their forces (in the British case, in particular of the navy, the most powerful and successful in the world) was matched by a strategic advantage stemming from their ability to deploy considerable resources and from a base that it was difficult to conquer. The extent of these resources was important, because the scale of warfare, and the simultaneity of commitments (a product of 'tasking') and operations on many fronts, were such that war posed formidable demands on the countries and states involved. The response to these demands required not simply resources in aggregate, but also organisational developments and cooperation between governments and political élites. Again, this was not new, and could be seen over the previous centuries, but the greater scale of warfare was notable compared to the major conflicts in 1756–63 and 1775–83.

The problem of mobilising resources, however, was lessened by the widespread increase in the European population from the 1740s, a development that helped make Napoleonic warfare sustainable. Indeed, population increase was a key factor in aggregate Western military capability. Numbers helped states accommodate heavy casualties and yet continue fighting. Russia suffered possibly 660,000 military casualties between 1789 and 1814, many due to disease and poor diet, while its army may have received as many as two million recruits between 1802 and 1812. Despite suffering terrible losses in Russia in 1812, while also fighting an intractable and now unsuccessful war in Spain, Napoleon was able to raise fresh forces the following year, albeit at the cost of weakening his regime. Indeed, the consequences for the Napoleonic system of raising this manpower were an instance of war weakening the state, a frequent occurrence and one that contrasts with the general portrayal of war as strengthening states.

Britain and Russia represented extensive economic systems. Britain drew not only on its own resources, which had been considerably enhanced by population growth and agricultural, industrial and transport improvements, each generally termed revolutions, but also on the global trading system that it was best placed to direct and exploit thanks to naval strength and maritime resources. Russia similarly benefited from scale and resources, not least in grain production and its metallurgical industry, although administrative sophistication, entrepreneurial initiative and fiscal capability and efficiency were far less in evidence than in Britain. Moreover, geopolitically, each state was able to repel Napoleon, as the British showed with the affirmation of their naval mastery in 1805, culminating in victory at the battle of Trafalgar, and the Russians in their unbroken and ultimately successful resistance to the invasion by Napoleon and his allies in 1812.

Subsequently, Britain and Russia saw off Napoleon, exploiting his inability to provide lasting stability in Western and Central Europe, and thus thwarted the last attempt before the age of nationalism to remodel Europe. Britain won at Waterloo, but Russia was the long-stop last resort to block Napoleon. Their success ensured the reversal of the trend toward French hegemony, which had reached its height in 1812, by which time France had been greatly expanded – Rome, for example, was annexed in May 1809 and Hamburg in December 1810 – while large parts of Europe were under French satellites and allies, such as Bavaria and Saxony.

The success of Britain and Russia was to define Europe and the postwar world. Britain remained the leading maritime and imperial power until succeeded by the United States in the 1940s, with Russia the dominant state on the Eurasian landmass for the remainder of the nineteenth century and until the crises of 1905–20, although Prussian victory over France in 1870–71 lessened Russian relative power. The British and Russian armies had an ability to engage in conflict not simply with other Western states but also with non-Western powers. As a result, Britain and Russia made major territorial gains in the quarter-century beginning in 1790 and also thereafter, setting the basis for their future competition in the 'Great Game' for dominance of South Asia and neighbouring regions, a process that still continues, albeit in a different form.

In 1814–15, Europe was returned by Napoleon's victorious opponents to the multiple statehood that distinguished it from so many of the other heavily populated regions of the world, most obviously China. This return was as much a consequence of Napoleon's political failure as of the absence of a lasting military capability gap in favour of France. These, however, were structural factors that took on meaning in war and on the battlefield. Whatever their disadvantages by 1815, Napoleon and France still had to be defeated, and Waterloo was both place and cause of this defeat.

IO.

WATERLOO AND NINETEENTH-CENTURY

WARFARE

'ITS RAPID CHANGES, AND the memorable battle which at once overthrew an imperial throne, and consigned its possessor to perpetual imprisonment on a rock in the midst of a distant ocean, were incidents singularly adapted to work upon the universal passion for wonder and novelty.'[1] The prediction in *The Annual Register* for 1815 was to be proved accurate. Napoleonic warfare dominated much of the Western historical imagination for the century after Waterloo. This dominance was a reflection of commemoration, but also of need and opportunity. The need was a reflection of Napoleon's repeated success in the 1790s and 1800s, and the wish to understand the basis of this success in order to try to repeat it or to know how best to avoid suffering from its repetition. In short, there was a clear obligation to understand Napoleon.

This obligation appeared more relevant because the European great-power system did not change substantially for several decades. Indeed, France was to find itself at war, separately, with Russia, Austria and Prussia, within fifty-five years of Waterloo, in 1854–56, 1859 and 1870–71, respectively. The battlefields in the wars with Austria and Prussia, those of northern Italy and eastern France, were those fought over under Napoleon. Figures from the

Napoleonic wars, such as Wellington, Soult and Josef Radetzky, remained prominent in their country's military establishments, Soult serving again as minister for war in 1830–34 and 1840–45. Less prominently, D'Erlon was governor of Algeria in 1834–35. So Napoleon seemed relevant, and particularly so because weaponry changed relatively little in the 1820s and 1830s.

Opportunity to consider the impact of Napoleon arose thanks to the availability of sources. The key rule master, or, rather, one who had that role thrust upon him, the Swiss-born Antoine-Henri de Jomini (1779–1869), had followed Napoleon as chief of staff to Marshal Ney but, from 1813, served in the Russian army, being made a lieutenant general by Alexander I. Jomini's influential works, which included the *Traité des grandes opérations militaires* (1805–09) and the *Précis de l'art de la guerre* (which appeared first in 1810 as the conclusion to the *Traité*), aimed to find logical principles at work in warfare, which was seen as having timeless essential characteristics. In particular, he sought to explain the success of Frederick the Great, the subject of his *Traité,* and, then, of Napoleon, who was treated in his *Vie politique et militaire de Napoléon* (1827).

Jomini, like Carl von Clausewitz, wrote in the shadow of Napoleon and had to address his sweeping success and his complete failure. A linkage of military objectives to political and policy goals was applauded by Clausewitz, the Prussian officer whose posthumous *On War* (1832) was to be the nineteenth-century work on warfare most praised by twentieth-century commentators, and so far, also, by those of the twenty-first century. Jomini, in contrast, enjoyed more influence in the nineteenth century. Jomini's focus was operational, and, to him, the crucial military point was the choice of a line of operations that would permit a successful attack. Napoleonic operational art was discussed in terms of envelopment – the use of 'exterior lines' – and, alternatively, the selection of a central position that would permit the defeat in detail (separately) of opposing forces, a position that was described in terms of interior lines.

By focusing on decisive battles, especially Austerlitz (1805) and

Jena (1806), rather than on the more intractable battles of 1809 and 1813, especially Wagram and Leipzig, let alone defeat at Waterloo, Jomini emphasised French battle-winning as decisive, rather than the wider consequences of social, economic and technological change. Jomini's influence was widespread, not least in Britain and the United States, including on Henry Halleck's *Elements of Military Art and Science* (1864), the first major American textbook on war, although the extent of this influence has also been questioned. A translation of the *Art de la guerre* was published in Philadelphia in 1862, when the American Civil War and the mass armies it led to provided an enhanced market for writings on war.

The habit of looking back was well engrained. In Britain, the legacies of Nelson at sea and Wellington on land proved potent and were kept alive in celebration, not least on occasions such as the Waterloo banquets, held annually in Downing Street and celebrated by William Salter in his painting of the 1836 banquet, a work that took Salter five years and was exhibited in London in 1841 to great public interest. An engraving of the painting, published in 1846, was very popular. In 1854, Lord Raglan, the British commander in the Crimea, was praised by comparison with his former patron, Wellington:

> If the poor old Duke had lived to see your triumph, how justly proud he would have been of victories won by his pupil and by his dearest and most trusted friend. Indeed he still lives in the army which he trained and in the general whom he taught to conquer. . . . This is indeed treading in the steps of your great master.[2]

There was also a confidence that the Napoleonic period was crucial to the grand narrative of Western history and that this narrative was the central topic for those working on state-building and conflict.

For the twentieth century, this relevance seemed self-evident, as warfare between major states dominated attention, and such warfare was the basic theme of Napoleonic conflict. The applicability of this model, however, appears less apparent from the perspective of the early twenty-first century. Now the focus is on a wider range of conflict and international relations, which reflects the trajectory of both in recent decades. Two spheres are of particular importance: first, conflict between Western and non-Western powers and, second, the dialectic of insurrectionary and counterinsurrectionary warfare. Yet both these elements were present in the Napoleonic Wars, and, partly as a result, they are more relevant to modern conflict than some appreciate.

In some respects, although coming close to Gettysburg in 1863, Waterloo was closer in character to the Battle of Pavia of 1525 than it was to the battle of Kursk of 1943. As Charles Esdaile has pointed out, Waterloo gave generals and others the conviction that a single battle could settle wars, a belief that was to help lead to tragedy in 1914, when the First World War was not decided by the opening campaign.[3] Yet the military context in 1815 was not only traditional. In practice, already by 1815, victory in an individual battle or even campaign seemed of scant weight beside the massive resources deployed against France by the Seventh Coalition. The scale was different from that of the challenge faced by Frederick the Great in the mid-eighteenth century, as was the 'miracle' required.

The difference in scale of resources also reflected the transition in Napoleonic warfare, from the battles of 1792–1807, when, to a considerable extent, the French had engaged opponents using more traditional tactics and force structures, to those of 1809–15, when the opposing forces were similar but France was faced with more extensive deployment of resources by them. Moreover, the political will that was critical was not only that of Napoleon, but also that of the French population, much of which was politicised as a result of the Revolution and its consequences. In 1815, Napoleon discovered that support from the population was fragile.

There was also much that was traditional at Waterloo. A closely deployed British force relied on the musket to defeat attackers whose tactics and weaponry were far from novel. Although the formations were different, the infantry squares that resisted Ney's cavalry looked back nearly half a millennium to Crécy (1346), where English longbowmen had defeated attacking French cavalry, firepower again bringing low physical force. Waterloo was not a battle decided by artillery, which played a far smaller role than in the battles of the First World War. Instead, it was infantry firepower that was crucial at Waterloo, although this firepower was somewhat different from that of the earlier longbowmen, and Napoleonic battles lasted longer. The British victories over the French in the Battle of Aboukir in Egypt in 1801, at Maida in Calabria in 1806, and, repeatedly, in the Peninsular War, can be attributed to superior infantry firepower, although there is considerable debate about this. General John Moore noted of the battle of Aboukir, 'We have beat them without cavalry and inferior in artillery.'[4] Though there were British cavalry at Waterloo, the situation was not too different there.

The French themselves enjoyed great success in the two major operations their army attempted in Europe in the two decades after Waterloo. These successes throw light on Napoleon's failure, which emerges clearly in comparison with these successes, a comparison that is generally neglected. In the case of each of these operations, the political conjuncture was crucially different. In Spain, civil conflict between liberals and supporters of Ferdinand VII was resolved by an invasion of the country on behalf of Ferdinand by 56,000 French and 35,000 Spanish troops, a large operational force for the period. The opposing liberal Spanish army, short of supplies and unpaid, was affected by extensive desertion and retreated.

Assisted by divisions among the liberals, and needing to do little fighting, the French, who invaded in April under the command of the Duke of Angoulême, made rapid progress, although they were handicapped by poor logistics. There was some resistance in Catalonia, where, indeed, there were echoes of the Napoleonic Wars: Catalonia was conquered by IV Corps under Bon-Adrien-Jeannot de Moncey, who had been made a marshal by Napoleon, and, in 1815, had refused to serve on a military tribunal to try Ney. At the city of Barcelona, which was blockaded for several months, he found himself in conflict with General Francisco Espoz y Mina, who had been a successful guerrilla leader in the Peninsular War, defeating French units in 1812.

The main French drive was on the capital, Madrid, which the army entered on 23 May 1823, and then, via Córdoba, to Cádiz, from which the liberal Cortes had fled. The city had been unsuccessfully besieged by the French during the Peninsular War. Now, in contrast, it was besieged by land and also (unlike during the Peninsular War, when the British fleet had restricted French activities) was blockaded by sea, surrendering on 1 October. There was fighting elsewhere, but the French were successful and the opposing generals capitulated: Morillo in Galicia on 10 July and Ballesteros in Andalusia on 4 August. Resistance ended when the garrison of Alicante surrendered on 5 November.[5]

The 1823 operation was a successful example of how foreign intervention could tip the balance in a domestically divided state. French action was accepted by the Holy Alliance of leading European conservative states, although Britain was opposed to the step and Austria uneasy about it. A comparison with French failure in Spain in 1808–13 would have repaid the attention of military commentators in subsequent decades, but warfare such as that in 1823 was not regarded by them as exemplary, and there were no battles to command attention. The 1823 campaign also did not satisfy the interest, seen in particular with the writings of Jomini, in producing formulaic guidance to operational effectiveness. More specifically, the 1823 operation, like that of the Austrians in Italy two years earlier, demonstrated the value of having forces able to fight limited wars for particular ends. This task rewarded professionalism, as well as relatively small forces with modest logistical requirements and only limited pressure on the roads. There was no need for a levée en masse, and, indeed, because of its radical potential, that was what was most feared.

Moreover, in 1831, the French successfully intervened in the Belgian crisis. This crisis had begun the previous year with a rebellion in Brussels against rule by the Dutch William I. The Dutch army failed to suppress the uprising, and the Belgians declared independence. However, in August 1831, the Dutch invaded Belgium. A force of 36,000 troops and seventy-two cannon under William, Prince of Orange, who himself had been wounded at

Waterloo, met poorly organised opponents. Invading from a different direction than Napoleon in 1815, the prince, like him, also faced two opposing forces, but they were far weaker and less experienced than those of Wellington and Blücher. Unlike Napoleon, Orange was able to exploit the gap between these forces and to drive them back. Nevertheless, the Dutch stopped their advance in the face of Anglo-French pressure that, crucially, included a French army. Its commander, Marshal Étienne Gérard, had been a corps commander under Napoleon, pressing Grouchy on the day of Waterloo to march from Wavre to the sound of the guns. In 1832, Gérard went on to besiege Dutch-held Antwerp successfully.

Different politics thus led to very contrasting outcomes. Napoleon had been the problem in 1815, but, once he was gone, it was possible for France to take a more assertive role in international relations. This role, however, involved cooperation with leading European powers, as in Spain and Belgium. Moreover, the army was intended as a support for political order and social stability within France. In 1818, the year in which the Army of Occupation left France, conscription was reintroduced by Gouvion Saint-Cyr, the minister of war, who had been a Napoleonic marshal. Yet only 40,000 out of the 290,000 eligible men were selected annually (by lot), and it was possible to arrange a substitute by means of payment. The conscripts served six years in theory, but in practice for fewer years. The introduction of this limited conscription was preceded by heated debates in which concern was voiced about the political challenge allegedly posed by the 'nation in arms'.

This emphasis on loyalty, however, was linked to a growing conservatism in the military establishment, as well as a gap between army and society and the absence of a trained national reserve, all of which served to vitiate the possibilities for effective wartime expansion of the military. The choice of force structure has been seen as sacrificing the future, in the shape of serious defeat at the hands of the Prussians in 1870, to the present concern to create a loyal military establishment.[6]

This new French army was not used in a fashion likely to offend other European powers, neither by the Bourbon monarchy nor by the

'July Monarchy' of the Orleanist candidate, Louis-Philippe, which succeeded it after a revolution in 1830. However, in 1848, another revolution led to the overthrow of the Orleanist monarchy and the creation of the Second Republic, with Louis-Napoleon, the third son of Louis Bonaparte, a brother of Napoleon I, as president. In turn, after a radical insurrection was crushed in Paris, Louis-Napoleon used an army-backed coup in December 1851 to strengthen his grip on power, to replace the elected presidency, and to suppress opposition. This success enabled Louis-Napoleon in 1852 to become the Emperor Napoleon III.

Napoleon III was to fight three of Napoleon I's major opponents: Russia in 1854–56, Austria in 1859, and Prussia in 1870. Napoleon III also sent an army to Mexico in an unsuccessful attempt to establish a protégé as emperor there. To his critics, at home and abroad, he threatened to revive the aggression of his namesake, and notably so as he attacked Napoleon I's opponents. Would Waterloo have to be fought again? Had the victory been in vain?

Napoleon III certainly campaigned more extensively than Napoleon I had done in 1815, and his forces were successful at the expense of Russia and, even more, Austria, before falling to total defeat at the hands of Prussia. Yet Napoleon III had also owed his relative success to the extent to which the job of Waterloo had been well done. Far from a new Napoleon focusing and dominating the anxieties of Europe, he was able to find allies: Britain and Piedmont against Russia in the Crimean War of 1854–56, and Piedmont and the liberal cause of Italian unification (the Risorgimento) against Austria in 1859. Strong British anxieties about Napoleon III, expressed in a serious naval race in 1859–65 as well as extensive fortifications on the south coast, especially near Portsmouth, did not lead to conflict.

The Franco-Prussian War of 1870–71 offered some interesting comparisons and contrasts with that of 1815. The French forces initially advanced into Germany, but due to the rapid deployment of the Prussians, failed to sustain the initiative and fell back. Thus, the attempt to gain the strategic advantage by taking the first steps was mishandled, although in a different way from Napoleon at Waterloo.

French staff-work was poor in both campaigns, but in 1870, it was the Prussians who were able to outmanoeuvre their opponents and to defeat the two main French armies separately. Napoleon III, a broken reed, abdicated after defeat at Sedan led to revolution in Paris, but, unlike the case of 1815, the Prussians had to fight on, because Napoleon III was replaced by a Government of National Defence, which was determined not to surrender territory and also discovered a role through continued resistance. This resistance led to a Prussian siege of Paris that winter and to fighting across much of northern and eastern France that, however, finally resulted in France accepting Prussian terms.

The contrast between 1815 and 1870–71 is instructive. The rapid collapse of the Napoleonic regime in 1815 and the restoration of a government willing and able to negotiate terms with the Allies, combined with the willingness of the latter not to insist on punitive terms, such as the cession of Alsace (which was considered), led to an essentially benign postwar situation, albeit one secured by an Allied occupation of much of the country that compromised Louis XVIII's popularity. In contrast, the terms insisted on in 1871 – occupation, indemnity, and also the cession of most of Alsace and much of Lorraine – ensured that there would be no postwar reconciliation of France and Germany to match that between Germany and Austria after their war in 1866. Victory also enabled Prussia to transform her hegemony within Germany into a German empire ruled from Berlin, an empire proclaimed at Versailles on 18 January 1871, in what was a major humiliation for the French.

This contrast underlined the value of Allied moderation in 1815, but also helped strengthen the reputation of Napoleon I, for his defeat did not lead to the humiliating and divisive aftermath that followed that of Napoleon III, an aftermath that included the radical Paris Commune and its brutal suppression by French forces. Moreover, Napoleon III's regime had played up Napoleon I's reputation as a way of claiming legitimacy and affirming normative standards, and if this process ceased to be the case with the establishment of the Third Republic in 1870, nevertheless Napoleon I's battles served as a source of national pride. Indeed, the fall of

Napoleon III and the end of the Napoleonic dynasty – his son, the prince imperial, was killed while fighting with the British against the Zulus in 1879 (his overly tight trousers prevented him from leaping onto a horse and escaping) – ensured that these battles could work for national pride without risking political partisanship.

Although a defeat, Waterloo played a role in this French depiction of a glorious military past because it was interpreted in terms of the fortitude and heroism also employed by the British in their depiction of the battle. The bravery of men advancing under heavy fire, especially the cavalry and the Guard, was played up, while, correspondingly, the French superiority in artillery was ignored, as were the command failures, notably of Ney and Napoleon. Paintings such as Hippolyte Bellangé's of the last stand of the Guard around their Eagle depicted heroic resolution. The return of Napoleon's remains to France from St. Helena in 1840 proved a festival of national commemoration.

Even radicals opposed to Napoleon III, such as Victor Hugo, who spent his reign in exile, could present Napoleon I in a positive light. Hugo visited the battlefield of Waterloo in 1852, guided by the colonel and historian Jean-Baptiste-Adolphe Charras. His poem 'L'Expiation', part of the anthology Les Châtiments (1853), begins with the famous verse 'Waterloo! Waterloo! Waterloo! Morne plaine!' (Gloomy plain). On 7 May 1861, Victor Hugo settled in the village to achieve his masterpiece, the novel Les Misérables (1862), in which the battle is described once again and the emperor is presented as a man of destiny and soul brought down by a methodical gradgrind, a portrayal echoed in the 1970 film Waterloo. The manuscript of the novel ends 'J'ai fini "Les Misérables" sur le champ de bataille de Waterloo et dans le mois de Waterloo, aujourd'hui 30 juin 1861, à 8h 30 du matin, jour de la kermesse [festival] de Mont-St-Jean, un dimanche.' The novel had a great impact on contemporaries. Four years later, the poet Charles Baudelaire visited Waterloo, slept in Victor Hugo's hotel, and asked to be served Hugo's preferred dishes. In 1865, Émile Erckmann and Alexandre Chatrian, two popular writers using the pseudonym of

Erckmann-Chatrian, deployed genuine descriptive power in their novel *Waterloo*.

In contrast, the Germans were directed to applaud the successes of the Wars of German Unification in 1864, 1866 and 1870–71 – particularly the last, the Franco-Prussian War, as it saw the Germans fight united under the leadership of Prussia. Waterloo, in comparison, was a far less happy memory, as the British had borne much of the fighting while many of the German units had fought in Wellington's army. Clausewitz had already criticised Wellington, who had diplomatically replied that there was glory enough for both Britain and Prussia. Despite this, the Prussian role in 1815 was not an appropriate backdrop for the new German empire. Ironically, Waterloo served as a model both for the Prussian victory over the Austrians at Sadowa in 1866 and also for the Prussian form of command, the idea that corps, division, and brigade commanders can function more or less independently without the constant supervision of the high command. More generally, there was a process of disassociation of Waterloo from its context, as the battle was used to resonate with, or indeed serve, current political concerns.

II.

CONCLUSION: LOCATING WATERLOO

IN CONCLUSION, IT IS important to return to the point made at the outset of Chapter 1, and to broaden this point out in order to consider Waterloo, the battle, and its consequences as a litmus test for standard assumptions about modernity and modernisation. In the standard linear accounts of history, modernity and modernisation were part of a narrative that was organised, if not defined, in terms of a series of revolutions that were discerned in the century 1750–1850. The presentation of this century in terms of revolution may seem obvious, not least with so many individual revolutions vying for attention, including the agricultural, American, Atlantic, consumer, French, industrial and transport, to offer a by no means comprehensive list. At the same time, there are both specific problems with several of these designations and a more general issue about the use of the term 'revolution' to describe change.

In part, the latter stems from the Marxist reading of the Hegelian understanding of change as occurring through conflict between coherent tendencies or bodies, which, in fact, greatly underplays the extent of interpenetration both between such bodies – for example the nobility and the 'middle class' – and between change and continuity. There is also a more profound liberal disinclination to accept the capacity of conservative societies and states to accept and manage change. As a consequence, a revolutionary process is seen as necessary for change to occur. This concept is related to another misleading idea, namely that great events have great causes, a thesis that leads to an unfortunate search not only for major and determining aspects of instability within the European ancien régime, but also to a characterisation of it as inherently weak.

As there can be no greater event than the onset of modernity, its onset must apparently be accompanied by a revolutionary disruption. The treatment of the century 1750–1850 as the turning point to modernity was also part of its appropriation by scholars concerned to locate the age in terms that made sense of themselves, in short making their own work on the period appear topical and therefore important, an issue that also affects military historians.

However, the intellectual agenda and analysis underlying the connection between modernisation and revolution can be challenged, not least by questioning the rate and impact of change, as well as the causal links that are generally drawn. This questioning provides a way to discuss the military history of the period, because it is still necessary to consider how best to locate it in terms of modernisation, a location that is important to the contextualisation of Waterloo. One of the most promising ways is to consider the century not as modern and/or revolutionary, but, instead, as the last of the premodern centuries. This approach can be adopted in part by emphasising the resilience of ancien régime ideas, structures, societies and solutions, including military means.

The wider context was certainly one of general continuity. The technological and organisational changes summarised by the phrase Industrial Revolution were still restricted in their impact. The major transformations in theoretical and applied science in most fields, whether transportation, the generation and distribution of power, medicine, contraception, or agricultural yields, were yet to come. The wealth had not yet been created that would make it feasible to suggest that man's lot on earth could be substantially improved. However radical their politics by contemporary standards, in practice the states of the period lacked the wealth and tax base to support an effective and generous national welfare system.

This was a world where an appeal to precedent, to history, and to previous modes of conduct were still central to legitimating behaviour as far as most people were concerned. Without economic growth, secular philosophies of change and improvement could only be limited in their impact, and it is not surprising that most radical thinkers in the eighteenth century were sceptical about the appeal of their views to the bulk of the population. Whatever their stated belief in the sovereignty of the people, radicals tended to be hostile to what they viewed as popular superstition and conservatism.[1] This hostility was fatally to compromise the appeal of radicalism across most of Europe in the 1790s. As a result of the failure of radicalism, the rise of Napoleon to replace the French Revolution was in some respects an understandable consequence both in France and as far as French expansion was concerned. Yet this rise left the French state overly dependent on Napoleon's personality and capability.

Questioning the extent of radical support in the late eighteenth century and the Napoleonic period can be matched by underlining the extent to which conservative or reactionary regimes in the first half of the nineteenth century rested on popular backing and not on coercion.[2] Indeed, an emphasis on popular conservatism represents an important continuity across the century 1750–1850, one that serves not only as an ironic counterpoint to the usual stress on liberalism, but also as a counter to the argument that the politics of the age has to be understood as essentially a counterpointing between radical change and despotic reaction.[3] An important element in continuity was that of the Long Reformation from the sixteenth to the eighteenth centuries, a process of religious renewal that led to both Protestantism and the Catholic Reformation and that helped explain hostility to the French Revolution and its foreign echoes.

To some of those fighting at Waterloo, this would still have been a resonance: the war with Napoleon was that against a new Satan. In political terms, there was also much continuity with late-medieval circumstances, not least a 'multipolar' system of a number of European states opposed to hegemonic pretensions, whether of Holy

Roman Emperors, such as Charles V, or rulers of France, for example, Louis XIV and Napoleon. Indeed, like Emperor Wilhelm II of Germany and Hitler, Napoleon was an aggressive imperialist within Europe. This fact undermines suggestions that a compromise settlement could have been negotiated with Napoleon, or, indeed, Hitler. As a result, counterfactuals based on Napoleonic victory at Waterloo are correctly challenged by the true characteristics of his leadership, especially his fantasies of endless military conquest.[4] The struggle against imperialism was given edge by the exactions inflicted by French forces. Those in Germany helped explain the greater brutality to French prisoners shown by the Prussians as opposed to the British.

Stress on continuity provides an important context for the Napoleonic Wars and Waterloo, but consideration of the period also highlights the extent to which the potential for change was best represented not by Napoleon, whose Caesarism made him essentially a destructive force, but by the capability of the impersonal state in the shape of Britain. Indeed, it was especially apt that the British monarch at the time of Waterloo was the elderly, blind, deaf and mentally confused George III. Britain did not need the king to fulfill the roles discharged by Napoleon, a meritocratic monarch in the sense that he seized power as a result of his own actions, but a destructive one; and indeed a key aspect of the British political system was that George III and his eldest son, the self-indulgent prince regent, did not seek to fulfill these roles.

Political modernity, in the shape of effective constitutional government within Britain (though not many of its colonies) capable of coping with the issues posed by the largest empire in the world, was matched by the economic modernisation characterised by Britain's leadership of the Industrial Revolution. The direct links between this situation and the British army at Waterloo were tenuous, and certainly less striking than those seen with the sophisticated administrative system that underlay the Royal Navy. Yet the nature of Britain in 1815, as state, economy and society, helps explain the extent to which Waterloo should be seen not simply as a national triumph, but, instead, as a victory that was important to the development of Europe, and thus to world history.

Despite the strong vested interest that historians of France have in arguing the importance of their subject, Napoleonic power was a dead end, the goals and process of which followed those of the French Revolution in proving very destructive to France and to Europe. Indeed, French attempts to insert Napoleon into the modern European history being advanced by the federalists of the European Union seriously neglect the extent to which European unity under Napoleon was a vehicle for French imperialism.

In contrast, British power was not without major problems and inequalities (for Britain as well as the rest of the world), both of which excite considerable, indeed too great, interest at present.[5] Nevertheless, if modernisation and progress are to be useful themes, they can be seen with the victors of Waterloo, those in Wellington's army who endured the hard hours of French attack, before joining the Prussians in putting the French to rout.

POSTSCRIPTS

IT SEEMS APPROPRIATE THAT the standard British image of Waterloo is of fortitude, the fortitude of soldiers in line and square resisting French attacks. This was the fortitude commemorated on canvas. Thus *The Battle of Waterloo* by Denis Dighton, who was appointed military draftsman to the prince regent in 1815, showed French cavalry attacking a resolute British square. Dighton's other paintings included *Waterloo, Defence of Hougoumont*. Foreign painters, in contrast, understandably took other themes, notably the Allied commanders, as in Jan Willem Pieneman's *The Battle of Waterloo* (1824).

The fortitude of defence was the key British note, and not, in contrast, the triumphant advance at the close of the battle. This defence spoke to something in the national character or, at least, self-image, although such abstractions have to be employed with considerable care. To nineteenth-century Britons, Waterloo was thus of a pattern with Sir John Moore's victorious checking of Soult's attack at Corunna in 1809, with that of the British against the Russians in the Crimean War in 1854, especially at Inkerman, the 'thin red streak tipped with a line of steel,' in the journalist W. H. Russell's memorable phrase, and with the defence of Rorke's

Drift against Zulu attack in 1879, an episode that could be compared to the defence of Hougoumont in 1815.

Heroism in defence is scarcely solely a British theme, as the Spartans bravely fighting to the end against Persian attack at Thermopylae in 480 B.C. amply demonstrate, but this heroism in defence provided the key master narrative for Waterloo and one that linked the British to similar efforts of classical endeavour. Waterloo was thus a modern epic, with multiple resonances from the past actively sought by contemporaries interested in measuring themselves against classical heroes. Clearly bravery was also shown by the French, the Prussians and the Allied contingents in Wellington's army, but the British narrative was least complicated by politics, as there was no equivalent to the ambivalence about Napoleon and, to a lesser extent, Prussia that existed in France and Germany, respectively.

The Prussians did not devote the same attention as the British to Waterloo, a battle, after all, in which they had only played a secondary role, and this omission was particularly the case after the Wars of German Unification (1864–71) had provided them with exemplary victories for which they could claim the entire credit. Indeed, for Napoleon III, defeat at Sedan in 1870 had the fatal impact of that of Waterloo for his uncle. Unlike Napoleon I, however, Napoleon III was able to find exile in Britain, with which he had earlier allied against Russia.

Despite the limited role of commemoration in Prussia, for Blücher, who was born in Rostock, there is an impressive bronze statue in the Universitätsplatz. It depicts the field marshal and carries a relief showing Waterloo. Blücher is also commemorated by a statue on Unter den Linden in Berlin, the walkway of Prussian greatness.

In Hanover, the Guelphic Order was established to mark the officers of the KGL who fought at Waterloo, as well as exemplary civilian service to the kingdom of Hanover. A memorial, erected between 1826 and 1832 in the Waterlooplatz in the city of Hanover, pays tribute to the casualties. However, the resonance of Hanover's role faded with the conquest and absorption of Hanover by Prussia in 1866. Nassau, where a memorial obelisk to Waterloo was erected, was also conquered and absorbed by Prussia.

Outside Germany, the role of the Prussians, however, shrank into insignificance, not least as the battle was simplified and person- alised into an Anglo-French struggle between Wellington and Napoleon. Moreover, the German role at Waterloo was not one that was stressed in the first half of the twentieth century, a period of Anglo-German confrontation and conflict. The British attitude to Napoleon was also affected by alliance with France in both world wars, although, on the French part, the establishment of the Vichy regime in 1940 provided occasion for the deliberate propagation of an anti-British historical myth. This myth, however, focused on Joan of Arc, a Catholic heroine, not on Napoleon.

The impression of the battle as an Anglo-French struggle between the two war leaders has proved most persistent and has lent itself to modern demotic representations, as in the *Blackadder History of the World,* produced for the Millennium Dome in London in 2000, which makes fun of the respective leaders, diminishing them to comic-book characters, with Wellington killed when a time machine lands on him; or the most famous rendition, ABBA's extremely popular song 'Waterloo'. This begins, inaccurately, 'My my, at Waterloo Napoleon did surrender', and continues by describ- ing a modern relationship in terms of conflict, with Waterloo the occasion of defeat.

Doubtless ridiculous and possibly undeserving of mention, ABBA's song shows that, for history to be resonant in a modern populist culture, it has to take different forms. As an example of the contrary, admittedly of a battle that was far less prominent or influ- ential in its impact, 2008 saw the tricentennial of the total victory of John, first Duke of Marlborough, over a French army at Oude- naarde, not far from Waterloo. Whereas this battle played a promi- nent role in the historical writings of Churchill and Trevelyan and would have been known, or at least taught to, generations of British schoolboys, now it is as one with the works of Ozymandias, in Shel- ley's poem of that name:

Nothing beside remains. Round the decay

Of that colossal wreck, boundless and bare
The lone and level sands stretch far away.

Shelley was a bitter critic of the Liverpool ministry, notably in *The Mask of Anarchy* (1819), but the point in his poem about the passage of greatness was as radical.

The change has been rapid. Waterloo was iconic for the Victorians. Painters commemorated it with zeal. Sir William Allan, president of the Royal Scottish Academy and limner to Queen Victoria in Scotland, exhibited the *Battle of Waterloo from the English Side* in 1843, selling it to Wellington, although his view of Waterloo from the French side, exhibited in 1846, lost out to Daniel Maclise's *The Meeting of Wellington and Blücher After Waterloo* in the competition to decorate the new Houses of Parliament, as did Thomas Sydney Cooper's painting of a cavalry action at Waterloo. The role of cavalry at Waterloo proved particularly attractive for painters, as in the *Charge of the Cuirassiers at Waterloo. The Sunken Road of Ohain* (1894) by the English painter Stanley Berkeley. Meanwhile, W. S. Gilbert's lyrics for the Gilbert and Sullivan comic operetta *Iolanthe* (1882) had the chorus of members of the House of Lords declare:

> *Yet Britain set the world ablaze*
> *In good King George's glorious days!*

The battle remained iconic for the first two-thirds of the twentieth century, partly because there was no disruption to national heritage and collective memory comparable to the defeats and revolutions that affected Russia, Germany, France and Italy between 1917 and 1945. In *1066 and All That* (1930), a highly successful comic account of the conventional approach to British history, Waterloo served the authors, Walter Sellar and Robert Yeatman, with standard resonances and established quotes:

> This utterly memorable battle was fought at the end of a
> dance, on the Playing Fields of Eton, and resulted in the
> English definitely becoming top nation. It was thus a very

Good Thing. During the engagement the French came on
in their usual creeping and crawling method and were
defeated by Wellington's memorable order, 'Up Jenkins and
Smashems.'[1]

G. M. Trevelyan, the most distinguished British historian of
midcentury, gave the readers of his *History of England,* which first
appeared in 1926, with a third edition in 1945 and a new impression in 1960 from which I am quoting, an account that presented
Britain as the moral centre:

> The fortunate brevity of this last war was due to the prompt
> and courageous action of the British Government in declar-
> ing war at once, and sending over Wellington to defend
> Holland and Belgium in alliance with Blücher and his
> Prussians, till the allied armies from the East could arrive in
> overwhelming numbers. The decisive character of the great
> battle put a sudden end to the war, because France was half-
> hearted in her desire that it should be renewed.[2]

Thus Britain's victory was in accordance with European destiny.
One of the major history books I had as a boy, *The Living World of
History* (1963), offered the reproduction of *Scotland Forever,* Lady
Butler's famous painting of the charge of the British cavalry, as the
endpapers. This book made no mention of the European Economic
Community, which the government had sought to join, and,
instead, presented the Victorian period as the great age of British
achievement.

By the start of the new millennium, Waterloo, however, had a precarious status. Membership in the European Union led to uneasi-
ness about celebrating triumphs over France, but there were more
profound cultural, political, social and chronological changes that
undercut the long inheritance of national history and the understanding of national identity bound up in it. The key land battle of
imperial Britain appears faded with the empire, while moving into
the twenty-first century has made the nineteenth seem very distant.

   Changes in presentation are far distant from the struggles of men
under the heavy cloud of the battle day, but they also capture the
extent to which the significance of these struggles was highly varied and would continue to be so. This situation is true of most
major battles, but is particularly the case with Waterloo. As with
such episodes as the sinking of the *Titanic* in 1912, the battle has
served to encapsulate contrasting narratives and analyses of behaviour.[3] No author can escape this; whatever he might try to do, he
will be seen by others, at least in part, in terms of their presupposi-
tions. A British writer praising the British effort in 1815 appears
especially partisan, but the Anglo-Prussian victory was of importance and value not only for Britain but also more generally; and,
however imperfectly, this importance was captured by the wide
composition of the Seventh Coalition and of the Allied forces both
on the battlefield and marching toward and into France.
Napoleonic success at Waterloo would simply have committed
Europe to a lengthier war and France to eventual defeat and probably harsher peace terms. These terms would have left a degree of
bitterness that would have fed pressure for revanche.

   The rapid defeat and overthrow of Napoleon were therefore a
general good as far as Europe was concerned. A lengthy war there
also might have made European expansion elsewhere in the world
over the subsequent three decades less likely. Britain might not
have fought, or fought successfully, the Marathas in 1818–19,
Burma in 1824–26, and China in 1839–42; invaded Afghanistan in
1839 and Sind in 1843; nor annexed Aden in 1839; nor, in 1840,
stopped the northward advance of Egypt in Syria and Palestine. The
Netherlands would not have been able to advance in Java and
Sumatra in the 1820s. Russia might not have risked war with Per-
sia in 1825–28 and the Ottoman Empire in 1828–29, each of
which led to territorial gains. France would not have been able to
focus on the conquest of Algiers from 1830, nor seize Gabon in
1844. More positively, Spain would not have been able to mount its
unsuccessful efforts to retain its empire in Latin America.

   These points now seem inconsequential, if not worse. Indeed, in
many respects Waterloo can now be seen not as the 'end of history'

for the nineteenth century with the defeat of Napoleon, but, instead, as an aspect of the reconceptualisation or attempted reconceptualisation of history. In particular, this reconceptualisation entails the assault on nationalism in Europe and the concern with a new twenty-first-century history. These points can be seen not only in criticism of the British empire, but also in the changing treatment of Napoleon. The response to the successful presidential bid by Nicolas Sarkozy in 2007 was instructive. Frequent references to Napoleon reflected not only Sarkozy's willingness to strike that echo, in both approach and language, in which he echoed his one-time rival on the right and prime minister, Dominique de Villepin, a biographer of Napoleon, but also a general habit of discussing French history in terms of a set cast of individuals. Thus, the influential German weekly *Stern* fronted its issue of 10 May 2007 with a photo of Sarkozy and the title 'The New Napoleon'.

Yet for a German weekly to refer to the French President in this fashion did not mean that it was suggesting any comparison with Napoleonic aggression in the early nineteenth century, nor that it is drawing on any deep well of popular anxiety on this head. Indeed, the detaching of historical reference from historical anxiety can be taken as a sign of maturity. Conversely, it can be suggested that this episode simply reflects the conditionality of historical reference. Germany scarcely has to fear French opposition. If, in contrast, a prominent French weekly had greeted a German electoral result with the cover headline 'The New Hitler', then the situation would have been different. The reference would have been to a more recent episode, and, more crucially, it would have drawn on a stronger anxiety.

The passage from contention to history is also at play. The term 'Bonapartism' was applied to Charles de Gaulle by his critics, but Napoleon's legacy has become considerably less contentious than it was in the nineteenth century. Then the legacy was strong, thanks, first, to Napoleon III's repeated references to his uncle and then to the Third Republic's self-validation and its concern about the possibility of a military coup, for example in 1888 by Georges Boulanger, a charismatic former general. At the same time, a liberal legend about Napoleon as a man of the people was pushed by prominent politicians such as Adolphe Thiers, president of the Third Republic from 1871 to 1873 and, earlier, author of *Histoire du consulat et de l'empire* (1845–62).[4]

By the 1960s, the political situation within France was very different. References to de Gaulle as a new Bonaparte lacked traction, and that was even more true of 2007. If this was the case due to the impact of a new history, one in which the crucial issue and frame of reference for France was Vichy and for Germany the Nazi regime and the Holocaust, then this new history was part of a reshaping of the past in which nationalism seemed redundant and anachronistic. This view of nationalism did not provide the best basis for recalling nineteenth-century battles, not least because France is a key member of the European Union, and dwelling on battles like Leipzig or Waterloo is seen as evidence of an unwelcome and anachronistic nationalism, a throwback to the age of nationalism that culminated in the First World War.

There are parallels in the changing treatment of Waterloo on screen. Several silent films tackled the battle, including *The Battle of Waterloo* (1913), an early 'spectacular' produced by the British and Colonial Kinematograph Company. This film was a historical reconstruction reportedly employing thousands of extras, including a squadron of lancers. The following year, a spoof of the film appeared under the title *Pimple's Battle of Waterloo*. Starring the music-hall comedian Fred Evans, this film was one of a series of skits of popular books, films and plays in which he played the character of Pimple.

The most influential silent account was Abel Gance's seventeen-reel epic *Napoléon* (1927), an impressionist film, sponsored by the French Société Générale de Films, that was praised critically but lost money due to the coming of sound. This film was followed by *Waterloo* (1928), a German work directed by Karl Grune that presented Blücher as playing the key role in securing victory. Napoleon was treated as an eminent historical figure, not a villain. The two main sound films were *The Iron Duke* (1934), a British account focused on Wellington, and the Italian-Soviet epic *Waterloo* (1970), a darker work of epic proportions directed by Sergei Bondarchuk and produced by Dino de Laurentiis. The second film very much presented the battle in terms of the clash between Napoleon and Wellington. The latter tells the Duchess of Richmond that Napoleon was not a gentleman, while Napoleon, facing pressure for abdication from his marshals in 1814, declares, 'Why is it always Wellington?' a remark that greatly exaggerates the Duke's importance at that stage. Waterloo has also played a role in television history, and in *Sharpe's Waterloo* (1997), the hero organises the defence of La Haie Sainte while the incompetence of a Dutch commander is emphasised.[5]

A reshaping of the past away from nationalism affected the contents and methods of academic military history. In place of a stress on battles came that on war and society, with an interest, in particular, in social groups who played a key role on the home front. This approach proved possible for the two world wars, where it was characterised by an interest in the contribution of women to the war effort. As a result, a focus on battles appeared dated and unwelcome. This approach, however, is seriously mistaken, as, more generally, is the attempt to demilitarise military history and, in particular, to leave out the fighting.[6]

The strength of the war and society approach in academic history, however, helps explain the mismatch between Waterloo, a battle that continues to attract massive popular interest, and its far more modest role in academic engagement and public history. Indeed, in 1965, the one hundred fiftieth anniversary of the battle was not celebrated by an issue of commemorative stamps, unlike, that year, the twentieth anniversary of the United Nations and International Cooperation Year, or, for example, the Commonwealth Arts Festival. In contrast, during Margaret Thatcher's period as prime minister (1979–90), portraits of Nelson and Wellington were deliberately hung in the dining room at 10 Downing Street, her residence and office, in order to impress foreign visitors.[7] Thatcher displayed a robust, historicised nationalism that the Labour governments of Tony Blair and Gordon Brown have failed to match.

The experience of Trafalgar may well be indicative of more recent developments. The government of Tony Blair bent over backwards at the time of the bicentennial in 2005 to avoid offending France and, indeed, in order not to make any unwelcome reference, the naval re-creation of the battle was between a red and a blue fleet, a much derided choice of titles. The government largely ignored the bicentennial and was very surprised by the intensity of public interest.

It is probable that the same will be true of Waterloo at the time of its bicentennial in 2015. Internationalism is a clear theme of the forthcoming Waterloo bicentennial. In his address at the launch of Waterloo 200, the official British guide and focal point for all organisations who wish to participate in the bicentennial events, Richard Holmes, a prominent military historian and a member of the committee, declared, 'We are celebrating the brave men of all sides, not just the British. . . . Such an event deserves to be com-memorated internationally.' Holmes is also chairman of Project Hougoumont, a project to preserve the farm, and during the official launch on 18 June 2008, he declared:

> In seeking to preserve this iconic spot we do not simply
> remember the British troops who held it. We also applaud
> the courage of the German infantry who fought for the
> wood in front of it, of the brave Frenchmen who came so
> close to taking it and turning the fortune of the day, and of
> the cavalry whose charges swirled up and down the slopes
> within sight of its ancient walls. . . . This is not a question
> of national pride or regimental commemoration.

Yet in 2008, Military-Genealogy.com asked, 'Have you a hero on your family tree that fought at Waterloo?' as it drew attention to the ability to search the Waterloo Medal Roll.

Meanwhile, in France, the Victor Hugo poem 'L'Expiation' had been 'hijacked' by René Goscinny (1926–77), the scenarist of the comic book *Astérix chez les Belges* (1979), which had an ironic credit to Victor Hugo on the title page. The book ends with a big battle opposing the Romans to the Belgians and the Gauls, with pastiches of the poem placed in cartouches 'captioning' the images. As usual with Goscinny, several verses were also reused, in a less prominent way, in dialogue throughout the book, the most notable being 'Waterzooie! Waterzooie! Waterzooie! Morne plat' [Gloomy dish, waterzooie being a traditional Belgian dish]. In the 1995 reenactment of the battle, more reenactors were willing to serve in the French army than with its opponents. Moreover, Napoleon appeared to be popular with the Belgian spectators of this reenactment, which presumably reflected the extent to which his memory has been annexed to Walloon assertiveness in Belgium. In this case as in others, the political context of 1815, therefore, is ignored or misunderstood.

This process suits both modern political agendas and also military historians who prefer not to think about politics. Thus, the argument, in 2001, in a piece on Napoleon and leadership, that Napoleon 'would have won the battle, except for the arrival of Blücher and 60,000 Prussians' (a problematic view from the point of the fighting itself, as Wellington would not have fought there but for the promise of Prussian help), ignores the key political point that the Prussians were in Belgium because Napoleon's political strategy in 1815 was a nonsense.[8] Whatever the military skill, and such skill was not in conspicuous display either operationally or tactically, his was leadership toward a dead end. Those who study Napoleon as a military commander need to remember this point.

The widespread lack today of Western commitment to national accounts of military history is matched by a hostility to the idea of imperialism, not only in Britain but also in the leading world power, the United States. It is not now fashionable to regard the overseas expansion of European empires, such as occurred in 1815–45, as a cause for congratulation, but, in terms of the values of the early nineteenth century, the failure of such expansion might have proved very serious. As far as the world-historical issue of the rise of the West is concerned, the 'tipping point' toward the triumph of the West was very much that of these decades, not least insofar as relations with China were concerned.

In 1815, aside from defeating Napoleon, Britain was also victorious in separate struggles in Sri Lanka, where the kingdom of Kandy was captured, and against the Gurkhas of Nepal. The ability to mount such campaigns would have been gravely undermined had Wellington been defeated in 1815 and a greater effort been necessary thereafter to support British interests in Europe. Indeed, on 29 March 1815, Henry, the third Earl Bathurst, the secretary of state for war and the colonies, had noted British vulnerabilities, observing, 'The British troops in the Mediterranean are at present unequal to do more than garrison certain fortresses, which are so distant from each other, and unconnected in their interests and systems of defence.'[9]

Had Napoleon been victorious in Europe, then he would have been in a position to challenge British interests farther afield. Thus Waterloo, and notably Britain's crucial role there, guaranteed a European settlement that was a key condition for the Western world order that dominated the nineteenth century and, albeit with many more difficulties and serious divisions, has essentially prevailed to the present.

Indeed, Waterloo can be seen as the culmination of the first of three great episodes – the Napoleonic Wars, the First World War and the Second World War – in each of which Britain played a key role against tyranny. That suggestion might sound vainglorious in the modern culture of relativism, but there is a central truth in this argument about Britain's role, and it is not one of British self-congratulation. Instead, as the American international relations specialist Paul Schroeder pointed out, Napoleon's return was 'one great self-serving imposture . . . the first staging of a third-world melodrama' and an attempt 'to seize power – nothing more.'[10] Napoleon's France, indeed, was the first of the modern 'rogue states', and its defeat was crucial to the creation of a nineteenth-century world order in which European liberal capitalism, whatever its faults, was to transform the world, in many ways for the better. Waterloo is thus symbolic: of a key moment in history and of the struggle against the unreason of tyranny.

SELECTED FURTHER READING

THERE IS A MASS of scholarship on the battle, and there is not the space to be more than heavily selective. The intention here is to offer a guide. The focus will be on more recent works, as earlier literature can be followed through its notes and bibliographies, but certain earlier works are noted. Alongside books, it is important to appreciate the range of periodical material. The *Waterloo Journal* is of special value.

Adkin, Mark. *The Waterloo Companion*. 2002.
Barthorp, Michael. *Wellington's Generals*. 1978.
Becke, A. F. *Napoleon and Waterloo*. 1914; repr. 1995.
Bowden, Scott. *Armies at Waterloo*. 1983.
Brett-James, Antony. *The Hundred Days*. 1966.
Chalfont, Lord, ed. *Waterloo: Battle of Three Armies*. 1979.
Chandler, David. *The Campaigns of Napoleon*. 1966.
———. *Napoleon's Marshals*. 1987.
———. *Waterloo: The Hundred Days*. 1980.
Chesney, Charles. *Waterloo Lectures*. 1907; repr. 1997.
Corrigan, Gordon. *Wellington: A Military Life*. 2001.
De Bas, F., and de Wommerson, J. *La Campagne de 1815*. 1908.

The Duke of Wellington, ed. *Supplementary Despatches, Correspondence and Memoranda of Field Marshal Arthur, Duke of Wellington.* 15 vols. 1858–72.

Elting, J. R. *Swords Around a Throne.* 1988.

Fletcher, Ian. *A Desperate Business: Wellington, the British Army and the Waterloo Campaign.* 2001.

————. *Galloping at Everything: The British Cavalry in the Peninsular War and at Waterloo.* 1999.

————. *Wellington's Regiments: The Men and their Battles from Roliça to Waterloo, 1805–1815.* 1994.

Forrest, Alan. *Napoleon's Men: The Soldiers of the Revolution and Empire.* 2002.

Gardner, D. *Quatre Bras, Ligny and Waterloo.* 1982.

Gash, N., ed. *Wellington: Studies in the Military and Political Career of the First Duke of Wellington.* 1990.

Gurwood, Colonel, ed. *The Dispatches of Field Marshal the Duke of Wellington.* 8 vols. 1844.

Hamilton-Williams, David. *Waterloo: New Perspectives.* 1993.

Haythornthwaite, Philip. *Waterloo Men: The Experience of Battle.* 1999.

Hofschröer, Peter. *1815: The Waterloo Campaign – The German Victory.* 1999.

Houssaye, H. *1815: Waterloo.* 1900.

Keegan, John. *The Face of Battle.* 1976.

Kennedy, Sir James Shaw. *Notes on the Battle of Waterloo.* 1865.

Linck, Tony. *Napoleon's Generals: The Waterloo Campaign.* 1994.

Longford, Elizabeth. *Wellington: The Years of the Sword.* 1969.

Mercer, Cavalié. *Journal of the Waterloo Campaign.* 1927; repr. 1995.

Nash, David. *The Prussian Army, 1808–1815.* 1972.

Navez, Louis. *Le champ de bataille et le pays de Waterloo en 1815.* 1908.

Nofi, Albert. *The Waterloo Campaign.* 1998.

Nosworthy, Brent. *Battle Tactics of Napoleon and his Enemies.* 1995.

Paget, J. and Saunders, D., *Hougoumont.* Barnsley, 1992.

Pivka, Otto von. *The Black Brunswickers.* 1973.

————. *The King's German Legion.* 1974.

Roberts, Andrew. *Napoleon and Wellington.* 2001.

————. *Waterloo.* 2005.

Siborne, Herbert, ed. *The Waterloo Letters.* 1891; repr. 1993.

Siborne, William. *History of the War in France and Belgium 1815.* 1848.

Uffindell, Andrew. *The Eagle's Last Triumph: Napoleon's Victory at Ligny.* 1994.

————. *Waterloo: The Battlefield Guide.* 2003.

Uffindell, Andrew, and Corum, Michael. *On the Fields of Glory: The Battlefields of the Waterloo Campaign.* 1996.

Ward, S.G.P. *Wellington's Headquarters.* 1957.

Weller, Jac. *On Wellington: The Duke and His Art of War.* 1998.

————. *Wellington at Waterloo.* 1967; repr. 1993.

Young, Peter. *Blucher's Army.* 1973.

NOTES

BL refers to the British Library.

Preface

1 Hill to Rev. Jacob Ley, 7 July 1815, Hill papers. I am grateful to Enid Case for granting access to this collection.
2 J. R. Freedman, *Whistling in the Dark: Memory and Culture in Wartime London* (Lexington, Ky., 1999).
3 J. Selby, ed., *The Recollections of Sergeant Morris* (Moreton-in-Marsh, 1998), p. 33.
4 R. Muir, *Salamanca 1812* (New Haven, Conn., 2001), pp. xi, 141.

Chapter 1

1 A. Ferrill, *The Origins of War: From the Stone Age to Alexander the Great* (London, 1985).
2 Sackville to Earl of Holdernesse, 10 Sept. 1758, BL. Egerton Mss. 3444 fol. 66; Fawcett to James Lister, 5 Dec. 1759, Halifax, Calderdale Archives Department SH: 7/FAW/58.
3 A. Starkey, *War in the Age of the Enlightenment, 1700–1789* (Westport, Conn., 2003).
4 Richard to Jeremy Browne, 14 Aug. 1759, BL. RP. 3284.
5 Fawcett to Lister, 24 Oct. 1760, Halifax, Calderdale Archives SH: 7/FAW/60.
6 Jenkinson to his father, Lord Hawkesbury, 25 July 1792, Oxford, Bodleian Library, Bland Burges papers vol. 37 fol. 62.

7 Chauvelin to Lebrun, French Foreign Minister, 9 Oct. 1792, Paris, Ministère des Relations Extérieures, Correspondance Politique Angleterre 582 fol. 318.

Chapter 2

1 C. Telp, *The Evolution of Operational Art 1740–1813: From Frederick the Great to Napoleon* (London, 2005).
2 G. E. Rothenberg, *The Art of Warfare in the Age of Napoleon* (Bloomington, Ind., 1978), p. 70.
3 O. Connelly, *Blundering to Glory,* 2nd ed. (Wilmington, Del., 1999).
4 A. Blin, *Iéna* (Paris, 2003); F. C. Schneid, *Napoleon's Conquest of Europe: The War of the Third Coalition* (Westport, Conn., 2005).
5 C. Telp, 'The Prussian Army in the Jena Campaign', in A. Forrest and P. H. Wilson, eds., *The Bee and the Eagle: Napoleonic France and the End of the Holy Roman Empire, 1806* (Basingstoke, 2009), pp. 155–71.

Chapter 3

1 J. Gore, ed., *Creevey* (1948), pp. 141–42.
2 C. Oman, *Wellington's Army* (London, 1912), p. 79.
3 I. Robertson, *A Commanding Presence: Wellington in the Peninsula, 1808–1814, Logistics, Strategy, Survival* (Stroud, 2008).

Chapter 4

1 A. Roberts, *Napoleon and Wellington* (2001), p. 178.
2 M. Leggiere, *The Fall of Napoleon,* vol. 1, *The Allied Invasion of France, 1813–1814* (Cambridge, 2007).
3 L. S. Kaplan, 'France and Madison's Decision for War, 1812', *Mississippi Valley Historical Review* 50 (1964): 652–71.

Chapter 5

1 E. de Waresquiel: *Cent Jours. La tentation de l'impossible, mars–juillet 1815* (Paris, 2008).
2 Wellington to Lord Stewart, later third Marquess of Londonderry, 8 May 1815, BL. Dept. of Manuscripts, Loan 105 fol. 9.
3 J. Hussey, 'Preparing to Invade France May into June 1815', *First Empire* (Mar.–Apr. 2009): 12–19.
4 J. Hussey, 'Orange and Nassau: A Multinational Complication in 1815', *First Empire* (Nov.–Dec. 2008): 28–32.
5 J. H. Rose, 'Sir Hudson Lowe and the Beginnings of the Campaign of 1815', *English Historical Review* 16 (1901): 517–27.
6 Wissell to ———, 18 Dec. 1829, BL. Add. 34703 fols. 101–2. See also P. M. Friedman, 'Respectable Spies!', *First Empire* (Jan.–Feb. 2009): 7.
7 P. P. Jones, ed., *In Napoleon's Shadow: Complete Memoirs of Louis-Joseph Marchand, 1811–1821* (1998), p. 249.
8 P. Hofschröer, *1815: The Waterloo Campaign: Wellington, His German Allies, and the Battles of Ligny and Quatre Bras* (Mechanicsburg, Penn., 1998).

9 National Army Museum, London, 1968-07-344-1, pp. 6–7.

10 Anonymous account of conversation with Jérôme, 10 May 1823, BL. Add. 34703 fol. 66.

11 National Army Museum, London, 1968-07-344-1, pp. 8–9.

12 Anonymous memorandum, 21 June 1815, BL. Add. 34703 fol. 33.

13 Account of conversations with Count Henri Bertrand, 2–3 Aug. 1824, BL. Add. 34703 fols. 67–69.

14 A. Mombauer, *Helmuth von Moltke and the Origins of the First World War* (Cambridge, 2001).

15 Marquess of Anglesey, *One-leg: The Life and Letters of Henry William Paget, First Marquess of Anglesey* (London, 1961), p. 133.

Chapter 6

1 Goulbourn draft memoirs, quoted in N. Thompson, *Earl Bathurst and the British Empire* (Barnsley, 1999), p. 97.

2 P. Barber, ed., *The Map Book* (London, 2005), p. 250.

3 Memorandum by Robert Manners, 12 Jan. 1830, BL. Add. 34703 fol. 105.

4 National Army Museum, London, 1968-07-344-1, p. 93.

5 D. Gates, *The Napoleonic Wars 1803–1815* (London, 1997), p. 268.

6 Anonymous account, 10 May 1823, BL. Add. 34703 fol. 65.

7 Clayton to Siborne, 9 Nov. 1834, BL. Add. 34703 fol. 201.

8 Anonymous memorandum, 21 June 1815, BL. Add. 34703 fol. 32.

9 Humphrey Senhouse to his wife, Elizabeth, 15 July 1815, Hull, University Library, Hotham papers DDHO/7/13.

10 C. J. Esdaile, 'Recent Books on Britain in the Napoleonic Wars', *History* 89 (2004): p. 73; A. Roberts, *Napoleon and Wellington* (London, 2001).

11 For a more positive assessment, A. Dellevoet, 'Cowards at Waterloo? A Reexamination of Bijlandt's Dutch-Belgian Brigade in the Campaign of 1815', *Napoleon* 16 (Summer 2000): 18–36.

12 Francis, Earl of Ellesmere, *Personal Reminiscences of the Duke of Wellington* (London, 1903), p. 240.

13 Anonymous memorandum, 22 June 1815, BL. Add. 34703 fol. 34.

14 J. S. Kennedy, *Notes on the Battle of Waterloo* (London, 1865), p. 51; cf. p. 54.

15 Wellington to Bathurst, 19 June 1815, *Wellington Dispatches,* VIII, 146–50.

16 Wellington to J. W. Croker, 8 Aug. 1815, *Wellington Dispatches* VIII, 231–32.

17 Stanhope to Duke of York, 19 June 1815, BL. Add. 34703 fol. 23.

18 Anonymous account of conversation, 10 May 1823, BL. Add. 34703 fol. 65.

19 J.-P. Bertaud, D. Reichel, and Jacques Bertrand, *Atlas de la révolution française,* vol. 3, *L'armée et la guerre* (Paris, 1989), pp. 69–70.

20 D. Chandler, *The Art of Warfare on Land* (London, 1974), p. 154; G. Rothenberg, *The Art of Warfare in the Age of Napoleon* (London, 1977), pp. 123–24.

21 National Army Museum, London, 1968-07-344-1, pp. 9–10.

Chapter 7

1   Wellington, *Supplementary Despatches,* X, pp. 530–31.

2   For other comparisons between the Waterloo campaign and battles of the Second World War, D. Fraser, *Wellington and the Waterloo Campaign* (Southampton, 1995), pp. 8, 12, 21.

3   D. Gardner, *Quatre Bras, Ligny and Waterloo* (London, 1882), p. 284.

4   *Supplementary Despatches,* X, 531.

5   Private John Marshall to his father, 11 July 1815, *United Services Journal* (1831), p. 315.

6   Apsley to Earl Bathurst, 19 June 1815, Historical Manuscripts Report, *Report on the Manuscripts of Earl Bathurst* (London, 1923), p. 357; Stanhope to Duke of York, 16 June 1815, anonymous memorandum, 21 June 1815, BL. Add. 34703 fols. 22, 31; Castlereagh to George Canning, 22 June 1815, Marquess of Londonderry, ed., *Memoirs and Correspondence of Viscount Castlereagh,* 3rd ser. (London, 1853), 2: p. 363.

7   Account of conversation on 2 Aug. 1824, BL. Add. 34703 fol. 66.

8   Account of conversation on 3 Aug. 1824, BL. Add. 34703 fol. 70.

9   N. Gash, 'Wellington and the Waterloo campaign', in C. M. Woolgar, ed., *Wellington Studies* (Southampton, 1999) II: p. 216.

10 Gardner, *Quatre Bras, Ligny and Waterloo,* p. 284.

11 Stanhope to Duke of York, 19 June 1815, BL. Add. 34703 fol. 22.

12 Howard to Siborne, 22 Nov. 1834, BL. Add. 34703 fol. 318.

13 R. Gronow, *The Reminiscences and Recollections of Captain Gronow* (Frome, 1984), p. 190.

14 C. Divall, *Redcoats Against Napoleon: The 30th Regiment During the Revolutionary and Napoleonic Wars* (Barnsley, 2009), p. 168; Stendhal, *The Charterhouse of Parma* (London, 1958), p. 59.

15 M. Duffy, '" . . . All Was Hushed Up": The Hidden Trafalgar', *Mariner's Mirror* 91 (2005): 216–40.

16 Apsley to Earl Bathurst, 19 June 1815, *Report on the Manuscripts of Earl Bathurst,* p. 357.

17 Stanhope to York, 19 June 1815, BL. Add. 34703 fols 22–23.

18 Kennedy, *Notes on the Battle of Waterloo,* p. 23.

19 Ibid., p. 71.

20 P. J. Haythornthwaite, *Napoleon's Military Machine* (New York, 1988), p. 158.

21 J. Black, *What If? Counterfactualism and the Problem of History* (London, 2008).

22 Kennedy, *Notes on the Battle of Waterloo,* pp. 24–25.

23 Garland to Siborne, 4 Dec. 1834, Add. 34704 fol. 1.

24 Lowe to Colonel Bunbury, 20 Oct. 1813, BL. Add. 37051 fols 157, 162.

25 Anonymous account of conversations, 10 May 1823, BL. Add. 34703 fol. 65.

26 Ibid.

27 Anonymous, 'A French Infantry Officer's Account of Waterloo', *United Services Journal,* Jan. 1879, p. 67; R. Muir, *Tactics and the Experience of Battle in the Age of Napoleon* (New Haven, Conn., 1998), p. 103.

28 Manners to Siborne, 12 Jan. 1830, Memo of movements of 10th Royal Hussars, BL. Add. 34703 fol. 106.
29 William Sharpire to Siborne, 6 Dec. 1834, BL. Add. 34704 fol. 16.
30 Captain J. R. Budgeon to Siborne, 17 Dec. 1834, Gawler to Siborne, 22 Dec. 1834, BL. Add. 34704 fols 57–58, 94.
31 Anonymous memorandum, 21 June 1815, BL. Add. 34703 fols 31–32.
32 Clayton to Siborne, 9 Nov. 1834, BL. Add. 34703 fol. 201.
33 Lieutenant Colonel Wissell to ———, 18 Dec. 1829, BL. Add. 34703 fol. 100.
34 *Supplementary Despatches,* X, p. 513.
35 *Supplementary Despatches,* X, p. 531–32.
36 Stanhope to York, 19 June 1815, BL. Add. 34703 fol. 23.
37 Memorandum by Robert Manners, 12 Jan. 1830, BL. Add. 34703 fol. 107.
38 Anonymous memorandum, 21 June 1815, BL. Add. 34703 fol. 33.

Chapter 8

1 Anonymous to Sir Thomas Acland, undated, Exeter, Devon CRO. 1148 Madd/36/91.
2 P. W. Schroeder, *The Transformation of European Politics 1763–1848* (Oxford, 1994), p. 551.
3 A. Arneth, *Johann Freiherr von Wessenberg* (Vienna, 1898), II: pp. 1–2.
4 I. Gale, *Four Days in June* (London, 2006), p. 368.
5 C. Hibbert, ed., *The Wheatley Diary* (London, 1964), p. 65.
6 Wellington to General Beresford, 2 July 1815, *Despatches* XII, p. 529.
7 Conversation with Bertrand, 2 Aug. 1824, BL. Add. 34703 fol. 66.
8 A. Corvisier, ed., *A Dictionary of Military History* (rev. English ed.) (Cambridge, Mass., 1994), p. 859.
9 National Army Museum, London, 1976-07-34-1.
10 National Army Museum, London, 1968-07-213, p. 32.
11 *The Diary of Frances, Lady Shelley* (London, 1912), I: p. 102.
12 E. Owen, ed., *The Waterloo Papers: 1815 and Beyond* (Tavistock, 1997), p. 34.

Chapter 9

1 Anonymous memorandum, 21 June 1815, BL. Add. 34703 fol. 31.
2 J. Fortescue, ed., *The Note-books of Captain Coignet* (London, 1928), p. 280.
3 Anonymous memorandum, BL. Add. 34703 fols. 73–74.
4 Castlereagh to George Canning, 22 June 1815, Marquess of Londonderry, ed., *Correspondence of Viscount Castlereagh,* 3rd ser. (London, 1853) 2: 383.
5 J. Colville, *The Portrait of a General* (Salisbury, 1980).
6 London, National Army Museum, 1975-09-62-1; K. Hagemann, 'Francophobia and Patriotism: Images of Napoleon and "the French" in Prussia and Northern Germany at the Period of the Anti-Napoleonic Wars, 1806–1815', *French History* 18 (2004): 404–25; 'Occupation, Mobilization, and Politics: The Anti-Napoleonic Wars in Prussian Experience, Memory, and Historiography', *Central*

European History 39 (2006): 580–610; ' "Desperation to the Utmost": The Defeat of 1806 and the French Occupation in Prussian Experience and Perception', in A. Forrest and P. H. Wilson, eds., *The Bee and the Eagle: Napoleonic France and the End of the Holy Roman Empire, 1806* (Basingstoke, 2009), pp. 191–213.

7 Cathcart to Castlereagh, 21 June 1815, *Correspondence of Viscount Castlereagh* 2: p. 382.

8 *Annual Register* 57 (1815): 46.

9 A. Grab, 'Army, State and Society: Conscription and Desertion in Napoleonic Italy', *Journal of Modern History* 67 (1995): 53–54; M. Broers, *The Politics of Religion in Napoleonic Italy: The War Against God, 1801–1814* (London, 2002).

10 F. C. Schneid, *Napoleon's Italian Campaigns, 1805–1815* (Westport, Conn., 2002), pp. 145–53.

11 Viscount Keith to Hotham, 10 July 1815, Hull, University Library, Hotham papers DDHO/7/8; cf. 20 July.

12 Bertrand to Hotham, 9 and 14 July, Senhouse to his wife, 15 July 1815, Hull, University Library, Hotham papers DDHO/7/13.

13 Maitland to J. W. Croker, Secretary of the Admiralty, 14 July 1815, Hull, University Library, Hotham papers DDHO/7/13.

14 J. Willms, *Napoleon and St. Helena* (London, 2008), p. 68.

15 M. Glover, *A Very Slippery Fellow* (New York, 1978), p. 150.

16 H. H. Kaplan, *Nathan Mayer Rothschild and the Creation of a Dynasty: The Critical Years, 1806–1816* (Stanford, Calif., 2006), p. 146, correcting N. Ferguson, *The House of Rothschild*, vol. 1, *Money's Prophets, 1798–1848* (New York, 1998).

17 N. Harding, *Hanover and the British Empire 1700–1837* (Woodbridge, 2007), p. 261.

18 T. D. Veve, *The Duke of Wellington and the British Army of Occupation in France, 1815–1818* (New York, 1992).

19 Anonymous memorandum, 21 June 1815, BL. Add. 34703 fol. 33.

20 Lecture at Brooklyn, 1 Nov. 1859, from his *Speeches* (1880).

21 L. Colley, *Britons: Forging the Nation, 1707–1837* (New Haven, Conn., 1992), p. 191.

22 N. Thompson, *Wellington After Waterloo* (London, 1986).

23 N. Rogers, *The Press Gang* (London, 2007), pp. 104–5, correcting Colley, *Britons*, p. 365.

24 A. Cunningham, *The Life of Sir David Wilkie*, 3 vols. (London, 1843), II: pp. 71–77.

25 P. Usherwood and J. Spencer-Smith, *Lady Butler: Battle Artist, 1846–1933* (Gloucester, 1987).

26 P. Sinnema, *The Wake of Wellington: Englishness in 1852* (Athens, Ohio, 2006).

27 H. Garlick, 'The staging of death: iconography and the state funeral of the Duke of Wellington', *Australian Journal of Art* 9 (1991): 58–77; C. Pearsall, 'Burying the Duke: Victorian mourning and the funeral of the Duke of Wellington', *Victorian Literature and Culture* 27 (1999): 365–93.

28 L. Leete-Hodge, *Curiosities of Somerset* (Bodmin, 1985), p. 67.

Chapter 10

1 *Annual Register* 57 (1815), p. iv.
2 Sir James Graham, First Lord of the Admiralty, to Fitzroy, Lord Raglan, commander of the British land forces sent to the Black Sea, 8 Oct., 22 Nov. 1854, BL. Add. 79696 fols 131, 135.
3 C. J. Esdaile, 'Waterloo', in J. Black, ed., *The Seventy Great Battles of All Time* (London, 2005), p. 197.
4 Moore to his father, 25 Mar. 1801, BL. Add. 59281 fols 74–75.
5 A. Nicole, 'Ouvrard and the French Expedition in Spain in 1823', *Journal of Modern History* 17 (1945): 193–201.
6 R. Holroyd, 'The Bourbon Army, 1815–1830', *Historical Journal* 14 (1971): 551.

Chapter 11

1 D. Andress, ' "A Ferocious and Misled Multitude": Elite Perceptions of Popular Action from Rousseau to Robespierre', in M. Crook, W. Doyle, and A. Forrest, eds., *Enlightenment and Revolution: Essays in Honour of Norman Hampson* (Aldershot, 2004), pp. 169–86.
2 D. Laven, *Venice and Venetia Under the Habsburgs, 1815–1835* (Oxford, 2002).
3 For a critique of this argument, R. Alexander, *Re-Writing the French Revolutionary Tradition* (Cambridge, 2003).
4 A. Horne, 'Ruler of the World. Napoleon's Missed Opportunities', and C. Carr, 'Napoleon Wins at Waterloo', in R. Cowley, ed., *What If? The World's Foremost Military Historians Imagine What Might Have Been* (London, 2001), pp. 218, 220–21.
5 J. Black, *The Curse of History* (London, 2008).

Postscripts

1 W. C. Sellar and R. J. Yeatman, *1066 and All That* (Stroud, 1993), pp. 102–3.
2 G. M. Trevelyan, *History of England,* 3rd ed. (London, 1960), p. 585.
3 S. Biel, *Down with the Old Canoe: A Cultural History of the* Titanic *Disaster* (New York, 1996).
4 J. Tulard, *Le Mythe de Napoléon* (Paris, 1971); S. Hazareesingh, *The Legend of Napoleon* (London, 2004).
5 J.-P. Matei, *Napoléon et le cinéma* (Ajaccio, 1998); U. Jung, ' "A Truly Fatherlandish Epic"? Karl Grune's *Waterloo* (1928)', in L. Engelen and R. V. Winkels, eds., *Perspectives on European Film and History* (Ghent, 2007), pp. 133–56.
6 J. Black, *Rethinking Military History* (London, 2004).
7 M. Thatcher, *The Downing Street Years* (London, 1993), p. 24.
8 D. D. Horward, 'Napoleon and Leadership', *Consortium on Revolutionary Europe, 1750–1850* (2001), p. 321.
9 *Supplementary Despatches,* X, p. 6.
10 P. W. Schroeder, *The Transformation of European Politics, 1763–1848* (Oxford, 1994), p. 550.

INDEX

ABOUT THE AUTHOR

JEREMY BLACK is professor of history at the University of Exeter and is one of the world's leading military historians. A past council member of the Royal Historical Society, Black is a senior fellow of the Foreign Policy Research Institute. In 2008, he received the Samuel Eliot Morison Prize of the Society for Military History.